HEALTH AND HUMAN DEVELOPMENT

MENTAL HEALTH FROM AN INTERNATIONAL PERSPECTIVE

HEALTH AND HUMAN DEVELOPMENT

JOAV MERRICK - SERIES EDITOR –

NATIONAL INSTITUTE OF CHILD HEALTH AND HUMAN DEVELOPMENT,
MINISTRY OF SOCIAL AFFAIRS, JERUSALEM, ISRAEL

Adolescent Behavior Research: International Perspectives
Joav Merrick and Hatim A. Omar (Editors)
2007. ISBN: 1-60021-649-8

Complementary Medicine Systems: Comparison and Integration
Karl W. Kratky
2008. ISBN: 978-1-60456-475-4

Pain in Children and Youth
P. Schofield and J. Merrick (Editors)
2008. ISBN: 978-1-60456-951-3

Obesity and Adolescence: A Public Health Concern
Hatim A Omar, Donald E. Greydanus; Dilip R. Patel and Joav Merrick (Editors)
2009. ISBN: 978-1-60692-821-9

Poverty and Children: A Public Health Concern
Alexis Lieberman, and Joav Merrick (Editors)
2009. ISBN: 978-1-60741-140-6

Living on the Edge: The Mythical, Spiritual, and Philosophical Roots of Social Marginality
Joseph Goodbread
2009. ISBN: 978-1-60741-162-8 (Hardcover)
2011. ISBN: 978-1-61470-192-7 (E-book)
2013. ISBN: 978-1-61122-986-8 (Softcover)

Social and Cultural Psychiatry Experience from the Caribbean Region
Hari D. Maharajh and Joav Merrick (Editors)
2011. ISBN: 978-1-61668-506-5

Challenges in Adolescent Health: An Australian Perspective
David Bennett, Susan Towns and Elizabeth Elliott and Joav Merrick (Editors)
2009. ISBN: 978-1-60741-616-6

Children and Pain
P. Schofield and J. Merrick (Editors)
2009. ISBN: 978-1-60876-020-6

Alcohol-Related Cognitive Disorders: Research and Clinical Perspectives
Leo Sher, Isack Kandel and Joav Merrick (Editors)
2009. ISBN: 978-1-60741-730-9

Bone and Brain Metastases: Advances in Research and Treatment
Arjun Sahgal, Edward Chow and Joav Merrick (Editors)
2010. ISBN: 978-1-61668-365-8

Chance Action and Therapy: The Playful Way of Changing
Uri Wernik
2010. ISBN: 978-1-60876-393-1

International Aspects of Child Abuse and Neglect
Howard Dubowitz and Joav Merrick (Editors)
2010. ISBN: 978-1-61122-049-0

Behavioral Pediatrics, 3rd Edition
Donald E. Greydanus, Dilip R. Patel, Helen D. Pratt and Joseph L. Calles Jr. (Editors)
2011. ISBN: 978-1-60692-702-1

Advances in Environmental Health Effects of Toxigenic Mold and Mycotoxins
Ebere Cyril Anyanwu
2011. ISBN: 978-1-60741-953-2

Rural Child Health: International Aspects
Erica Bell and Joav Merrick (Editors)
2011. ISBN: 978-1-60876-357-3

Principles of Holistic Psychiatry: A Textbook on Holistic Medicine for Mental Disorders
Soren Ventegodt and Joav Merrick
2011. ISBN: 978-1-61761-940-3

International Aspects of Child Abuse and Neglect
Howard Dubowitz and Joav Merrick (Editors)
2011. ISBN: 978-1-60876-703-8

Positive Youth Development: Evaluation and Future Directions in a Chinese Context
Daniel T.L. Shek, Hing Keung Ma and Joav Merrick (Editors)
2011. ISBN: 978-1-60876-830-1

Alternative Medicine Yearbook 2009
Joav Merrick (Editor)
2011. ISBN: 978-1-61668-910-0

Understanding Eating Disorders: Integrating Culture, Psychology and Biology
Yael Latzer, Joav Merrick and Daniel Stein (Editors)
2011. ISBN: 978-1-61728-298-0

Advanced Cancer, Pain and Quality of Life
Edward Chow and Joav Merrick (Editors)
2011. ISBN: 978-1-61668-207-1

Positive Youth Development: Implementation of a Youth Program in a Chinese Context
Daniel T.L Shek, Hing Keung Ma and Joav Merrick (Editors)
2011. ISBN: 978-1-61668-230-9

Environment, Mood Disorders and Suicide
Teodor T. Postolache and Joav Merrick (Editors)
2011. ISBN: 978-1-61668-505-8

Chance Action and Therapy: The Playful Way of Changing
Uri Wernik
2011. ISBN: 978-1-61122-987-5

Public Health Yearbook 2009
Joav Merrick (Editor)
2011. ISBN: 978-1-61668-911-7

Child Health and Human Development Yearbook 2009
Joav Merrick (Editor)
2011. ISBN: 978-1-61668-912-4

Narratives and Meanings of Migration
Julia Mirsky
2011. ISBN: 978-1-61761-103-2

Self-Management and the Health Care Consumer
Peter William Harvey
2011. ISBN: 978-1-61761-796-6

Sexology from a Holistic Point of View
Soren Ventegodt and Joav Merrick
2011. ISBN: 978-1-61761-859-8

Clinical Aspects of Psychopharmacology in Childhood and Adolescence
D. E. Greydanus, J. L. Calles Jr., D. P. Patel, A. Nazeer and J. Merrick (Editors)
2011. ISBN: 978-1-61122-135-0

Drug Abuse in Hong Kong: Development and Evaluation of a Prevention Program
Daniel TL Shek, Rachel CF Sun and Joav Merrick (Editors)
2011. ISBN: 978-1-61324-491-3

Climate Change and Rural Child Health
Erica Bell, Bastian M. Seidel and Joav Merrick (Editors)
2011. ISBN: 978-1-61122-640-9

Rural Medical Education: Practical Strategies
Erica Bell and Craig Zimitat and Joav Merrick (Editors)
2011. ISBN: 978-1-61122-649-2

Understanding Eating Disorders: Integrating Culture, Psychology and Biology
Yael Latzer, Joav Merrick and Daniel Stein (Editors)
2011. ISBN: 978-1-61470-976-3

Positive Youth Development: Evaluation and Future Directions in a Chinese Context
Daniel T. L. Shek, Hing Keung Ma and Joav Merrick (Editors)
2011. ISBN: 978-1-62100-175-1

The Dance of Sleeping and Eating among Adolescents: Normal and Pathological Perspectives
Yael Latzer and Orna Tzischinsky (Editors)
2011. ISBN: 978-1-61209-710-7

Randomized Clinical Trials and Placebo: Can You Trust the Drugs Are Working and Safe?
Søren Ventegodt and Joav Merrick
2011. ISBN: 978-1-61470-151-4 (E-book)
2012. ISBN: 978-1-61470-067-8 (Hardcover)

Child and Adolescent Health Yearbook 2009
Joav Merrick (Editor)
2012. ISBN: 978-1-61668-913-1

Applied Public Health: Examining Multifaceted Social or Ecological Problems and Child Maltreatment
John R. Lutzker and Joav Merrick (Editors)
2012. ISBN: 978-1-62081-356-0

Adolescence and Chronic Illness. A Public Health Concern
Hatim Omar, Donald E. Greydanus, Dilip R. Patel and Joav Merrick (Editors)
2012. ISBN: 978-1-60876-628-4

Translational Research for Primary Healthcare
Erica Bell, Gert P. Westert and Joav Merrick (Editors)
2012. ISBN: 978-1-61324-647-4

Child and Adolescent Health Yearbook 2010
Joav Merrick (Editor)
2012. ISBN: 978-1-61209-788-6

Child Health and Human Development Yearbook 2010
Joav Merrick (Editor)
2012. ISBN: 8-1-61209-789-3

Public Health Yearbook 2010
Joav Merrick (Editor)
2012. ISBN: 978-1-61209-971-2

The Astonishing Brain and Holistic Consciousness: Neuroscience and Vedanta Perspectives
Vinod D. Deshmukh
2012. ISBN: Vinod D. Deshmukh

Treatment and Recovery of Eating Disorders
Daniel Stein and Yael Latzer (Editors)
2012. ISBN: 978-1-61470-259-7 (Hardcover)
2013. ISBN: 978-1-62808-248-7 (Softcover)

Alternative Medicine Yearbook 2010
Joav Merrick (Editor)
2012. ISBN: 978-1-62100-132-4

Building Community Capacity: Minority and Immigrant Populations
Rosemary M Caron and Joav Merrick (Editors)
2012. ISBN: 978-1-62081-022-4

Human Immunodeficiency Virus (HIV) Research: Social Science Aspects
Hugh Klein and Joav Merrick (Editors)
2012. ISBN: 978-1-62081-293-8

AIDS and Tuberculosis: Public Health Aspects
Daniel Chemtob and Joav Merrick (Editors)
2012. ISBN: 978-1-62081-382-9

Public Health Yearbook 2011
Joav Merrick (Editor)
2012. ISBN: 978-1-62081-433-8

Alternative Medicine Research Yearbook 2011
Joav Merrick (Editor)
2012. ISBN: 978-1-62081-476-5

Textbook on Evidence-Based Holistic Mind-Body Medicine: Basic Principles of Healing in Traditional Hippocratic Medicine
Søren Ventegodt and Joav Merrick
2012. ISBN: 978-1-62257-094-2

Textbook on Evidence-Based Holistic Mind-Body Medicine: Holistic Practice of Traditional Hippocratic Medicine
Søren Ventegodt and Joav Merrick
2012. ISBN: 978-1-62257-105-5

Textbook on Evidence-Based Holistic Mind-Body Medicine: Healing the Mind in Traditional Hippocratic Medicine
Søren Ventegodt and Joav Merrick
2012. ISBN: 978-1-62257-112-3

Textbook on Evidence-Based Holistic Mind-Body Medicine: Sexology and Traditional Hippocratic Medicine
Søren Ventegodt and Joav Merrick
2012. ISBN: 978-1-62257-130-7

Textbook on Evidence-Based Holistic Mind-Body Medicine: Research, Philosophy, Economy and Politics of Traditional Hippocratic Medicine
Søren Ventegodt and Joav Merrick
2012. ISBN: 978-1-62257-140-6

Building Community Capacity: Skills and Principles
Rosemary M Caron and Joav Merrick (Editors)
2012. ISBN 978-1-61209-331-4

Our Search for Meaning in Life: Quality of Life Philosophy
Soren Ventegodt and Joav Merrick
2012. ISBN: 978-1-61470-494-2

Health and Happiness from Meaningful Work: Research in Quality of Working Life
Soren Ventegodt and Joav Merrick (Editors)
2013. ISBN: 978-1-60692-820-2

Pediatric and Adolescent Sexuality and Gynecology: Principles for the Primary Care Clinician
Hatim A Omar, Donald E. Greydanus, Artemis K., Dilip R. Patel and Joav Merrick (Editors)
2013. ISBN: 978-1-60876-735-9

Conceptualizing Behavior in Health and Social Research: A Practical Guide to Data Analysis
Said Shahtahmasebi and Damon Berridge
2013. ISBN: 978-1-60876-383-2

Adolescence and Sports
Dilip R. Patel, Donald E. Greydanus, Hatim Omar and Joav Merrick (Editors)
2013. ISBN: 978-1-60876-702-1

Human Development: Biology from a Holistic Point of View
Søren Ventegodt, Tyge Dahl Hermansen and Joav Merrick (Editors)
2013. ISBN: 978-1-61470-441-6

Building Community Capacity: Case Examples from Around the World
Rosemary M. Caron and Joav Merrick (Editors)
2013. ISBN: 978-1-62417-175-8

Managed Care in a Public Setting
Richard Evan Steele
2013. ISBN: 978-1-62417-970-9

Alternative Medicine Research Yearbook 2012
Søren Ventegodt and Joav Merrick (Editors)
2013. ISBN: 978-1-62808-080-3

Health Promotion: Community Singing as a Vehicle to Promote Health
Jing Sun, Nicholas Buys and Joav Merrick (Editors)
2013. ISBN: 978-1-62618-908-9

Public Health Yearbook 2012
Joav Merrick (Editor)
2013. ISBN: 978-1-62808-078-0

Health Risk Communication
Marijke Lemal and Joav Merrick (Editors)
2013. ISBN: 978-1-62257-544-2

Building Community Capacity: Case Examples from Around the World
Rosemary M. Caron and Joav Merrick (Editors)
2013. ISBN: ISBN: 978-1-62417-175-8

Bullying: A Public Health Concern
Jorge C. Srabstein and Joav Merrick (Editors)
2013. ISBN: 978-1-62618-564-7

Advanced Cancer: Managing Symptoms and Quality of Life
Nemica Thavarajah, Natalie Pulenzas, Breanne Lechner, Edward Chow and Joav Merrick (Editors)
2013. ISBN: 978-1-62808-239-5

Health Promotion: Strengthening Positive Health and Preventing Disease
Jing Sun, Nicholas Buys and Joav Merrick (Editors)
2023. ISBN: 978-1-62257-870-2

Pain Management Yearbook 2011
Joav Merrick (Editor)
2013. ISBN: 978-1-62808-970-7

Pain Management Yearbook 2012
Joav Merrick (Editor)
2013. ISBN: 978-1-62808-973-8

Food, Nutrition and Eating Behavior
Joav Merrick and Sigal Israeli (Editors)
2013 - 4th Quarter.
ISBN: 978-1-62948-233-0

Public Health Concern: Smoking, Alcohol and Substance Use
Joav Merrick and Ariel Tenenbaum (Editors)
2013 - 4th Quarter.
ISBN: 978-1-62948-424-2

Mental Health from an International Perspective
Joav Merrick, Shoshana Aspler and Mohammed Morad (Editors)
2013 - 4th Quarter.
ISBN: 978-1-62948-519-5

Suicide from a Public Health Perspective
Said Shahtahmasebi and Joav Merrick
2014 - 1st Quarter.
ISBN: 978-1-62948-536-2

HEALTH AND HUMAN DEVELOPMENT

MENTAL HEALTH FROM AN INTERNATIONAL PERSPECTIVE

JOAV MERRICK
SHOSHANA ASPLER
AND
MOHAMMED MORAD
EDITORS

NOVA BIOMEDICAL
New York

For permission to use material from this book please contact us:
Telephone 631-231-7269; Fax 631-231-8175
Web Site: http://www.novapublishers.com

Library of Congress Cataloging-in-Publication Data

ISBN: 978-1-62948-519-5

Library of Congress Control Number: 2013952578

Published by Nova Science Publishers, Inc. † New York

Contents

Introduction

Mental health is "a state of well-being in which the individual realizes his or her own abilities; can cope with the normal stresses of life; can work productively and fruitfully; and is able to make a contribution to his or her community". Mental illness is defined as "collectively, all diagnosable mental disorders" or "health conditions that are characterized by alterations in thinking, mood, or behavior (or some combination thereof) associated with distress and/or impaired functioning." Mental disorders, especially depressive disorders, are related to many chronic diseases like diabetes, cancer, cardiovascular disease, asthma and obesity. In recent years, there has been an alarming number of school shootings with youth or adults involved who are seriously mentally disturbed. There has also been an increase in suicides and mental pathology in the military and in fact, many professionals perceive that the increase in psychiatric drugs negatively impacts our population. In spite of more people receiving psychotropic medication at a large expense to the individual and society, it does not seem that people are getting better on the whole. As a result, there is a need to re-evaluate our policy and interventions, but also a need for more accurate data and information.

In: Mental Health from an International Perspective
Editors: J. Merrick, S. Aspler and M. Morad
ISBN: 978-1-62948-519-5

Chapter 1

Mental health issues

***Joav Merrick, MD, MMedSc, DMSc**[*1,2,3,4], **Shoshana Aspler, RN, BScN, MPH**[1,2] **and Mohammed Morad, MD, FRCP (Edin), MRCPS(Glasg)**[1,4,5]*

[1]National Institute of Child Health and Human Development, Jerusalem
[2]Office of the Medical Director, Health Services, Division for Intellectual and Developmental Disabilities, Ministry of Social Affairs and Social Services, Jerusalem
[3]Division of Pediatrics, Hadassah Hebrew University Medical Center, Mt Scopus Campus, Jerusalem, Israel
[4]Kentucky Children's Hospital, University of Kentucky, Lexington, United States of America
[5]Yaski Medical Center, Clalit Health Services, Department of Family Medicine, Faculty of Health Sciences, Ben Gurion University of the Negev, Beer-Sheva, Israel

Mental health is "a state of well-being in which the individual realizes his or her own abilities, can cope with the normal stresses of life, can work productively and fruitfully, and is able to make a contribution to his or her community", while mental illness is defined as "collectively all diagnosable mental disorders" or "health conditions that are characterized by alterations in thinking, mood, or behavior (or some combination thereof) associated with distress and/or impaired functioning." Mental disorders, especially depressive disorders, are related to many chronic diseases, like diabetes, cancer, cardiovascular disease, asthma, and obesity. In recent years there have been an alarming numbers of school shootings with youth or adults involved, who are seriously mentally disturbed. There are also an increase in suicides and mental pathology in the military and in fact many professionals perceive that the increase in psychiatric drugs negatively impact upon our population. In spite of more people receiving psychotropic medication at a large expense to the individual and society it does not seem that people are getting

* Correspondence: Professor Joav Merrick, MD, MMedSci, DMSc, Medical Director, Health Services, Division for Intellectual and Developmental Disabilities, Ministry of Social Affairs and Social Services, POBox 1260, IL-91012 Jerusalem, Israel. E-mail: jmerrick@zahav.net.il

better on the whole. There is therefore a need to re-evaluate our policy and interventions, but also a need for more accurate data and information.

Introduction

Mental health is “a state of well-being in which the individual realizes his or her own abilities, can cope with the normal stresses of life, can work productively and fruitfully, and is able to make a contribution to his or her community” (1).

Mental illness is defined as “collectively all diagnosable mental disorders” or “health conditions that are characterized by alterations in thinking, mood, or behavior (or some combination thereof) associated with distress and/or impaired functioning” (2).

Mental disorders, especially depressive disorders, are related to many chronic diseases, like diabetes, cancer, cardiovascular disease, asthma, and obesity. Together with this connection there is also many associated risk behaviors like physical inactivity, smoking, excessive drinking, and insufficient sleep. Mood disorders are among the most pervasive of all mental disorders like major depression, where the individual commonly reports feeling, for a time period of two weeks or more, sad or blue, uninterested in things previously of interest, psychomotor retardation or agitation, and increased or decreased appetite, since the depressive episode ensued.

Children and mental health

Many children are living with mental health disorders and for example in the United States it is estimated that the total annual cost is $247 billion (3). A total of 13-20% of children living in the United States experience a mental disorder in a given year and surveillance during 1994–2011 has shown the prevalence of these conditions to be increasing (3). Suicide, which can result from the interaction of mental disorders and other factors, was the second leading cause of death among children aged 12-17 years in 2010 (3).

Attention deficit hyperactivity disorder (ADHD) (6.8%) was the most prevalent diagnosis among children aged 3-7 years, followed by behavioral or conduct problems (3.5%), anxiety (3.0%), depression (2.1%), autism spectrum disorders (1.1%) and Tourette syndrome (0.2% among children aged 6-17 years) (3). An estimated 4.7% of adolescents aged 12-17 years reported an illicit drug use disorder in the past year, 4.2% had an alcohol abuse disorder in the past year and 2.8% had cigarette dependence in the past month. The overall suicide rate for persons aged 10-19 years was 4.5 suicides per 100,000 persons in 2010 (3). Approximately 8% of adolescents aged 12-17 years reported ≥14 mentally unhealthy days in the past month (3).

Children with mental health disorders are more likely to have chronic health conditions like asthma, diabetes and epilepsy and the disorders can also carry into adulthood, increasing risk for decreased productivity, substance use and injury and substantial costs both to the individual and society.

A public health concern

In recent years there has been an alarming number of school shootings with youth or adults involved, who are seriously mentally disturbed. There is also an increase in suicides and mental pathology in the military, in fact many professionals perceive that the increase in psychiatric drugs negatively impacts our population.

On December 14, 2012, Adam Lanza, a shy, bright 20-year old murdered 27 people (most of them children), including his mother and himself. The toxicology report from his autopsy has been withheld, but close friends of Adam's mother indicated that he was taking one or more psychotropic drugs to manage issues related to emotional disturbance.

Since 1982, 61 mass murders involving firearms have occurred throughout the United States and if you would investigate all the cases you will find that most of the murderers were taking psychiatric medications or withdrawing from them.

American soldiers have never been more medicated than they are today with about 20% of active-duty military taking medications the military considers "high risk" for suicide. From 2001 to 2009, the Army's suicide rate increased more than 150 percent while orders for psychiatric drugs rose 76 percent over the same period. In the first 155 days of 2012, 154 soldiers committed suicide—about one per day – compared to the 139 soldiers who died in combat in the same period.

With so much spend on psychotropic medication the question should be raised "why are people not getting better?" and with the increase in suicide during treatment and even violent episodes "is the medication doing something we still do not understand and comprehend?" and should we change mental health intervention from medication to psychotherapy?

A need for surveillence

Not only for children, but for the whole population, we need standard case definitions of mental disorders to ensure comparability and reliability of estimates across surveillance systems and better documentation of the prevalence of mental disorders.

More comprehensive surveillance is needed to develop a public health approach that will both help prevent mental disorders and promote mental health and also relate mental health disorders to chronic disease and disability.

References

[1] World Health Organization. Strengthening mental health promotion. Geneva: World Health Organization, Fact sheet 220, 2001.

[2] US Department of Health and Human Services. Mental health: A report of the Surgeon General. Rockville, MD: US Department Health Human Services, Substance Abuse Mental Health Services Administration, Center Mental Health Services, National Institutes Health, National Institute Mental Health, 1999.

[3] Perou R, Bitsko RH, Blumberg SJ, Pastor P, Ghandour RM, Gfroerer JC, et al. Mental health surveillance among children. United States, 2005–2011. MMWR Suppl 2013;62(02):1-35.

SECTION ONE:
MENTAL HEALTH ISSUES

In: Mental Health from an International Perspective
Editors: J. Merrick, S. Aspler and M. Morad
ISBN: 978-1-62948-519-5

Chapter 2

Mental health policy development

Said Shahtahmasebi, PhD*

School of HealthCentre for Health and Social Practice, WINTEC, Hamilton, New Zealand, Good Life Research Centre Trust, Rangiora, New Zealand and Division of Adolescent Medicine, Kentucky Children's Hospital, University of Kentucky College of Medicine, Lexington, Kentucky, United States of America

In recent years public wellbeing has been central to the mental health policy debates. Mental wellbeing is subjective and is dependent on individual traits, socio-economic, political and environmental factors. The question is whether or not the policy development process is able to translate subjective wellbeing into appropriate policies. In this chapter, I explore policy documents on mental health from WHO, New Zealand, United Kingdom and Australia and discuss the policy ideology in relation to evidence for policy action. Method: An internet search for mental health policy documents retrieved documents on mental health policy from WHO, United Kingdom, Australia and New Zealand. Results: The documents were analysed for their policy statements and recommended actions. Discussion: I argue that there is always an unresolvable conflict between policy statements and policy actions due to often subjective public wellbeing and the complex interactions of the many variables affecting human behaviour and decision making (e.g., politics, economy, and social). Therefore, it is plausible that objective and clinical scales e.g., rates of morbidity, mortality, services utilization, and a variety of clinical scales measuring mental wellbeing should be used to measure public quality of life and wellbeing. This is a highly contentious issue requiring a clinical interventional approach which translates into an increase in psychiatric and mental health intervention services. Conclusion: We can expect well-intended policies to be translated into 'more of the same' policy actions, when evidence-based information is lacking.

* *Correspondence:* Said Shahtahmasebi, PhD, Director; The Goodlife Research Centre Trust, 975A South Eyre Road, RD 1, Rangiora. New Zealand. E-mail: radisolevoo@gmail.com.

Introduction

The World Health Organisation (WHO) defines mental health as 'a state of well-being in which every individual realizes his or her own potential, can cope with the normal stresses of life, can work productively and fruitfully, and is able to make a contribution to her or his community'. WHO is appealing to countries to increase their support for mental health services. The appeal, which was published in the Lancet (1), see also http://www.who.int/mental_health/en/), is part of a series of six reviews on global mental health. Policy statements made by various governments post WHO's appeal may resonate the core element of the appeal and place a higher emphasis on mental health. For example, in the UK, the government recently launched its mental health care policy entitled 'no health without mental health' (2). While, in New Zealand, the Commission for Mental Health tendered a literature review (3) and the Mental Health Foundation of New Zealand based their strategy vision for 2009-15 entirely on the premise that 'flourishing' people do better in life (4). However, such documents commonly tend to present a simplistic but deterministic view of cause and effect. For example, a statement may declare that increasing access to mental health services will lead to a higher service uptake and therefore will improve outcomes for a particular mental health issue. In this context, 'access' is multi-dimensional and can be related to physical and geographical factors (e.g., transport), and the appropriateness of services being offered. Thus, the terminology and the language of the strategy documents may imply an elective approach to policy development, where, supporting information is sought subsequent to the policy implementation (5).

One of the main issues in the context of evidence-based decision making is the role of information. What constitutes evidence? Who decides which information can be classed as evidence and which to ignore? Can the public's overall wellbeing be clinically contextualised and determined? In this chapter, I argue that 'evidence' and 'knowledge' should be critically assessed, and policy formation needs to be informed by a *broader range* of evidence rather than selectively. Therefore, a fresh approach to policy development is well overdue.

Background

Mental health problems are prevalent in the general population with 20% of New Zealanders experiencing a mental disorder at any one time (6). This figure is much higher for specific populations such as youth, Maori and Pacific Peoples. According to WHO (7), prevalence is increasing, and by 2020, depression will be the most common long term disability worldwide.

Mental health issues are poorly understood, and as many as 60% of people experiencing a mental health issue do not have their problems recognized: as many as 80% of people with alcohol issues remain untreated (6). Suicide rates in New Zealand are unacceptably high when compared with other OECD countries.

Furthermore, 36% of people presenting to GP (General Practitioner) surgeries in New Zealand meet the criteria for mental disorder at the time of consultation (8). Many mental health problems can be treated effectively within primary care, however, there are a number of barriers to accessing primary care which need to be addressed. They include, but are not limited to, cost to the service user, stigma, lack of understanding about mental health issues from both community and clinicians, lack of culturally appropriate models of care and lack of time within a fee for service model (9) .

In some health care systems, primary care is the gateway to secondary and clinical care services. The Evaluation of Primary Mental Health Initiatives (10) suggests evidence that funding primary mental health initiatives produces significant improvement in health outcomes for people experiencing mild to moderate mental health issues. However, primary care clinicians still require both the opportunity to upskill around the management of mental health issues and need more support from specialist mental health clinicians. The consequences of undiagnosed or unnoticed mental illness on the economy are also reported in the literature e.g., loss of productivity, long-term unemployment, and premature retirement e.g., see (11). The economic aspect of mental health is frequently acknowledged by various governments. For example, the New Zealand Government (12), quotes results from a study by The London School of Economics which appears to demonstrate that any funding spent to increase the availability of evidence-based talking therapies will pay for itself.

The dynamics of policy formation may influence the outcome through a feedback effect i.e., the policy, its implementation and its outcome(s). The issues relevant to policy development and analysis appear to be around the definition and the identification and *critical* assessment of the evidence (13). Often, evidence obtained in a clinical setting will not be appropriate evidence in a social or primary care environment (13). There is no real value in review after review of the literature to inform policy if 'evidence' is frequently misunderstood and mis-interpreted. As the gate keepers, primary health care services must be concerned about the factors or parameters that are most likely to govern 'health' and be preventative in nature. In this chapter, I explore policy documents on mental health from WHO, New Zealand, the United Kingdom (UK) and Australia and discuss the policy ideology in relation to evidence for policy action. Whilst it would be interesting to know what kind of mental disorders are most prevalent in the population, the focus of this discussion is on the approach and attitude to mental health service development.

Review

In this chapter it is assumed that governments, following a consultation process, produce a policy document stating the direction of mental health care provisions. Often, policy documents contain statements of intent (policy statements) that are translated into priority areas with recommended actions (policy actions). Clearly, policies developed by any government will be specific to the needs of their population but there will be variations in health outcomes between the socio-economic groups. The WHO's work, in the main, has focused on harmonising health care delivery to reduce variations in health outcomes due to poverty. It is, therefore, plausible to assume that WHO's role in health policy development may be as a trend setter: different governments may take notice or be influenced by WHO's work to develop policies that are aimed at reducing gaps in health outcomes due to socio-economic variations in populations.

In this context, I am interested in exploring published intention of policy action in the context of published policy statements. I am not interested in the version retold by policy analysts working in governments or private policy units. In other words, I am interested in the relevance of the language/syntax used within the strategy documents to indicate policy intentions and actions. The intention of this discussion is to review national policy documents that have been developed after a call for a policy change. In this case, policy documents released following WHO's appeal to countries to increase their support for mental health services. A full critique of mental health policy documents from English speaking countries is beyond the scope of this chapter. Therefore, to stimulate discussion in this area, the review was limited to New Zealand (NZ), Australia and United Kingdom (UK).

Document access

The simplest and easiest method of accessing policy documents independently is via the internet. The following government internet sites were visited: www.dh.gov.uk, http://www.health.gov.au, http://www.mentalhealth.org.nz, and http://www.who.int/mental_health.

Document analysis

Documents were analysed in terms of the relationship between the strategy policy statement and the action policy. In this context the analytical method was to examine the policy documents for the language/syntax they used to express justification for their stated intents and the actions recommended to achieve the outcomes.

Findings

The Global Mental Health movement was launched in September 2007, London, UK amid rising concerns that despite the attention that is paid to mental health in western countries mental illness is neglected and deeply stigmatised (1). WHO's appeal to the world to invest more to support mental health services was part of six reviews on global mental health which was published in the Lancet (1). Based on its definition of mental health, through the project Mental health Improvements Nations (MIND) WHO supports countries to develop and implement programs that effectively deliver mental health services to all people who need them. The MIND project has four thematic areas: action in countries; mental health policy and service development; mental health and human rights and legislation; mental health and poverty and development (mental health core to planning) (http://www.who.int/mental_health/policy/en/). The assumption, here, is that WHO is setting direction for global mental health policy and service planning.

The UK Government's mental health strategy 'no health without mental health' (2) published in 2011 has proposed six objectives with a promise of a shared vision with partner agencies and across government departments for mental health. The objectives include: more people will have good mental health; more people with mental health problems will recover; more people with mental health problems will have good physical health; more people will have a positive experience of support and care; fewer people will suffer avoidable harm; fewer people will experience stigma and discrimination.

The Australian strategy for mental health is a commitment to improve the lives of people with mental illness. It aims to promote the mental health of the Australian community; to reduce the impact of mental disorder on individuals; to promote recovery from mental illness; and, to assure the rights of people with mental illness (14). The Australian strategy, which was endorsed in 2008 (14), declares five priority areas: 'Social inclusion and recovery; Prevention and early intervention; Service access, coordination and continuity of care; Quality improvement and innovation; and, Accountability - measuring and reporting progress'.

The New Zealand action plan is more direct and to the point (15). In the foreword, the Associate Minister of Health declares the Government's ongoing commitment to better access to mental health and addiction services that address the health needs of the people they serve. The Associate Minister goes on to suggest that clinical networks would be fundamental to achieving this commitment. The strategy proposes four priority areas with an action plan for each area. These areas are: increase access to mental health and addiction services; enhance communities' mental health and wellbeing; tackling alcohol and other drug related harm; integrating efforts across government.

A common trend in the approach to mental health is evident from the mental health strategy documents. These strategies appear to place the emphasis on the wellbeing of their respective populations in their strategy documents. However, this raises a number of issues.

Discussion

One of the major issues with the above strategies is translating public 'wellbeing' into a plan of action. Wellbeing is a state of mind that is influenced by individual characteristics and circumstances, which are, in turn, governed by other socio-economic, socio-political and socio-environmental parameters. Furthermore, wellbeing is relative to other individual and social standards and norms (16) e.g., elderly people assessing their own health as good/all right despite poor health (17). Therefore, an individual's and society's notion of wellbeing will change over time with or without changes in an individual's circumstances or the social environment. The net effect of attempting to achieve 'more people with good mental health (2)' will be on how outcomes are measured e.g., the inclusion of a mental health scale in the census to measure population mental health outcomes (2). In other words, inevitably a clinical approach to measuring 'wellbeing' outcomes will be employed. Therefore, the first priority together with the remaining priority areas which are related to accessibility to mental health services and interventional care, impress a clinical approach to a set of subjective but well motivated objectives.

The Australian strategy and New Zealand strategy documents approaches to improving public mental health are not too dissimilar. The Australian strategy was first implemented in 1992 and boasted priority areas of social inclusion, recovery, prevention and access to services. This strategy was endorsed in 2008 to continue to 2014 (14). The latest report on the progress since 1992, over and above the increases in financial expenditure on mental health services, suggests that epidemiological and survey studies were also undertaken including a repeat survey in 2007 (18). Interestingly, a study by the Australian Department of Health and Aging reported: 'The findings from these surveys highlighted that mental health issues reach into the fabric of Australian society, and for many, into our own families. As in other Western countries, mental illness is common in the Australian population.' ((18), page 25). The findings of the report are very serious, and raise questions about the effectiveness of increased *access* to clinical interventions in order to prevent and treat mental ill health.

Similarly, the focus of the New Zealand strategy documents is for all New Zealanders to lead longer, healthier and more independent lives. Unsurprisingly, the projected actions needed to achieve this are merely by increasing/improving access to interventional clinical services e.g., 'moving health resources to increase access to mental health and addiction services and improve health outcomes'. Very clearly, taken for granted is the assumption that increased access to mental health services will lead to commensurate improvements in health outcomes.

There is confusion, however, about the population. For the New Zealand strategy, the action plan to improve wellbeing is seen as improving access to mental health services for all New Zealanders when they need it. This means either operating an impressive model that anticipates incidence of mental illness or an ambitious plan that places clinical intervention in every home. In other words, we may expect an increase in the number of specialist clinics – unsurprisingly this is a stated outcome. So does the word 'population' refer to the entire population or those who at any given time have mental health issues? It appears that the New Zealand authorities are preparing to respond to a symptom rather than preventative preparation by providing more of the same interventional clinical care. An action plan that aims to increase services for the main purpose of improving access to them is an interventional plan within the framework of a clinical care philosophy. Often, the incidence and prevalence of mental health issues have been associated with access to interventional services. This assumption appears to be based on the shortfalls in other aspects of health care. For example, the lack of service uptake has been associated with socio-economic background of individuals as well as their residential area (19, 20), and, with GPs and primary care services not being equipped to diagnose mental illness (21-23). Indeed, some have called for improved access to clinical services for those in low socio-economic groups e.g., (24) and upskilling GPs to better recognise mental health issues e.g., (25,26). The assumption of a strong correlation between a lack of service uptake and access to services indicates a clinical approach to a mental health strategy and action plan. Access to services may be improved through increased service provision. However, service uptake will only improve if service provision is relevant and appropriate to the needs of the population. Thus, it is not wise to assume that overall wellbeing of the population will improve as stated in the strategy documents.

Inferential statements are common syntax used within strategy documents to justify a proposed action. For example, the following statement infers mental health problems are due to a lack of access which will be improved by redistributing resources: 'improving the wellbeing of all New Zealanders by moving health resources to increase access to mental health services'. The assumption of a causal link between a policy statement and a desired outcome appears to have caused confusion in the developing of strategies for mental health in New Zealand. The strategy document on mental health information (27) declares ten priority areas for the period 2005 to 2010 and signals a shift in emphasis from information collection to local and national use of mental health information. It is not clear how this shift will lead to desired mental health outcomes in particular when issues relevant to information are still unresolved, e.g., what constitute information. Furthermore, the whole philosophy behind the shift appears flawed because of the conflict between data utilisation and most of the stated priority areas which require data collection. For example, most of the identified priority areas such as 'Extend the coverage of mental health data to primary health care', and 'Fill data gaps and improve quality data' involve data collection.

The importance of information and other issues including the creation of a *unified* database to assist with ill-health prevention are discussed elsewhere (28, 29). Furthermore, the New Zealand suicide prevention strategy 2006-16 (30) declared seven goals. These goals include:

- Promote mental health and well-being, and prevent mental health problems
- Improve the care of people who are experiencing mental disorders associated with suicidal behaviour
- Improve the care of people who make non-fatal suicide attempts
- Reduce access to the means of suicide
- Promote the safe reporting and portrayal of suicidal behaviour by the media
- Support families/whānau, friends and others affected by a suicide or suicide attempt
- Expand the evidence about the rates, causes and effective interventions.

These goals, although commendable and impressive, are highly complex and, therefore, vague in terms of measurement outcomes due to policy actions. For example, the first goal suggests at least three areas for action: to promote mental health, to promote wellbeing, and prevent mental health problems. There are actions that individuals, families and communities can take to improve and maintain a reasonable level of wellbeing. There are actions that governments can take through health and social policies, law and order policies, economy and environmental policies to create an environment conducive for individuals/families decision making. Promotion of mental health and wellbeing could be interpreted as a series of media advertisements that mental illness is no longer a social taboo, encouraging the public to seek professional help. In other words, the check-box for the first goal can be ticked despite rising unemployment, a weak local and global economy, and unresolved law and order issues and so on. Two years after the launch of the suicide prevention strategy 2006-2016, the New Zealand Government launched its associated action plan 2008-2012 (31). The policy action document (31) proposes the following strategies to achieve the first goal: 'Strengthen mechanisms for interagency collaboration and co-operation to ensure that issues relating to suicide are recognised and incorporated into both policies and programmes, and their evaluation'; 'Develop structures to ensure that all policies and programmes are appropriate and effective for Maori'; 'Include a focus on reducing inequalities in policies and programmes that may contribute to suicide prevention'. The proposed strategies are equally vague. These strategies refer to complex human behaviour processes with inter-relating patterns and influences. Thus, it will be difficult to interpret the strategies into a series of actions to achieve the first goal, without sufficient insight into the dynamics of human behaviour.

It is not surprising that in 2013 the New Zealand government launched an action plan (2013-16, see http://www.health.govt.nz/our-work/mental-health-and-addictions/suicide-prevention/suicide-prevention-strategy-and-action-plans) based on the 2006-2016 suicide prevention strategy. The Action Plan includes actions designed to:

- address the impact of suicide on families, whānau and communities by strengthening support for family, whānau and communities
- build the evidence base, specifically around what works for Māori and Pasifika
- extend existing services, specifically addressing geographical gaps in the coverage of services
- strengthen suicide prevention targeted to high risk populations who are in contact with agencies.

The action plan (2013-16) was published one year after the expiry of the previous action plan (2008-2012), and eighteen months after the intervention by the Chief Coroner (32) calling for new suicide prevention methods. As it can be envisaged above, the new action plan offers very little new or different action to previous action plan and basically offers 'more of the same'. The action plan (2013-16) does not address suicide prevention. By suggesting the above actions, e.g., to build evidence-base around what works, and targeting high risk populations, the strategy and the action plan (2013-16) are completely oblivious to suicide trends and temporal dependencies due to health and social policies such as the aforementioned suicide prevention policies (33). In other words, suicide rates appear to follow a cyclic trend with added complexities that there are lagging effects in suicide trends of various groups (e.g., different age groups, males, females). For example, in New Zealand male suicide rates on average appear almost a full cycle ahead of the female rates, so when the male suicide rate is high, the female suicide rate is low.

On the other hand, the relationship between mental health and suicide is vague. For example, there is ample evidence to suggest that more than two-thirds of suicide cases do not come into contact with mental health services and do not have a psychiatric record (34-36). It is not clear why *access* to mental health services is more important than access to *appropriate* mental health services. In other words, why does such a large proportion of suicide cases *avoid* seeking help (also see (37-41)). One possibility is that the *uncritical* use of research/evidence has informed the development of strategies and action plans. For example, in suicide research, Beautrais (42-44) claims that depression and mental illness are the causes of suicide, Khan et al. (45) claim that antidepressants do not reduce suicide and may increase the risk of suicide while Hall et al. (46) claim that antidepressants reduces suicide rates. A critical assessment may reveal that these studies have failed to address the methodological issues related to the design, data collection and analysis, thus resulting in misleading conclusions (41). Interestingly, prescription data for New Zealand over the last twelve years suggests that prescriptions for antidepressants had increased four-fold and yet suicide rates over the same period maintained an upward trend (33).

Moreover, the Mental Health Foundation of New Zealand's (4) overall goal is 'building a society where all people flourish'. The strategy document's main focus is 'flourishing'. The strategy document stresses that flourishing is more than an absence of mental illness: 'flourishing requires certain positive qualities in one's life to be cultivated over time, and within conducive social and political environments'. The strategy intends to conduct initiatives to raise the profile of 'flourishing' and its benefits to our mental health. The documents provide no discussion of what constitute 'flourishing' and how it will be measured, and therefore, how much reliance could be placed on its reported relationship, if any, with health outcomes. Like 'wellbeing', 'flourishing' is a complex subjective process outcome and dynamic. For example, a post suicide description of an adolescent suicide case as being happy, popular with peers and a high achiever (both in sport and academically) with no sign of physical or mental ill health (36) could be interpreted as a flourishing person.

It seems, therefore, that the lesson is only partly learnt in that the authorities can always find 'new' buzz words to describe an intention to do 'good'. In terms of action, the strategies appear to have led to more funding to do more of the same: more clinical interventional services. The approach of having more interventional services without appropriate preventional services may not work in preventing mental ill health and may actually exacerbate it (47).

Whichever spin is put on the approach to mental health the problems appear to be associated with translating a strategy (the buzz words) into actions. One explanation may be the suggestion that all is not well in the health sectors across the world (48). Given that strategy policies are developed to make the health sectors well again, the problem may lie with *vagueness* in the process of policy development. Experience and anecdotal evidence suggest that the national strategy policy documents are taken as template for local strategy. As mentioned earlier, policy statements, such as 'improving everyone's quality of life', are often broad and refer to human behaviour. One of the main issues is related to the measurement of policy outcomes. Commonly, ill-health outcomes are used as proxy for public well-being and quality of life such as aiming to lower mortality and morbidity rates. Often action may be quantified in terms of the number of GPs, hospital beds and resources, and the number of expected patients. In other words, the underlying principles for any policy action appear to be clinical intervention. For example, in the early 1990s the UK government identified health priority areas and introduced the Health of the Nation Targets (49). Experience suggests that the actions that followed the UK's White Paper included the creation of many 'Health of the Nation Targets' committees and sub-committees and the translation of national targets into local targets by the regional and district health authorities (e.g., see (50, 51)). The setting of targets for health outcomes suggests a clinical approach of intervention which emphasised the role of intervention being necessary in order to achieve the targets. In other words, the stakeholders lost a huge opportunity to gain additional insight into the process of disease development in order to inform the process of policy development. One of the outcomes of this era was the trend for practice and decision making to be 'evidence-based'. However, even evidence-based practice has become synonymous with clinical practice in the form of randomised clinical trials (RCT) which is of little value in non-clinical settings (13).

Similarly, in New Zealand, the Waikato District Health Board's vision is 'improving the health, independence and quality of life for the communities it serves by addressing the needs of the population and reducing health disparities' (52). This is translated into a five point action plan that Health Waikato Mental Health and Addictions Service will: 1) implement a recovery approach in practice; 2) be safe and effective; 3) be transparent and trustworthy; 4) provide culturally responsive services; 5) build leadership, recruit and retain a skilled workforce. Clearly, a 'recovery' based policy action implies the incidence and prevalence of mental illness, for which clinical interventions will be recommended. However, adapting interventional services to prevent ill-health will not be without adverse consequences. This means that preventional policies will attempt to intervene on assumed causal symptoms or precursors. For example, the prescribing of antidepressants has been common in suicide prevention including very young children (some under one year old) (37).

Conclusion

Beautiful words describing well intentioned public policies are not sufficient by themselves to do public good. National or public 'well-being' is a complex and subjective goal that will describe the wellbeing of a nation as a whole and thus will be governed by micro- and macro-economic, environmental, cultural and beliefs, health and social wellbeing while continuously under the influence from similar processes internationally. It is positive thinking to utilise the notion into developing a health strategy and the Office of National Statistics (UK) is carrying out public consultation on how to measure wellbeing (see http://www.ons.gov.uk/well-being). Given the dynamics of human behaviour and current world economic and environmental concerns, it will be difficult to measure public quality of life and any impact on public mental health and general health. Predictably, proxy measures such as the rate of morbidity and mortality and service uptake will be interpreted as a lack of access to mental health services and more services will be recommended as in the suicide prevention strategy in the US military (39, 40). However, these health outcomes are likely to be the influence of previous strategies and policies on the dynamics of human behaviour. If this is the case, we will have lost another fantastic opportunity to increase our insight into holistic health and/or ill-health development so that our health services will be more efficient and more sustainable.

However, in practice, given the current world economic status, increasing unemployment rates both in the UK and New Zealand and the respective Government's political conservative ideology, the beautifully worded strategies will translate into more of the same. In other words, actions from the strategy will include an increase in counselling, psychiatric units and so on, and a 'wellbeing' measure will be used to monitor improvements in mental health through increased access to mental health services.

Politics is one of the most important key processes in human behaviour that can help describe the bigger picture. Politics can also mean red-tape at higher levels of governance and conflict at the agency and individual level. For example, the establishment of a suicide prevention interagency steering group is the milestone/measure for the action 'strengthen the mechanisms for interagency collaboration...' (31). Politics, at least in part, also plays an important role in how policy statements are translated into actions. However, politics is also responsible, at least in part, for current health and social outcomes: committees or groups on their own are insufficient and ineffective in particular in an environment where continuous evaluation is absent (48). The possible adverse effects of past social, economic and health policies on health outcomes, e.g., through unemployment, has not been acknowledged. However, due to political processes the role of socio-economic, e.g., employment status, has only recently been acknowledged in the UK's mental health strategy (2). Therefore, by default, current mental health outcomes can be assumed to be partly due to past policy actions.

Operating within the framework of a 'clinical' philosophy is the main hurdle in developing effective preventional services that address the concerns that have given rise to strategy directions, such as 'Better, Sooner, More Convenient' (53) and 'no health without mental health' (2). The main issue is not clinical services but their appropriateness and effectiveness to prevent mental illness.

An interesting avenue for future research would be a time series analysis of policy documents from different countries. A time series study design would allow comparison of policy intent with policy action over time, between successive governments and as well as between countries. Such a study will assist identifying patterns in policy development through the time series memory (i.e., past behaviour predict future behaviour). The time series memory can be contextual (i.e., behaviour that will lead to more of the same) or historical (i.e., ability to self-learn). If a large time series study results in contextual memory, as suggested in this chapter, then this may mean that policy development process is not being informed by evidence other than past policy documentations. In this context, strategy policy titles such as 'Better, Sooner, More Convenient' and 'no health without mental health' or 'evidence-based practice/decision making' have no real meaning; for the service developers and providers it is business as usual. This chapter is about highlighting the dynamics of interpreting a policy statement for a policy action. In this context, the study is limited to policy documents that were publicly available at the time of the writing of this chapter. The critique of policy documents is based on an examination of the language/syntax used within policy documents. The suggested conflict is between a policy statement and a policy action that infers it will significantly improve public 'mental health' and 'wellbeing'. Health care services are used after an illness occurs. Furthermore, government priorities and policies change at every general election. Thus, public wellbeing measured by the number of patients utilising a health care service is very different to a reduced service uptake due to lowered incidence of illness. The latter is more relevant to the whole population while the former refers to the patient population. The implications of this study are for future research, policy development, and service planning that promotes health.

Indeed, despite strong opposition by authorities a number of community suicide prevention initiatives have been developed that promote a grassroots approach e.g., see (33, 54). In Australia, too, the idea of a combination of community development and public/population health to suicide prevention has attracted attention. Indeed, this was the conclusion of an evaluation of the youth suicide prevention strategy in Australia in the late 90's and early 2000's, "Valuing Young Lives" conducted by Dr. Penny Mitchell at the *Australian Institute of Family Studies*, 2000. The Australian *LIFE Framework* acknowledges this, as does the current national strategy (55).

References

[1] Lancet. Global mental health. URL: http://www.thelancet.com/series/global-mental-health.

[2] Department of Health. No health without mental health: A cross-government mental health outcomes strategy for people of all ages. London: HM Government 2011.

[3] Mental Health Commission. Request for proposal: Literature review: December 9-22. Wellington, NZ: Mental Health Commission, 2010.

[4] Mental Health Foundation of New Zealand. Strategic approach 2010-15. URL: http://www.mentalhealth.org.nz/file/Publications/mhf-strategic-approach-web-23-11-10.pdf.

[5] Short S. Elective affinities: Research and health policy development. In: Gardner H. Health policy in Australia. Melbourne: Oxford University Press, 1997.

[6] Mental Health Commission (MHC). Mental notes. New Zealand 2010. URL: http://www.mhc.govt.nz/sites/mhc.govt.nz/files/Mental%20Notes%July%202010.pdf.

[7] WHO. Mental health: Depression. World Health Organisation; 2011. URL: http://www.who.int/mental_health/management/depression/definition/en/.

[8] MaGPIE Research Group. The nature and prevalence of psychological problems in New Zealand primary healthcare: A report on mental health and general practice investigation (magpie). NZ Med J 2003;116:1171.

[9] NZGG. Identification of common mental disorders and management of depression in primary care. Wellington: New Zealand Guidelines Group, 2008.

[10] Ministry of Health. Evaluation of the primary mental health initiatives: Summary report 2008. Wellington: Ministry of Health, 2009.

[11] Insel TR. Assessing the economic costs of serious mental illness. Am J Psychiatry 2008;165(6):663.

[12] Ministry of Health. Towards optimal primary mental health care in the new primary care environment: A draft guidance paper. Wellington: Ministry of Health, 2009.

[13] Shahtahmasebi S, Villa L, Nielsen H, Graham-Smith H. Proposal of a holistic model to support local-level evidence-based practice. Scientific World Journal 2010;10:1520-9.

[14] Department of Health and Ageing. Fourth national mental health plan: An agenda for collaborative government action in mental health 2009-2014. Canberra: Commonwealth of Australia, 2009.

[15] Ministry of Health. Mental health and addiction action plan 2010 Wellington: Ministry of Health, 2010.

[16] Diener E, Fujita F. Social comparisons and subjective well-being. Health, coping, and well-being. In: Buunk BP, FX Gibbons. Health, coping, and well-being: Perspectives from social comparison theory. Mahwah, NJ: Lawrence Erlbaum, 1997:329–57.

[17] Shahtahmasebi S, Davies R, Wenger C. A longitudinal analysis of factors related to survival in old age. Gerontologist 1992;333:404-13.

[18] Department of Health and Ageing. National mental health report 2010: Summary of 15 years of reform in Australia's mental health services under the national mental health strategy 1993-2008. Canberra: Commonwealth of Australia, 2010.

[19] Haines MM, McMunn A, Nazroo JY, Kelly YJ. Social and demographic predictors of parental consultation for child psychological difficulties. J Public Health 2002;24(4):276.

[20] Maheswaran R, Pearson T, Jordan H, Black D. Socioeconomic deprivation, travel distance, location of service, and uptake of breast cancer screening in north Derbyshire, UK. J Epidemiol Commun Health 2006;60(3):208.

[21] Afana A, Dalgard OS, Bjertness E, Grunfeld B. The ability of general practitioners to detect mental disorders among primary care patients in a stressful environment: Gaza strip. J Public Health 2002;24(4):326.

[22] Biddle L, Donovan JL, Gunnell D, Sharp D. Young adults' perceptions of gps as a help source for mental distress: A qualitative study. Br J Gen Pract 2006;56(533):924.

[23] Shaw K, Wagner I, Eastwood H, Mitchell G. A qualitative study of Australian GPs' attitudes and practices in the diagnosis and management of attention-deficit/hyperactivity disorder (ADHD). Fam Pract 2003;20(2):129.

[24] Lorant V, Kunst AE, Huisman M, Costa G, Mackenbach J. Socio-economic inequalities in suicide: A European comparative study. Br J Psychiatry 2005;187(1):49.

[25] Boyd C, Aisbett D, Howard A, Filiades T. Detection and management of eating disorders by general practitioners in regional Australia. Adv Ment Health 2007;6(2):101-6.

[26] Malcolm H. A primary mental health care model for rural Australia: Outcomes for doctors and the community. Aust J Rural Health 2000;8(3):167-72.

[27] Ministry of Health. National mental health information strategy 2005-2010 Wellington: Ministry of Health, 2005.

[28] Shahtahmasebi S. Researching health service information systems development. In: Dwivedi A. Handbook of research on it management and clinical data administration in healthcare. Hershey: IGI Publishing, 2008:598-615.

[29] Shahtahmasebi S, & Millar R. A discussion of the future of health informatics. International Journal of Information Science (IJIS) 2013;3(3):70-9. DOI:10.5923/j.ijis.20130303.04.

[30] Associate Minister of Health. The New Zealand suicide prevention strategy 2006-2016. Wellington: Ministry of Health, 2006.

[31] Ministry of Health. New Zealand suicide prevention action plan 2008-2012: The summary for action. Wellington: Ministry of Health, 2008.

[32] Chief Coroner. Chief coroner releases nz suicide statistics. URL: http://www3newsconz/Chief-Coroner-releases-NZ-suicide-statistics/tabid/423/articleID/223638/Defaultaspx 2011;26 August.

[33] Shahtahmasebi S. De-politicizing youth suicide prevention. Front Pediatr 2013;1(8).

[34] Hamdi E, Price S, Qassem T, Amin Y, Jones D. Suicides not in contact with mental health services: Risk indicators and determinants of referral. J Ment Health 2008;17(4):398-409.

[35] Shahtahmasebi S. Suicides by mentally ill people. Scientific World Journal 2003;3:684-93.

[36] Shahtahmasebi S. Suicides in New Zealand. Scientific World Journal 2005;5:527-34.

[37] Shahtahmasebi S. Suicide research and adolescent suicide trends in New Zealand. Scientific World Journal 2008;8:287-302.

[38] Shahtahmasebi S. Can suicide be quantified and categorised? In: Sher L. Internet and suicide. New York: Nova Science, 2008:373-90.

[39] Shahtahmasebi S. Suicide prevention in a top-down society. In: Sher L, A Vilens. Suicide in the military. New York: Nova Science, 2009:121-36.

[40] Shahtahmasebi S. War, massive social change and suicide. In: Sher L. War and suicide. New York: Nova Science, 2009:27-42.

[41] Shahtahmasebi S, Shahtahmasebi R. A holistic view of suicide: Social change and education and training. J Altern Med Res 2010;2(1):115-28.

[42] Beautrais AL. Serious suicide attempts in young people: A case control study [PhD]. Christchurch: Christchurch School of Medicine, 1996.

[43] Beautrais AL. Suicides and serious suicide attempts: Two populations or one? Psychol Med 2001;31:837-45.

[44] Beautrais AL, Joyce PR, Mulder RT. The canterbury suicide project: Aims, overview and progress. Commun Ment Health NZ 1994;8(2):32-9.

[45] Khan A, Warner HA, Brown WA. Symptom reduction and suicide risk in patients treated with placebo in antidepressant clinical trials: An analysis of the food and drug administration database. Arch Gen Psychiatry 2000;57:311-7.

[46] Hall WD, Mant A, Mitchell PB, Rendle VA, Hickie IB, McManus P. Association between antidepressant prescribing and suicide in australia, 1991-2000: Trend analysis. BMJ 2003;326.

[47] Shahtahmasebi S, van den Berg L, Hermann F. What do you do when no health and social agency wants to care for you? Int J Child Health Hum Dev 2010;forthcoming.

[48] Jackson D, Darbyshire P. People not paper: Challenging document dependence and audit addiction in contemporary health care. J Clin Nurs 2011;20(3-4):301-2.

[49] Department of Health. The health of the nation: A strategy for health in England. London: HMSO, 1992.

[50] Bensely D, Shahtahmasebi S, Merrick D, Fryers P, Fryers PT. A census based view of the population and its health - statistical review. Harrogate: Yorkshire Regional Health Authority, 1994.

[51] Bensley D, Shahtahmasebi S, Fryers P, Merrick M. The health of the nation targets - first steps. Statistical Review, Public Health Report, Yorkshire Regional Health Authority 1993.

[52] Health Waikato Mental Health and Addiction Services. Strategic plan 2009-2014: Supporting people towards their own recovery. Waikato District Health Board 2009. URL: http://www.waikatodhb.govt.nz/file/fileid/16152.

[53] Ministry of Health New Zealand. Better, sooner, more convenient' primary health care. URL: http://www.moh.govt.nz/mohnsf/indexmh/phcs-bsmc 2009.

[54] Omar H. A model program for youth suicide prevention. Int J Adolesc Med Health 2005;17(3):275-8.

[55] Webster I. Appreciation of your recent article. Personal communication, 2013.

In: Mental Health from an International Perspective
Editors: J. Merrick, S. Aspler and M. Morad

ISBN: 978-1-62948-519-5

Chapter 3

Psychological well-being and life satisfaction among an adult population

Bruce D Kirkcaldy, MA, PhD, FBPsS*[*1], Adrian F Furnham, DPhil, DSc, DLitt[2] and Rainer G Siefen, MD, Dipl Psychol[3]

[1]International Centre for the Study of Occupational and Mental Health, Düsseldorf, Germany
[2]Department of Psychology, University College London, London, United Kingdom
[3]Department of Paediatrics, St Josef Hospital, Ruhr University Bochum, Bochum, Germany

1,276 European adults were administered a Checklist of Physical Complaints and an Inventory of Satisfaction with specific aspects of daily life and social relationships. Women were more anxious and complained more about diverse physical ailments, particularly tension headaches, sickness and nausea, mental fatigue, migraine, lack of appetite, muscular aches and pains and skin disorders than men. No gender differences were observed however, on chest pains, sexual problems and low/high blood pressure, nor were there any somatic ailments in which men reported higher scores than women. There were few gender differences in satisfaction on work and leisure issues with the exception of finances where women were significantly more satisfied than men. On all scales of social relationships e.g., working atmosphere, family and partnership, women yielded higher satisfaction scores than men. Specific somatic ailments were significant predictors of psychological health, explaining between 14-25% of the variance in health outcome variables for men and women. Overall, the association between somatic health and psychological ill-health was significant for both men and women, but tended to be more pronounced for women. The implications of these results are discussed within the framework of health and policy makers.

* Correspondence: Bruce David Kirkcaldy, MA, PhD, FBPsS, Haydnstr. 61, D-40593 Dusseldorf, Germany. E-mail: brucedavidkirkcaldy@yahoo.de.

Introduction

The *biopsychosocial* approach in medicine suggests we best understand chronic conditions by also understanding the patient, the physical, the social context of both *and* the health care system. We know about soma-psychic and psycho-somatic illness patients call for drugs and counselling. The healthy process occurs for three reasons according to this model: the self-healing properties of the body; the patient-doctor relationships; the medicines and treatments prescribed. Doctors offer cognitive, emotional and pharmaceutical care.

Historically physicians have always taken a patient's psyché (personality, beliefs, values) and their social circumstances and context into consideration when treating them. Osler, a great nineteenth century expert in internal medicine noted: "The good physician treats the disease but the great physician treats the patient who has the disease". Whilst the biopsychosocial approach to health and illness has always been articulated in one form or another the stunning success of pharmacotherapy over the last 20-30 years led to a resurgence of the *biomedical* model, which again is being challenged by the biopsychosocial model.

The biopsychosocial approach to health understands the nature/nurture interaction. It accepts conscious and unconscious influences on health and wellness. Most of all, it understands reciprocal determinism which accepts that social factors may influence psychological factors which change the psychological factors. In short it accepts that biological, psychological and social factors *all* play their part and interact to impact on health outcomes.

This study is primarily concerned with gender differences in physical, mental and social health. This topic has been one that has been addressed by specialists in many areas including anthropology (1, 2)) and psychology (3, 4). It is well known that there are sex differences in specific illnesses morbidity and that lay people also know this (5, 6).

A person's gender as well as their gender role orientation and attitudes have been key to understanding work, leisure and lifestyle effects on health (7). These differences occur for socio-cultural, economic and physiological reasons. Furthermore they can be determined very early. Sweeting and West (8) looked at health changes in over 2500 Scottish 11 to 15 year olds. They found that self-reported health deteriorated from age 11 and that the problems were greater for girls than boys. Girls reported more depression, 'malaise" headaches, stomach problems and dizziness than boys.

The 2002 EU report for health (9) revealed that almost one quarter (24%) of individuals reported very good health, 49% good health, 20% neither good or bad health, 6%bad health and 1% very bad health. The incidence of physical symptoms among the general European population is long-standing muscle, joint, bones ailments (22%), hypertension (22%), allergy (17%), migraine/headache (16%), chronic anxiety/depression (9%), asthma (7%), diabetes (6%), chronic bronchitis (5%), osteoporosis (5%), peptic/gastric ulcer (4%) and cancer (2%).The most frequent long term ailments that are expressed by patients are hypertension (36%), long standing trouble with muscles and joints (24%), diabetes (13%), chronic anxiety/depression (10%), asthma (9%), osteoporosis (8%), allergy (6%), migraine/headache (5%), cancer (4%) and peptic ulcers (3%).

Kirkcaldy et al. (10) reported rates of ailments among an adult German population attending medical care over the last six months: backaches (63.6%), headaches (55.7%), general fatigue (50.6%), mood swings (35.8%), sleeplessness (23.3%), constipation (14.2%), persistent colds (14.2%), eczema (13.6%), angina (9.7%), and gastric ulcers (8.0%). In a second article, Furnham and Kirkcaldy (11) explored gender differences in subjective reports of somatic complaints. Women displayed an average of 3.4 complaints in contrast to men 2.6, a difference which emerged as statistically significant. A detailed analysis revealed that 23.2% of men reported having headaches during the last 6 months, in contrast to 34.5% women. And 3.5% of men and 12.9% women have experienced constipation. General fatigue was also significantly more common among women (28.87%) than men (23.24%). Overall, more women than men reported physical ailments, more specifically psychosomatic complaints, a finding consistent with Clancy & Gove (12). However there is always the debate over whether this is a reporting issue vs. a physical issue. Women go to see their GP more often than men, and most take more of an interest in medical issues. There is some evidence that given the same acute and chronic symptoms women tend to seek more help and advice sooner and more comprehensively than men (5). Yet women seem to report higher happiness levels and life satisfaction scores than men. This has been explained in terms of women's social roles which specify more emotional responsiveness. The greater well-being among women was reported for married women compared to those living alone, although this benefit of married life on favourable well-being was less pronounced among men (13).

Clearly men and women show notable differences in the frequency and intensity of their reporting of their physical and mental health. This study intends to explore some of these differences in more detail.

Gender and life and social satisfaction

Sousa and Lyzmbomirsky (14) discuss the paradox of women displaying higher rates of depression than men, yet higher levels of (psychological) well-being. Moreover, studies generally show no gender differences in global life satisfaction (which appears primarily associated with cognitive assessment). They argued that women display a greater range of affect, both positive and negative, in terms of frequency and intensity. They further suggest that men and women differ in their source of life satisfaction. Drawing evidence from diverse studies it appears that social resources such as family and friends are more predictive of life satisfaction for women than men. In contrast, men's orientation towards personal goals e.g., athleticism, authorities, income and prominent ties, etc. were more related to life satisfaction and self-reported happiness.

In a recent Germany survey, Daig et al. (15) reported gender differences in domain-specific life satisfaction, revealing that women were more satisfied with their family life than men with men displaying more satisfaction in their leisure activities. They suggested this was consistent with other findings that life satisfaction in women is positively explained by perceived social support, with "Perceived availability of emotional support, reassurance, instrumental assistance, and companionship provided by social network partners such as a family have consistently been reported to be related to better life satisfaction" Daig et al. (15). Generally, women appear more susceptible to their social networks than are men. The authors further argue that the increased satisfaction of women in their family/social relationships may reflect traditional role concepts in which women are expected to expend more time in chid-rearing and family life in general. They further found age group differences in every life-satisfaction domain. And age x gender interaction emerged as significant in satisfaction with health, income and family life. Thus whilst there is evidence that there are numerous gender differences in health they interact with many other individual factors like age and socio-economic status.

Satisfaction and health: Age, marital and educational status

Diverse studies suggest that men benefit more from being married in terms of improved psychological health than women. Overall, married people tend to be happier and more satisfied than those who are divorced, unmarried or widowed, Moreover, there is evidence that unmarried men are less happy than unmarried women, indicating that men seem to get more out of a "secure relationship" such as marriage than women. Argyle (16) noted that women serve as better confidants and offer more secure social support than men.

Kalleberg and Loscocco (17) showed clear incremental changes in job satisfaction with increasing age. In a longitudinal study of life satisfaction over a 22 year period, Mroczek and Spiro (18) found both gains and losses could be observed: Life satisfaction increased up to the age of 65-70 years and thereafter diminished. Using growth-curve modelling, they found evidence of a complex, non-linear trend over time. They argued that impending death may be related to the decline in life satisfaction and this need not be due to a waning in physical health. The authors were cautious in warning that their sample had contained persons born between 1900-1945, a period marked by major societal upheavals such as the Great Depression, World War II and the Korean War. It remains speculative as to whether such a curvilinear trend would be found for later born populations.

In a recent German study, Beutel et al. (19), among a sample of just over 2500 women, life satisfaction and satisfaction with partnership and sexuality was found to decrease among the age group 50+. Life satisfaction was highest for the age group 31-40 years and declined among those aged 50 and over and was lowest among the 70+ age group. Satisfaction with health revealed a decline which began in early adulthood. Depression was highest in the oldest group whereas anxiety remained stable across ages. Life satisfaction was associated with resilience, presence of a partner/spouse, lower anxiety and depression, positive self-esteem, higher household income and religious affiliation. They further cite their work that age was related to increased physical ailments such as exhaustion, cardiovascular and musculoskeletal complaints, but not gastrointestinal ailments.

Daig et al. (15), they reported age x gender interactions for family life and partnership satisfaction. Women up to 30 years, and between 30 and 60 years of age, displayed more satisfaction with their family life than men. Conversely, men over sixty years showed greater satisfaction with their income than women, the latter displaying most "financial" satisfaction when they were under thirty or between 30-60 years. Diener and Suh (20) however, found little evidence that life satisfaction declines with age among some 40 nations.

On the other hand, a recent APA stress poll (21) revealed for the first time, that middle-aged men reported more stress – and presumably less satisfaction – regarding money, work and job stability compared to women. It has been argued that these gender differences may result from the current recession, with increasing layoffs in males dominated work domains such as manufacturing and industry (21).

Light et al. (22) found that those persons with higher educational status and higher income displayed higher satisfaction levels. Argyle (16) noted that in the United States among persons with high incomes education seems to have little difference on happiness (and presumably life satisfaction) but for those with low income it does. Campbell (23) has also shown that the better educated displayed greater happiness than persons with less, although this effect has declined over time. Education is a powerful predictor of job level, security and benefits which is often used as a proxy for socio-economic status.

This study which is part of a programmatic series focuses particularly on sex differences in mental and physical health in a representative European population sample. More specifically it addressed six big questions:

- What are the most prevalent physical ailments displayed among adults?
- Do men and women differ in their physical health problems?
- Are there any clear sex differences in the areas of personal, life and work satisfaction?
- To what extent do age differences moderate the impact of gender on health and life satisfaction?
- To what extent do socio-demographic variables e.g., educational status, marital status, gender and age determine physical and psychological ill-health?
- Are the somatic (ailment) determinants of "satisfaction with physical and psychological health" different for men and women?

Internet research

In a three month period, an internet exploratory research study was performed collating data from the new psychometric instrument. Recent studies suggest that comparative analyses about internet questionnaires reveal findings generalisable across presentation formats and not adversely affected by non-serious or repeat responders and produce results consistent with traditional methods of data collation (24). Internet certainly presents empirical researchers with tremendous opportunities for collecting large data bases on topics of contemporary interest (25). In addition to details of sickness during the last year, persons were required to respond on a 1-5 Likert scale the degree of endorsement of items associated with physical (somatic ailments) and psychological (emotions) health, satisfaction with specific areas of working and private life (family, partnership, work content, working relationships, physical health and mental health). The alpha-coefficients for the total scales were 0.85 for physical health, 0.93 for mental (ill-)health and 0.71 for life satisfaction. Moreover, a variety of questions were asked regarding socio-demographic data – age, gender, educational status, and marital status. The advantages of using an anonymous internet administration of questionnaires may allow us to get better estimates of actual compulsive thinking among European adult workers.

One of the difficulties inherent in such data collection involves the issue of the quality of such data. In order to ensure good quality data sets in this study, the data was double-screened, checked through visually and through descriptive analyses filtering out multiple responders and removing those respondents with incomplete data or those who exhibited obvious outliers or response sets. Individuals were provided with a special coded number after completion of the questionnaire enabling them to obtain their detailed profile scores if requested. Description statistics of the sample are provided in table below. Over a period of approximately 6 months, there were 1,275 persons who had completed the entire questionnaire in the complete sample. The average age was 35.54 years and average number of children – including those persons having "0" children - was 0.63 SD 0.99. The distribution of the demographic data and the size of the sample suggest that this data should yield meaningful and replicable results

Table 1. Description of sample. Socio-demographic factors

	%	n
Gender		
Male	65.8%	843
Female	34.2%	433
Age	Mean 35.54 SD 9.01	
<20 years	1.3%	16
21-30	34.0%	434
31-40	37.3%	476
41-50	20.4%	260
51-60	6.4%	82
>60 years	0.6%	8
Educational status		
Secondary	23.5%	298
GCE A level (12th grade)	22.3%	283
First degree	23.7%	300
Higher degree	24.0%	304
Other	6.5%	82
Marital status		
Single	30.6%	388
Married /cohabiting	61.7%	782
Divorced	4.3%	55
Separated	2.8%	36
Widowed	0.5%	6

Physical health

Figure 1 reveals the listing of all physical ailments and their frequency of occurrence. The most common ailment was backache, followed by muscular aches and pains, mental fatigue, sleeplessness, tension headaches and physical exhaustion. The least likely physical complaints were sickness/nausea, chest pains, allergies and migraine. These results are similar to those found in the EU report on health.

Table 2 shows the percentage of those reporting almost daily/weekly manifestation of physical ailments. Following this a detailed analysis of the sex differences was explored. An array of significant gender differences were observed with women reporting more frequent physical ill-health symptoms than males with the exception of chest pains, sexual problems and blood pressure disorders which were equivalent for men and women.

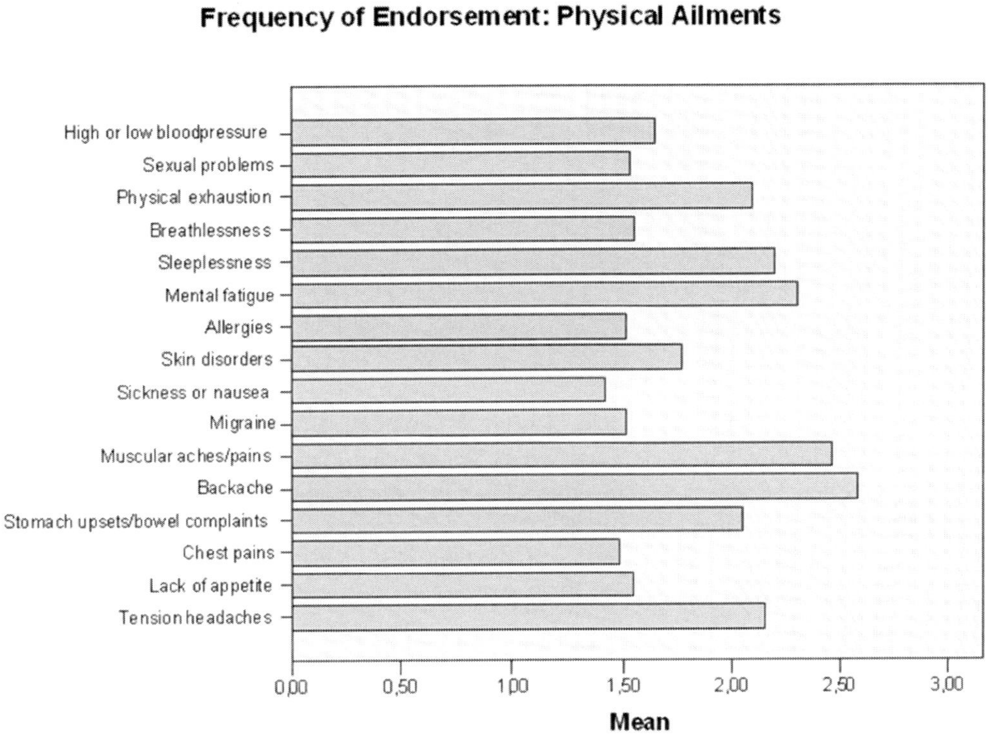

Figure 1. Incidence of somatic ailments.

Table 2. Frequency of physical ailments across gender

Physical ailments	% daily/weekly men	% daily/weekly women	Chi-squared
Tension headaches	11.0	**19.5**	63.41***
Lack of appetite	3.7	6.0	29.62***
Chest pains	4.4	4.6	4.35 n.s.
Stomach upset/bowel	10.0	14.7	20.92***
Backache	**22.2**	**29.0**	22.05***
Muscular aches/pains	**17.9**	**26.5**	19.82***
Migraine	4.2	7.4	35.22***
Sickness/nausea	2.2	5.3	52.38***
Skin disorders	9.1	13.6	20.33***
Allergies	5.9	8.5	19.17***
Mental fatigue	**14.3**	**26.0**	37.14***
Sleeplessness	**15.2**	**23.2**	14.04**
Breathlessness	5.8	8.8	10.19*
Physical exhaustion	**13.2**	18.5	14.10**
Sexual problems	6.1	9.0	4.56 n.s.
Problems with blood pressure	9.2	8.3	4.79 n.s.

Let *p>0.05, **p<0.01 and ***p<0.001

Bold print corresponds to those 5 ailments most commonly endorsed by men and women separately.

The magnitude of the gender differences were largest for tension headaches (chi-squared (4,1275)= 63.41, $p<0.001$), sickness and nausea (chi-squared (4, 1275)= 52.38, $p<0.001$), mental fatigue (chi-squared (4,1275)= 37.41, $p<0.001$), migraine (chi-squared (4,1275)= 35.22, $p<0.001$) and lack of appetite (chi-squared (4,1275)= 29.62, $p<0.001$).

In order to investigate which ailments best differentiated men and women a discriminant analysis was performed. If a linear discriminant analysis using stepwise procedures is computed, the physical ailment profiles differ significantly between men and women (eigenvalue = 0.09, Wilk's lambda = 0.92, chi-squared (5) = 113.43, $p<0.001$; $F(5, 1269)$= 23.70, $p<0.001$). The standardised canonical discriminant coefficients were significant for tension headache (0.56), chest pains (0.47), sickness or nausea (-0.59), mental fatigue (0.25) and skin disorders (0.33).

Table 2 shows the "collapsed" responses of those ailments experienced at least "weekly" if not "daily". In other words, backaches were most common among women (29%) and men (22.2%) on a daily/weekly basis. Tension headaches and fatigue were among the most frequently experienced physical complaints but again more so among women than men.

A MANOVA was computed looking at gender differences in physical health scores when introducing the covariate terms educational status and age. As previously the gender difference term was statistically significant (Pillai's trace = 0.036, $F(16, 1163)$ = 2.73, $p<0.001$) after controlling for covariates. The main effects due to age differences were also significant (Pillai's trace = 0.051, $F(16, 1163)$= 3.92, $p<0.001$) as was the effect due to educational status (Pillai's trace = 0.032, $F(16, 1163)$ = 2.39, $p<0.01$). There was no evidence of a gender x age effect ($F(16, 1163)$ = 1.08, $p>0.05$) but the gender x educational status interaction was statistically significant ($F(16, 1163)$ = 2.03, $p<0.01$).

Life satisfaction

In addition to the physical symptoms, the various facets of satisfaction with specific areas of life were assessed.

The domains were subdivided into a) general (job content, physical appearance, finances and leisure) and b) quality of social relationships (social friends, working atmosphere, family and partnership). The degree of satisfaction was highest for relationships. There was no significant sex difference in the responses to satisfaction with physical appearance, leisure and job content but on finances where women were surprisingly more satisfied than men, $p<0.03$). Conversely, all four rates of relationships revealed women were more satisfied than men (social friends, $p<0.001$; working atmosphere $p<0.03$; family $p<0.04$ and partnership<0.02).

When we examined the percentages who expressed feeling "very satisfied" in terms of social friends, 26% of women and 16.7% men reported that degree of satisfaction (chi-squared (2,4)=18.04, $p<0.001$). In terms of working atmosphere, 16.1% and 11.5% of women and men respectively (chi-squared (2,4)= 11.05, $p<0.03$; family, 40.7% and 33.6% for women and men respectively (chi-squared (2,4)= 10.15,$p<0.04$), and partnership, 32.0% and 23.7% (women: men, chi-squared (2,4)= 12.60, $p<0.02$).

Previous studies have shown how sex differences in health are affected by age. Hence, a MANOVA was computed exploring gender differences and age (3 categories) (controlling for educational and marital status as covariates) across the specific satisfaction scales scores. On this occasion the gender difference term was statistically significant across profiles (Pillai's trace = 0.019, F(8, 1169) = 2.81, p<0.01). The effects due to age differences were also significant (Pillai's trace = 0.036, F(16,2340)= 2.70, p<0.001) as was marital status (Pillai's trace = 0.20, F(8,1169)=37.51), p<0.001) but educational status was not (Pillai's trace = 0.010, F(8,1169) = 1.41, p>0.05). There was evidence of a gender x age effect (F16,2340) = 1.83, p<0.05). Since the scales of satisfaction were themselves interrelated (r=0.13-0.51, p<0.001), a series of univariate F-tests between scales were computed to identify which specific facets of life satisfaction differed between groups.

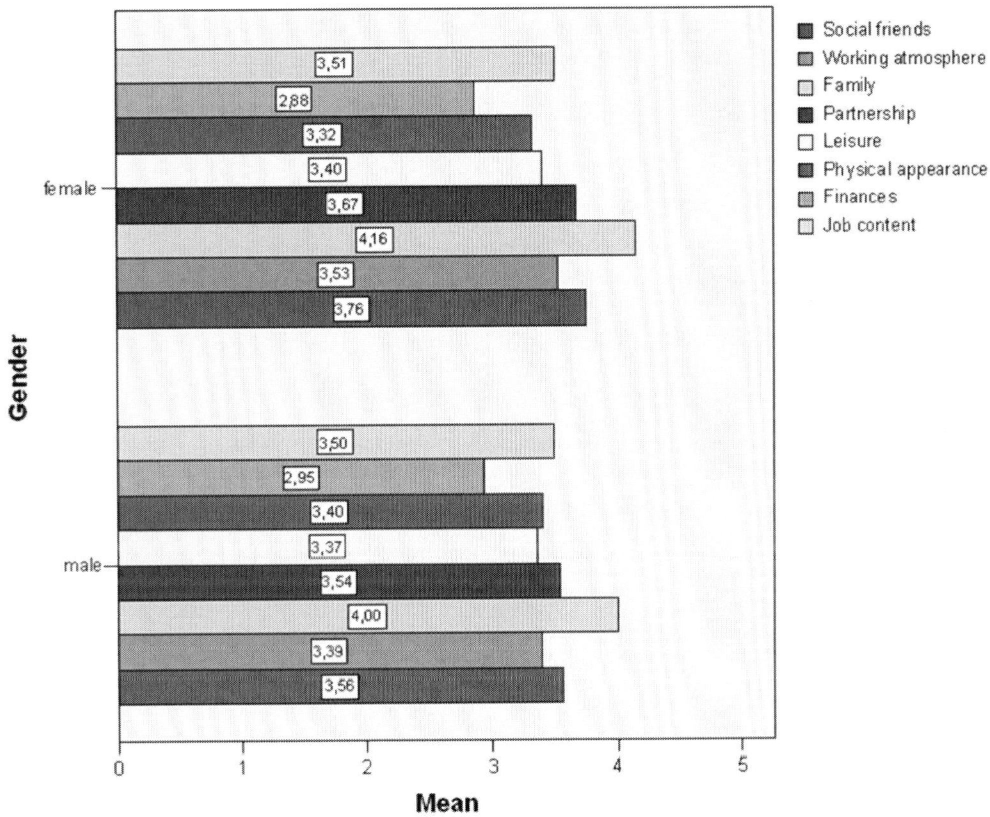

Figure 2. Mean levels of satisfaction across specific domains of work and private life for men and women. (lowest bar column represents social friends, above which is working atmosphere, etc)

Women displayed greater satisfaction with their relationship to friends and their family, but less satisfaction with their physical appearance. With increasing age persons were more likely to display dissatisfaction with their physical appearance (8.4% of young age group were very satisfied with their physical appearance and 6.3% of older group) and with their family and partnership (whereas 26.0% of younger age group reported satisfaction with friends, 20.7% intermediate aged group and 13.1% for older group) a finding consistent for men and women.

Some interesting age x gender interactions were observed for the domains of satisfaction, friends, work (colleagues) and to some extent job content (for younger group, women reported lower satisfaction than men with job content, but women reported higher levels of satisfaction for the older groups).

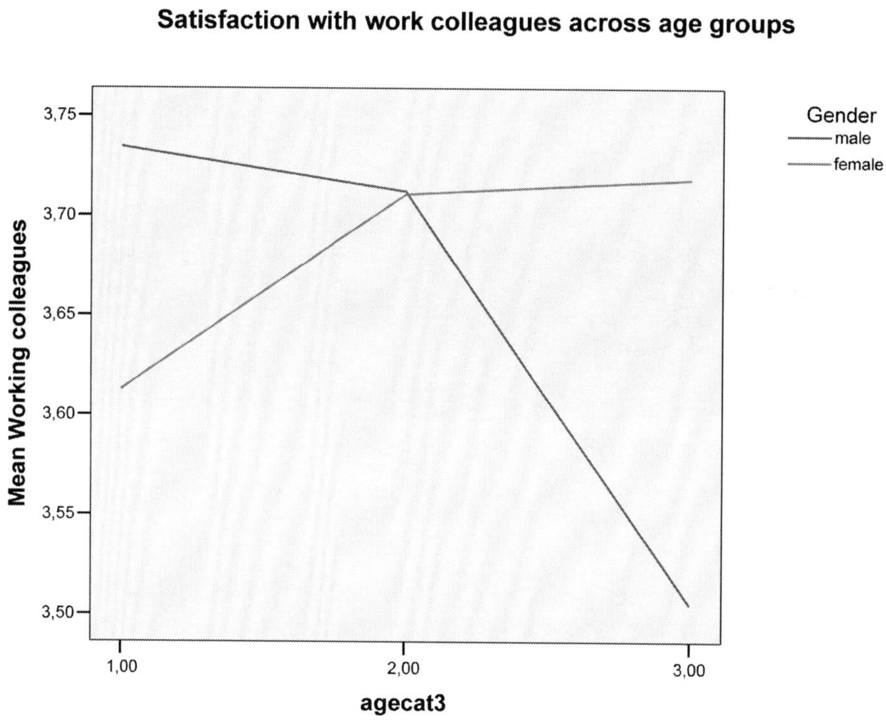

Figure 3. Satisfaction with work (colleagues) across age for men and women separately (age cat, 3 categories of ages).

There is abundant evidence that work satisfaction is a powerful component of life satisfaction, contentment and health. Further health effects productivity at work. The figure above reveals the evaluation of satisfaction at work (colleagues) as a function of age. Young men display more satisfaction with their work colleagues than women, but the mid-aged groups they converge – women displaying an increase in their satisfaction – and among the older men satisfaction at work drops dramatically, whereas women continue to display an improvement in their assessment of work with increasing age.

Social networks and the quality of friendship groups have been shown to be powerful predictors of adaptation. The figure below reveals the trend in satisfaction with friends across various age categories. Again, for women there is little change in their satisfaction which remains high throughout adulthood. Men display a progressive decline in their appraisal of their satisfaction with friends with increasing age, reaching its ebb for the oldest group.

Gender and age: Absenteeism during the year. A 2 x 3 ANOVA was computed using gender and age category (agecat3) as the main effect variables. Age categories were such that group "1" were the 16-29 year old (n=380), then mid-aged group "2" 30-38 years of age (n=465) and then older than 39 (-66 years. Group "3") (n=428). The dependent variables were "number of days ill off work during the last 12 months". There was no significant effect due to age differences ($F(2, 1260)=1.99$, $p>0.05$) but a significant gender effect (Mmen 5.65 SD 21.73, Mwomen 9.23 SD 28.11; $F(1, 1260)= 8.26$, $p<0.01$) showing that women took almost twice as many days ill per year as men. The figure reveals that whereas men the showed no clear linear increase of illness absenteeism with age, women did, although the interaction term gender x age was not statistically significant (F(2, 1260)=0.95, p>0.05) in part presumably because of the high degree of variability of "days ill" scores. Further analyses revealed significant gender differences in the total physical ill-health scores between men and women (F(1, 1260)=36.60, p<0.001) but no gender differences in terms of satisfaction with physical (F(1,1260)=1,44, p>0.05) or psychological health (F(1,1260)=1.06, p>0.05).

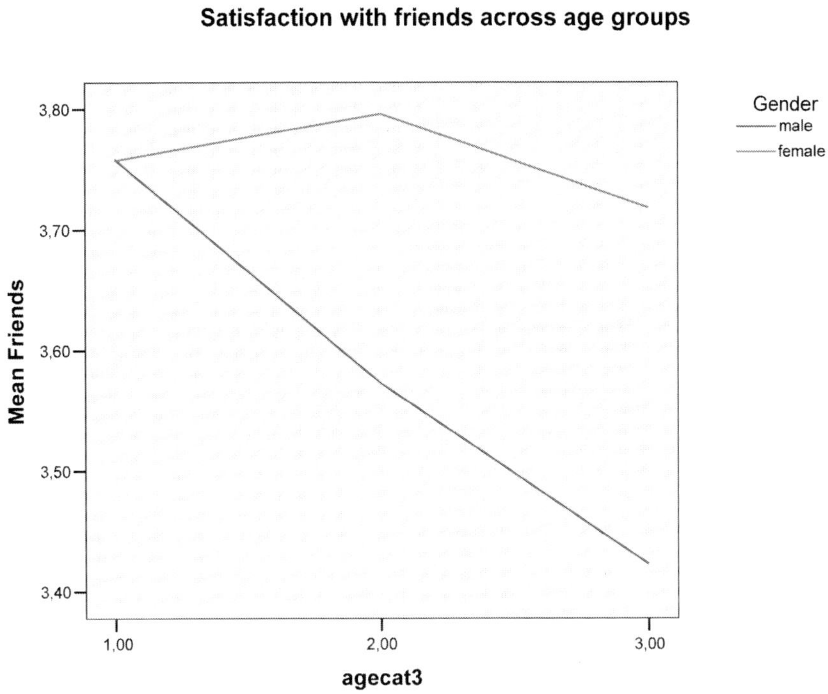

Figure 4. Satisfaction with friends across age for men and women separately (age cat, 3 categories of ages). (upper line – female; lower line male)

Table 3. MANOVA with age and gender as the between group difference factors and the scales of specific life satisfaction as the outcome variables controlled for effects of marital status and educational status

	Gender	*Age*	*Gender x age*
Satisfaction	F p	F p	F p
Friends	**7.62** **	1.86	**4.68** **
Leisure	0.14	0.19	1.25
Physical appearance	**4.10** **	**4.76** **	1.68
Finance	1.14	2.60	0.06
Work (colleagues)	0.07	2.11	**3.80** *
Job Content	0.30	0.93	2.35 (*)
Family	**6.58** **	**5.72** **	1.47
Partnership	2.63	**8.33** ***	0.07

Let *p<0.05, **p>0.01 and ***p<0.001

In order to specify exactly which scales of health and illness differed as a function of educational status, an analysis of variance was performed to see more clearly the effects of education on overall health (physical ailments and subjectively perceived satisfaction with health) and illness rates

Days taken off from illness were decreasingly less with higher levels of educational status, so that those with a first and higher degree were likely to be absent from work less than others. On the other hand, this cannot be attributed to actual physical illness, because there is no difference between groups (educational status) in terms of subjective reports of physical ailments. Those better educated reported greater satisfaction with their physical (and psychologically) health compared to those less educate, no doubt because education is a proxy for social class and social status.

Table 4. Differences in absenteeism, physical ailments, and satisfaction with physical and mental health

	secondary	University entrance	First degree	Higher degree	F(3,1180)
Illness rates	10.22 (29.46)	6.98 (20.00)	7.54 (33.76)	3.68 (8.12)	2.53*
Physical ill-health	39.97 (13.81)	39.25 (11.67)	37.77 (11.24)	39.20 (13.32)	1.61 n.s.
Satisfaction: physical health	3.29 (1.07)	3.39 (1.02)	3.30 (0.99)	3.50 (1.01)	2.66*
Satisfaction: mental health	3.46 (1.03)	3.56 (0.92)	3.61 (0.97)	3.68 (0.95)	2.63*

*p<0.05

Satisfaction and physical ill-health

Stepwise regression analyses revealed that four physical complaint scales were significant predictors of satisfaction with mental well-being. Mental fatigue and sexual problems were common determinants for both men and women, and chest pains and skin disorders emerged as significant predictors of mental well-being for men, but not women, for whom sleeplessness and stomach ailments were the main other determinants. Overall 14-25 percent of the variance in well-being was predicted by the physical ailments.

Separate block regression analyses revealed that for women, none of the other sociodemographic variables e.g., education, marital status or age influenced the relationship on satisfaction with mental health. Conversely, for men, age and educational status merged as significant predictors of satisfaction with mental health.

The above table shows the correlation coefficients between satisfaction with physical and mental health, somatic complaints and days taken ill during the last year. The magnitude of the degree of satisfaction with physical and psychological health was roughly equivalent for men and women. The relationship between full scale scores on the somatic ailment scales and satisfaction with health was significant for both men and women. Days taken off ill during the last year were significantly correlated to total somatic ailments for both men and women.

A further analysis incorporated the four main socio-demographic variables age, gender, educational status and marital status using the aggregate score all physical ailment scores (total somatic ill-health). The regression was statistically significant (R=0.20, adj. R2 = 0.04;

F(4, 1270) = 12.83, p<0.001) but only one of the variables – gender - emerged as a significant predictor of ill-health (beta = 0.19, t = 6.75, p<0.001).

Table 5. Socio-demographic and physical symptoms as determinants of health satisfaction for men and women

Mental well-being: satisfaction		
Men	F(4,834)=34.52***	R=0.38, adj. R2=0.14
	beta	P
Mental fatigue	-0.23	0.001
Chest pains	-0.12	0.001
Skin disorders	-0.11	0.001
Sexual problems	-0.09	0.05
	F(2,789)=7.52***	R=0.14, adj. R2=0.02
Age	-0.09	0.01
Educational status	+0.09	0.02
Women	F(4,429)=36.07***	R=0.50, adj. R2=0.25
Mental fatigue	-0.27	0.001
Sexual problems	-0.18	0.001
Sleeplessness	-0.14	0.01
Stomach aches/bowel	-0.09	0.05
	F(3,388)=0.52 n.s.	R=0.06, adj. R2=0.00

Let ***p<0.001

Table 6. Interrelationship between scales of ill-health (satisfaction with health), somatic ailments and illness (men and women)

	Physical health	Mental health	Somatic ailments	Illness days
Physical health		+0.38***	-0.27***	-0.13***
Mental health	+0.39***		-0.34***	-0.04**
Somatic ailments	0.38***	-0.44***		+0.16***
Illness days	-0.11***	-0.13***	+0.11*	

let **p<0.01 and ***p<0.001

Discussion

This was intended as a comprehensive survey to establish age and gender differences in specific domains of life satisfaction. It aimed to explore the relative relational strengths of socio-demographic variables e.g., age, marital status, educational status and gender, and physical health symptom predictors with the various facets of satisfaction.

This internet-data-based study has confirmed much of the previous literature on sex differences in mental and physical health namely that there are different patterns and correlates of mental and physical health between the sexes. Many studies done in different countries with different data sets and with different measures have shown that females report more minor physical and psychological health problems than men. There is also universal evidence in morbidity: Men die before women. Women consult doctors more frequently than men and have lower subjectively rated mental and physical health. The question is why? Different researchers have proposed different factors like biological factors, reporting differences, access to health care, exposure to risk, work stress. Certainly many suggest that one's social position in society which is, in part, dictated by gender is associated with many health promoting or damaging circumstances. Gender is related to educational opportunities and success which in part dictates the type of paid work one can get which does have an impact on many things like income, stress etc.

One way of trying to understand the gender differences in health is to look in detail at the symptoms both in physical and mental health. This study found the most common physical ailments reported by these European adults were aches and pains and mental and physical fatigue. Of the 16 complaints in only three women reported fewer problems than men and much more incidence of headaches, nausea, mental fatigue and lack of appetite. Some of these problems maybe stress based and/or seen as psychosomatic illnesses which may relate to the well established higher neuroticism scores among women compared to men.

This stress may also be as a function of women carrying more home based responsibilities than men and thus a poorer work-life balance as well as being in lower paid jobs. However it is possible to refute some of these hypotheses, as women were shown to be more satisfied than men by their working and family life.

Interestingly the regression analyses show that whilst similar problems predict overall mental well being for both sexes. Mental fatigue and sexual problems were, understandably, strong predictors of mental well-being for both men and women, but the pattern was more varied because for men, age and educational status played a major role whereas they were not significant predictors for women. Moreover, it was interesting that although clear gender differences had been observed in terms of various measures of somatic ailments (physical ill-health), there was no significant effect of gender on the subjective satisfaction of health (both physical and mental health).

Looking at life satisfaction domains, both men and women reported the most satisfaction with the family, friends and partnership, and least satisfaction with finance, physical appearance and leisure. On the other hand, we found evidence that women were much more satisfied with their family and friends relationships than men, although no differences were found for satisfaction in leisure, finance, working colleagues, job and partnership. This greater satisfaction with family life is in agreement with the survey from Daig et al. (15), consistent with the notion that women perceive life satisfaction more in terms of social support and social interactions.

We did not find any evidence to support the notion men displaying greater satisfaction in terms of work, finance or leisure compared to women (nb. Daig et al. (15) "Satisfaction with leisure activities was significantly more pronounced in men than in women. Engaging in leisure activities is a highly utilised strategy of getting away from the demands of work"). However gender differences in working relationships and friends were moderated by age. More specifically, males reported declining levels of satisfaction with their friends with increasing age, whereas women maintained high levels of satisfaction with their social relationships. Relationship satisfaction is also a function of personality (especially optimism) as well as living conditions and arrangements. Certainly there is abundant literature which shows that social support from good relationships buffers the effects of stress and leads to better health.

Whereas Daig et al. (15) reported age differences on every aspect of life satisfaction, we found differences due to age on the facets of physical appearance (8.4 and 8.3% of young and intermediate group were very satisfied with their physical appearance, but "only" 6.3% of the older group), partnership (29.7%, 25.2% and 25.1% reporting being very satisfied with their relationships across age), and friends (26.3% of young persons expressed extreme satisfaction with their friends, 20.7% for intermediate age group and 13.1% for oldest group). The latter finding may reflect the lack of opportunity of social interacting with increasing aging whether in the leisure or work domain. There was no indication of age exerting a major role on the other domains of satisfaction (e.g., leisure, work and finance). This maybe a function of this particular sample and requires replication.

The age x gender interactions suggested that men were more susceptible to the impact of increasing age on work and friend relationships. There were no significant interaction effects for satisfaction with leisure time and family life, again not consistent with Daig's et al. (15) finding in which they suggested older women become less satisfied with family life because the risk of being widowed or divorced may be higher, causing alienation and lonesomeness. Furthermore, the decrease in satisfaction with appearance with increasing age was not influenced by gender, that is, men and women were "equally affected". Our findings also failed to confirm a decrease in self-reported physical health across age nor was this influenced by gender differences.

Comparing our findings to the recent German survey (15) was helpful, but findings were not entirely consistent and this may be attributed to different categories of aging and differences inherent in sample regarding educational status (three-quarters of our sample had at least 13 years education, and over one half, that is, 54.2% had at least one university degree if not a higher academic qualification. This compares to 17.6% for Daig's survey (15)). We had a higher proportion of men (65% vs. 47% for Daig et al. (15)). Both studies were cross-sectional in nature and this seriously limits the generalisability of our findings.

Some sociodemographic variables such as educational status also were associated with subjective reports of health, and this may be more pronounced among men. Certainly, although better educated persons did not necessarily differ in terms of somatic ailments, their rates of illness (absenteeism) were lower among the better educated. Furthermore, the higher the educational status, the greater the satisfaction with one health – both physically and psychologically. This may be due to their being partly freed from material concerns which impact on health.

Our results tend to support the notion of a decline in satisfaction with increasing age, but only for certain domains of life satisfaction such as with respect to working colleagues and relationship to friends. Moreover, this is most pronounced among men and not women. Interestingly, the main effect of age was observed with satisfaction regarding family and partners/spouse and this does not appear moderated by gender. Here we see that with increasing age there are marked changes in reported satisfaction with ones immediate family unit. Although this study has focused on gender differences in self-reported health and well-being it should not be forgotten that there are probably more similarities than differences between the sexes. Health and happiness are a function of many things including inherited biology and personality as well as life style and factors like education, job status and social class. Furthermore as we have seen these interact with gender and particularly with age.

Our results underline the importance of health professionals to distinguish their treatment modality forms for men and women. Moreover, as a consequence of demographic changes in the general population, there will be an increased need to focus on the specific needs both in diagnostic assessment and treatment of an aging population. Research focussing on areas of life satisfaction may provide valuable insight which challenge stereotype concepts e.g details of sexual and body satisfaction among elderly persons.

One issue that perhaps remains is the clinical relevance of such findings. Why indeed focus on areas of life satisfaction in psychotherapy? In the early 90's "psychologists decried the exclusive emphasis on psychiatric symptoms of 'being ill' to the neglect of *positive* mental health ... leaders from opposing theoretical camps in clinical psychology, psychiatry, health psychology, and general medicine encourage the development on nonpathology oriented measures of QOL (*quality of life*) SWV *(subjective well-being),* life satisfaction, positive psychology, and 'positive mental health'..." (26, p. 47). Some suggest that subjective well-being may be a core criteria for evaluation of mental-health and a detailed assessment of personal strengths, resources and skills could be essential for effective therapy. Frisch (26) provides for example, a comprehensive array of core techniques focussing on quality of life including basic strategies as well as area-specific treatment strategies from facets of daily life e.g., visual quest exercise; my most feared obituary, and happiness per exercise. Clinical and health psychologists as well as medical physicians may do well from examining domains of life and work satisfaction in their tailoring of treatment for patients.

References

[1] Helman C. Culture health and illness. London: Hodder, 2007.

[2] Pollard T, Hyatt S, eds. Sex, gender and health. Cambridge: Cambridge Univ Press, 1999.

[3] Kirkcaldy BD. Sex differences in somatic and autonomic habituation responses. Psychologische Beiträge 1983;25(3/4):515-20. [German]

[4] Kirkcaldy BD, Furnham AF, Siefen RG. The effects of gender and migrant status on physical and psychological well-being. Int J Child Adolesc Health 2009;21(1): 61-72.

[5] Emslie C, Hunt K, Macintyre S. Gender differences in minor morbidity among full time employees of a British university. J Epidemiol Community Health 1999;53:465-75.

[6] Emslie C, Hunt K. The weaker sex? Exploring lay understandings of gender differences in life expectancy. Soc Sci Med 2008;67:808-16.

[7] Hunt K, Sweeting H, Keoghan M, Platt S. Sex, gender, role orientation, gender role attitudes and suicidal thoughts in three generations. Soc Psychiatry Psychiatr Epidemiol 2006;41:641-7.

[8] Sweeting H, West P. Sex differences in health at ages 11, 13 and 15. Soc Sci Med 2003;56:31-9.

[9] EU. The health of adults in the European Union. Special Eurobarometer. Brussels: Eur Commission, 2002.

[10] Kirkcaldy BD, Furnham A, Trimpop R, Knobloch J. Akzeptanz und Skepsis: Einstellungen und Verhalten von Patientin der Alternativ- und Schulmedizin. Z Gesundh 2001;9(2):57-66.

[11] Furnham A, Kirkcaldy BD. Age and sex differences in health beliefs and behaviours. Psychol Rep 1997;80:63-6.

[12] Clancy K, Gove W. Sex differences in mental illness: An analysis of response bias in self-reports. AJS 1974;80:205-16.

[13] Wood W, Whelan N. Sex differences in positive well-being. A consideration of emotional style and marital status. Psychol Bull 1989;106(2):249-64.

[14] Sousa LA, Lyumbomirsky S. Life satisfaction. In: Worrell J, ed. Encyclopaedia of women and gender. Sex similarities and differences and the impact of society on gender. New York: Acad Press, 2001;2.

[15] Daig I, Herschbach P, Lehmann A, Knoll N, Decker A. Gender and age differences in domain specific life satisfaction and the impact of depressive and anxiety symptoms: A general population survey from Germany. Qual Life Res, in press.
[16] Argyle M. The psychology of happiness. London: Methuen, 1987.
[17] Kalleberg AL, Loscocco KA. Aging, values and rewards: explaining age differences in job satisfaction. Am Sociol Rev 1983;48:78-90.
[18] Mroczek DK, Spiro A. Changes in life satisfaction during adulthood: Findings from the veterans Affairs Normative Aging Study. J Pers Soc Psychol 2005;88(1):189-202.
[19] Beutel ME, Glaesmer H, Decker O, Fischbeck S, Brähler E. Life satisfaction, distress and resiliency across the life span of women. Unpubl manuscript, 2009.
[20] Diener E, Suh E. Age and subjective well-being: An international analysis. Annu Rev Gerontol Geriatr 1998;17:304-24.
[21] American Psychological Association. The recession is stressing men more than women. Monit 2009;7:110.
[22] Light HK, Hertsgaard RE, Martin RE. Education and Income: Significant Factors in life satisfaction of farm men and women. JRRE 1985;3(1)7- 12.
[23] Campbell A. The sense of well-being in America. New York: McGraw Hill, 1981.
[24] Gosling SD, Vazire S, Srivastava S, John OP. Should we trust web-based studies? A comparative analysis of six preconceptions about internet questionnaires. Am Psychol 2004;59:93-104.
[25] Kraut RM, Olson J, Banaji M, Bruckman A, Cohen J, Couper M. Psychological research online: Report of Board of Scientific Affairs' Advisory Group on the conduct of research on the Internet. Am Psychol 2004;59(2):106-17.
[26] Frisch, MB. QOLT assessment, integrating QOL with traditional health assessment. In: Frisch MB, ed. Applying a life satisfaction approach to positive psychology and cognitive therapies. Chichester: John Wiley, 2005.

In: Mental Health from an International Perspective
Editors: J. Merrick, S. Aspler and M. Morad
ISBN: 978-1-62948-519-5

Chapter 4

Antenatal depressive symptomatology among Chengdu Chinese women

Ying Lau, RN, RM, IBCLC, PhD[*]
Alice Lee Centre for Nursing Studies, Yong Loo Lin School of Medicine,
National University of Singapore, Singapore

In this chapter we describe a total of 1,609 women recruited from four regional public hospitals to participate in a study using an exploratory cross-sectional design. This is the first study investigated the prevalence and correlates of antenatal depressive symptoms among Chinese women from Chengdu during their second trimester of pregnancy in mainland China. The women were identified as having depressive symptoms using the Edinburgh Postnatal Depression Scale. Marital conflict and parent-in-law conflict were assessed using the Dyadic Adjustment Scale and the Stryker Adjustment Checklist, respectively. The vulnerable factors of depressive symptoms were explored in terms of their demo-socio-economic, obstetric, and Chinese family relational aspects. The prevalence rates of mild to severe antenatal depressive symptoms were 35.9% (n = 578). The logistic regression analysis revealed that participants who had been married for a shorter time (aOR = 1.338), who had a single source of financial support (aOR = 1.407), who had a poor marital relationship (aOR = 2.347), and who had a poor mother-in-law relationship (aOR = 1.399) were more likely to have mild to severe depressive symptoms ($p < 0.05$). The findings provide important information to help in the reduction of antenatal depressive symptoms among the Chengdu population. The implications and limitations of these findings, and directions for future research, are discussed.

Introduction

Antenatal depression is very significant because research indicates that there is a risk of potentially devastating adverse consequences for mothers and their families (1). Studies show

* Correspondence:Ying Lau, Assistant Professor, Alice Lee Centre for Nursing Studies, Yong Loo Lin School of Medicine, National University of Singapore, 10 Medical Drive, Block MD11, Level 2 Clinical Research Centre, Sinapore 117597. E-mail: nurly@nus.edu.sg.

that depression during pregnancy is associated with spontaneous pre-term births (2), obstetric complications (3), adverse perinatal outcomes (4), and postnatal depression (5). The evidence also supports the proposition that antenatal depressive symptoms may have the potential to influence fetal immune development (6) and cause neonatal complications (7), and to have a generally deleterious effect on a child's neurological, cognitive, social, emotional, and developmental functioning (8, 9).

Inadequate treatment and inappropriate intervention in depression during pregnancy may be fatal because the risk of suicide is all too real (10). There is a general consensus that depression is at its most treatable when detected early (11). The identification of antenatal depressive symptoms is therefore significant in making possible early detection and intervention. However, none of the existing studies has explicitly explored the correlates associated with antenatal depressive symptoms among the mainland Chinese population. It is therefore difficult to interpret antenatal depressive symptomatology in this group, or to investigate the factors associated with depressive symptoms so as to determine what we need to know to offer appropriate treatment. Successful clinical management relies on a clear understanding of the relationships between the correlates of antenatal depressive symptoms to create effective therapeutic approaches for women who are affected.

Few depressive disorders are associated with a decrease in biological fertility, so the prevalence of all forms of such disorders at the time of conception is equivalent to that found in nonpregnant women of a similar age (12). There is a growing global literature on antenatal depression, but most research focuses on the western, developed countries, primarily in Europe and North America. Prevalence rates show considerable variation between countries, ranging between 10% and 52% (13). One reason for these disparate figures might be the inherent difficulties of conducting cross-cultural research (14).

Factors recently found to be associated with depressive symptoms during pregnancy include youth (15), low levels of education (16), being a newly-arrived immigrant (17), being single (18), suffering financial hardship (19), living in poor accommodation (20), and maternal employment (21). Furthermore, an unwanted (21) or a first (22) pregnancy, a first baby (23), late antenatal booking (24), and negative attitudes to breastfeeding (13) all increase the risk of suffering antenatal depressive symptoms. Although evidence for these risk factors has been found in many reviews of western literature, the applicability of these findings to mainland Chinese populations is still a matter of debate.

Marital conflict and antenatal depressive symptomatology

In traditional Chinese families, husbands are considered as the "heaven" (tian) and wives as the "earth" (di), an arrangement that has been heavily influenced by Confucian philosophy (25). The inferior role of women is succinctly reflected by rigid gender norms such as "three obediences and four virtues" (san cong sd de) and being "virtuous wives and good mothers" (xian qi liang mu) (26). Men, as the heads of household, preside over major decisions about family matters. It is common knowledge among Chinese population that the marital roles of men and women are greatly influenced by a domestic inequality originating in the gendered division of labor and the male-oriented patriarchal element of Chinese culture (27). However, the economic policies in place since the 1980s have transformed China into a market-based socialist economy, resulting in increased education and employment opportunities for women (25). Women can bring additional financial resources to their families as a result of their greater access to education and employment (28). As a result, they have begun to demand greater decision power in the family, a view that may challenge men's status as head of the household (27). Indeed, marital conflict is far more common today in China (26).

Becoming a mother is a life-changing experience that can make a woman feel uncertain, insecure, and unstable, contributing to symptoms of tension, anxiety, and distress (29). Studies suggest that couples experience a decline in marital satisfaction in the transition to parenthood (30), which might represent the first step in a deteriorating course of dyadic functioning (31). Research also shows that marital conflict has a significant effect on, and is a consistent risk factor for, depression in pregnant women (32, 33). However, there is little research data on marital conflict among pregnant mainland Chinese women. To establish the magnitude of the association between depression and marital conflict, it is important to provide a solid foundation for making recommendations for treatment of both marital conflict and the associated depression (34).

Parent-in-law conflict and antenatal depressive symptoms

Based on the Confucian paradigm, the most important relationships in Chinese culture involve the rule of hierarchy (35). The subordination of the daughter-in-law to the parents-in-law is reinforced by a Confucian ideology that prescribes a hierarchy in its doctrine of the separated spheres (25). The daughter-in-law is perceived as "an outsider" (wai ren) from another family and therefore must take the initiative to adjust to her "new" family. She is expected to show respect for, and obedience to, the older generation (36). The birth of a baby is not only a matter for the couple, but concerns the whole family; the grandparents are still the first choice as childcare providers (37). Indeed, the parents-in-laws see themselves as key providers of, and therefore decision-makers in, perinatal care practices (38). Previous studies show that all pregnant women claim to have heard about traditional practices from their parents-in-law (39). However, traditional practice is an active concept that changes gradually as it is transmitted from generation to generation (40). Tension and conflict between traditions and modernity may result because of incompatible value systems (41).

The study of in-law relationship conflict has received little research attention. Our research team has previously shown that higher levels of mother in law conflict are associated with antenatal depression among Hong Kong Chinese (33). In fact, the cultural and social contexts of Hong Kong and mainland Chinese families are quite different. Although the information is limited as a result, it is still of some use in considering the experiences of mainland women. The key issue is the centuries-old, adversarial in-law relationship, especially between mother- and daughter-in-law, that can be traced back to historical China, a patriarchal, patrilineal, and patrilocal society (36). One Chinese national survey has shown that mother-in-law conflict is the third most common stressful life event experienced by married women (42). A study conducted in rural China also revealed that mother-in-law conflict featured in nearly one-third of attempted suicides by young women (43). Although mother-in-law conflict may accordingly be perceived as one of the most important issues for pregnant Chinese women, there has been limited research on the topic.

Given the limited information on the demo-socio-economic status, obstetric variables, marital status and parent-in-law conflict associated with antenatal depressive symptoms in the Chinese population, this study aims to fill the gap. To our knowledge, this is the first large-scale study conducted in mainland China to focus on these issues. The findings will be beneficial for planning services and designing further interventions. More research is needed to increase our understanding before culturally sensitive therapy can be implemented. Thus, the following research questions may be asked. Among pregnant women living in Chengdu;

- What is the prevalence of antenatal depressive symptoms?
- What demo-socio-economic and obstetric factors are associated with antenatal depressive symptoms?
- Is the presence of marital conflict a risk factor of antenatal depressive symptoms?
- Is the presence of parent-in-law conflict a risk factor of antenatal depressive symptoms?

Our sample

In this study, antenatal depressive symptoms are mainly focus on cognitive and affective features of depression in this study for at least 1 week that included inability to laugh, inability to look forward to things with enjoyment, blaming oneself unnecessarily, anxious or worried, scared or panicky, inability to cope, difficulty sleeping, sad or miserable, crying, and thoughts of harming oneself (44) during the second trimester of pregnancy (12 weeks to 24 weeks of gestation). Marital conflict is defined as a woman's perception of dissatisfaction with a male partner with whom she is either married to or cohabiting with in four areas of dyadic adjustment that include dyadic cohesion, dyadic satisfaction, dyadic consensus, and dyadic affectional expression (45). Parent-in-law conflict is defined as daughter-in-law perception of experiences with the parent-in-law that has less intimacy and more tension (46). Chengdu Chinese is defined as people of Chinese ethnic origin who live in Chengdu and includes residents (with local household register 'hu kou'), immigrants, travelers, or visitors of Chinese origin from other places of mainland China, or other countries.

The research was exploratory, cross-sectional, and quantitative in nature. The study was approved in August 2007, and a pilot test carried out a month before the main study with 100 similar subjects in similar settings. The pilot aimed to examine the reliability, validity, and usability of the measurement methods in the target population. Based on the comments received, some of the demo-socio-economic items and obstetric items were revised to make them more accessible, without changing their meaning.

The research setting was Chengdu, a subprovincial city located in southwestern China and the capital of Sichuan province. Chengdu is one of the most important economic centers and transportation and communication hubs in this region, and has a population of over 11 million. The study was approved by the institutional review boards of four regional public hospitals in Chengdu – one university-affiliated and three regional hospitals – serving a combined population of over 2.75 million people and delivering about 30,000 babies per year.

Women being served by these hospitals under governmental support were identified as a representative group covering different demo-socio-economic classes of the Chengdu population. Nonprobabilistic convenience sampling was adopted because of resource constraints. The exclusion criteria included: (1) the woman did not supply written informed consent; (2) baby had an abnormality; and (3) the woman was not Chinese. The inclusion criteria included; (1) primiparas or multiparas; (2) the woman was having either a vaginal or instrumental delivery in one of the four participating hospitals.

The Edinburgh Postnatal Depression Scale (EPDS) (44) was used to screen for antenatal depressive symptoms because it has already been validated for this type of use (47). The EPDS is a 10-item self-rating instrument, with each item scored using a 4-point scale. The minimum and maximum total scores are 0 and 30. This scale focuses on the cognitive and affective features of depression. A Chinese version was used that has been tested in a Chinese population and demonstrated good reliability and validity (48). The EPDS scores are divided into three levels: 0-9, insignificant; > 9, mild to severe depressive symptoms; and > 14, severe depressive symptoms (49). Therefore, cutoff scores of 9/10 and 14/15 were used in this study. The Cronbach's alpha for the EPDS was 0.762, suggesting good internal consistency.

The Dyadic Adjustment Scale (DAS) (45) is a 32-item marital inventory with four subscales on "affectional expression," "dyadic consensus," "dyadic cohesion," and "dyadic satisfaction" that adequately demonstrate the level of adjustment in pair relationships (45). The range of scores on the DAS is 0 to 151. A lower score means more conflict in the marital relationship. The reliability and validity of the DAS are satisfactory when it is applied across cultures (45). The Chinese version of the DAS, which has a satisfactory reliability and validity as measured by Cronbach's alpha (50), was adopted in this study. The mean score is 101 among Chinese women (51). Thus, 101 was used as the cutoff point in this study: = 101 was defined as a poor relationship and < 101 as a better one. Our Cronbach's alpha coefficient for the DAS subscales was 0.881, suggesting good internal consistency.

The Stryker Adjustment Checklist (SAC) (46) was used to measure the relationships between women and their parents-in-law. The checklist consists of 40 true-false items measuring adjustment in terms of four categories; affection, intimacy, sympathy, and tension. Only two categories (intimacy and tension), comprising 20 items in total, were used in this study as they were more relevant to the purpose of the investigation. The items were added up to give a score for each subscale. The reliability and validity of the measurement has been confirmed (46). A higher score indicates poor adjustment and more conflict. A higher degree of parent-in-law conflict was present when the woman's perception of her experiences with them contained less intimacy and more tension. The Chinese version of the SAC was adopted (52) and achieved satisfactory reliability and validity. The mean score in this study is 8, so a score of 8/9 was used as the cutoff point because there is no relevant cutoff found elsewhere in the empirical evidence. A score of = 9 was defined as a poor relationship and < 9 as a better one.

Information on demo-socio-economic status and obstetric data was also collected. Demographic data included age, educational level, and socio-economic status (employment, total family income, and type and size of residence). The obstetric aspect included number of pregnancies, number of children, intention to be pregnant, and intention of breastfeeding.

The target population

The target population was Chinese pregnant women living in Chengdu. All women who attended antenatal clinics within the data collection period of August 2007 to March 2009 were eligible for entry into the study on the basis of their obstetric record. These women were screened, and the investigator then approached them individually to confirm that those who were eligible had satisfied the selection criteria before they were invited to participate. The data were collected at approximately 12-24 weeks' gestation. All of the women who were approached were given a full explanation of the study and informed of their right to refuse to participate. They completed the self-report instruments in approximately 20 to 25 minutes while waiting for their routine antenatal check-up at the hospital.

The SPSS for PC 18.0 software package was used for statistical analysis. Proportions of the groups were compared using a Chi-square (X2) test. All potential variables were chosen based on the preceding literature review using the dichotomized items. The main advantage of dichotomization is that it greatly simplifies the presentation of the results and produces meaningful findings that are easily understandable without causing a decrease in the measured strength of associations (53). The reliability of the subscales was measured using internal consistency (Cronbach's alpha). This study adopted the EPDS cutoff thresholds to identify mild to severe depression with depressive symptoms, by scores of > 9. Significant variables were used as input variables in multivariate stepwise logistic regression models to identify, separately, the factors predicting mild to severe and severe depressive symptoms. Statistical significance was set at $p < 0.05$. The strength of association between the independent variables used in the regression model was moderate for some pairs (| r | ? 0.4). Hence, the tolerance values of predictive variables were obtained in the logistic regression models. All of the tolerance values were about 0.9 or higher, which is greater than the common cutoff threshold of 0.1 (54). The multicollinearity between predictor variables was at an acceptable level. Hostmer and Lemshow's goodness-of-fit (HL-GOF) test was used to fit the model (55).

Findings

Two thousand Chinese Hong Kong women attending four regional hospitals were invited to join the study. Three hundred and ninety one women (19.5%) declined. The main reasons for refusal were busyness, tiredness, and reluctance to disclose information. The remaining 1,609 women (giving an overall response rate of 80.5%) completed the questionnaires. The demographic characteristics of the women who had declined and the participants were not significantly different. The percentages of women with an EPDS score > 9 was 35.9% (n = 578). Table 1 shows the demo-socio-economic status, obstetric characteristics, marital conflict score, and parent-in-law conflict scores of the participants sorted into different groups. The majority of participants were aged over 25 (80.7%), had attained at least a secondary level education (80.6%), and were married (99.2%). Significant differences in age, educational level, period of time living in Chengdu, length of marriage, employment, monthly income, source of financial support, type of residence, intention to breastfeed, marital conflict, parent-in-law conflict, and social support were found among the groups ($p < 0.05$).

Table 1. Demographic, obstetric characteristics and marital and parent-in-law conflicts of participants in Chengdu (n=1,609)

		Entire sample (n =1609)	Non depressed [EPDS ≤9] (n =1031) 64.1%	Mild to severe Depressed [EPDS >9] (n =578) 35.9%	p-value※
		N (%)	*N (%)*	*N (%)*	
Demographic characteristics					
Age	> 25	1298 (80.7)	851 (82.5)	447 (77.3)	.011
	≤ 25	311 (19.3)	180 (17.5)	131 (22.7)	
Educational Level	≥ Secondary	1297 (80.6)	858 (83.2)	439 (76.0)	<.000
	< Secondary	312 (19.4)	173 (16.8)	139 (24.0)	
Places of birth	Chengdu	824 (51.2)	531 (51.5)	293 (50.7)	.755
	Others	785 (48.8)	500 (48.2)	285 (49.3)	
Period of time in Chengdu	≥ 1 years	1527 (94.9)	991 (96.1)	536 (92.7)	.003
	< 1 year	82 (5.1)	40 (3.9)	42 (7.3)	
Marital status	Married	1569 (99.2)	1024 (63.6)	572 (99.0)	.440
	Cohabited/Unmarried/ Separated/Divorced	13 (0.8)	7 (0.7)	6 (1.0)	
Length of marriage	≥ 1 year	1265 (78.6	842 (81.7)	423 (73.2)	<.000
	< 1 year	344 (21.4)	189 (18.3)	155 (26.8)	
Employment Status	Full-time / Self-employment	1223 (76.0)	807 (78.3)	416 (72.0)	.005
	Part-time/Unemployment/ Housewife	386 (24.0)	224 (21.7)	162 (28.0)	
Partner's employment Status	Full-time / Self-employment	1549 (96.3)	1001 (97.1)	548 (94.8)	.021
	Part-time/Unemployment	60 (3.7)	30 (2.9)	30 (5.2)	
Monthly individual total income	> RMB $2000	1207 (75.0)	809 (78.5)	398 (68.9)	<.000
	≤ RMB $2000	402 (25.0)	222 (21.5)	180 (31.1)	
Main financial supporter of family	Couple sharing	1021 (63.5)	689 (67.7)	323 (55.9)	<.000
	One partner only	588 (36.5)	333 (32.3)	255 (44.1)	
Types of residence	Private House	479 (29.8)	272 (26.4)	207 (35.8)	<.000
	Others	1130 (70.2)	759 (73.6)	371 (64.2)	
Size of residence	≥50 meter square	1097 (68.2)	712 (69.1)	385 (66.6)	.311
	<50 meter square	512 (31.8)	319 (30.9)	193 (33.4)	
Obstetric characteristics					
Number of pregnancy	> First pregnancy	936 (58.2)	596 (57.8)	340 (58.8)	.692
	First pregnancy	673 (41.8)	435 (42.2)	238 (41.2)	
Number of baby	> First baby	320 (19.9)	197 (19.1)	123 (21.3)	.295
	First baby	1289 (80.1)	834 (80.9)	455 (78.7)	
Antenatal booking	Before 12 weeks gestation	1029 (64.0)	669 (64.9)	360 (62.3)	.296
	Between 12 to 28 weeks gestation	580 (36.0)	362 (35.1)	218 (37.7)	
Planning of pregnancy	Planned / neutral	1283 (79.7)	837 (81.2)	446 (77.2)	.054
	Unplanned / IVF/ Others	326 (20.3)	194 (18.8)	132 (22.8)	
	Yes	23 (1.4)	14 (1.4)	9 (1.6)	
Feeding intention of breastfeeding	Yes	1403 (87.2)	918 (89.0)	485 (83.9)	.003
	No or not sure	206 (12.8)	113 (11.0)	93 (16.1)	
Family conflicts					
Marital conflict [The Dyadic Adjustment Scale Total Score (DAS)]	Better couple's relationship (DAS ≥ 101)	1319 (82)	909 (88.2)	410 (70.9)	<.000
	Poor couple's relationship (DAS < 101)	290 (18.0)	122 (11.8)	168 (29.1)	
Father-in-law conflict [The Stryker Adjustment Checklist (SAC)]	Better father-in-law's relationship (SAC < 9)	847 (54.6)	593 (59.9)	254 (45.2)	<.000
	Poor father-in-law's relationship (SAC ≥ 9)	705 (45.4)	397 (40.1)	308 (54.8)	
Mother-in-law conflict [The Stryker Adjustment Checklist (SAC)]	Better mother-in-law's relationship (SAC < 9)	849 (54.0)	600 (59.7)	249 (43.9)	<.000
	Poor mother-in-law's relationship (SAC ≥ 9)	723 (46.0)	405 (40.3)	318 (56.1)	

EPDS = Edinburgh Postnatal Depression Scale,

※Chi-square Test, Values in boldface indicated p value < .05

Table 2. Adjusted odds ratios (95% CI) of logistic regression models of significant variables associated with antenatal depressive symptoms

		Mild to severe Depressed [EPDS > 9] (*n* =578)			
		aOR	95% CI		*p*-value
			Lower	Upper	
Demographic characteristics					
Age	≤ 25	1.162	.870	1.552	.310
Educational Level	≤ Secondary	.884	.647	1.207	.437
Period of time in Chengdu	< 1 year	1.639	1.001	2.684	.050
Length of marriage	< 1 year	1.338	1.014	1.765	.040
Employment Status	Part-time/Unemployment/ Housewife	.939	.708	1.246	.633
Partner's employment Status	Part-time/Unemployment	.994	.554	1.783	.984
Monthly individual total income	≤ RMB $2000	1.201	0.912	1.581	.191
Main financial supporter of family	One partner only	1.407	1.099	1.800	.007
Types of residence	Rented House	.814	.628	1.054	.119
Obstetric characteristics					
Number of pregnancy	First pregnancy	-	-	-	-
Feeding intention of breastfeeding	No or not sure	1.310	.949	1.808	.101
Family conflicts					
Marital conflict [The Dyadic Adjustment Scale Total Score (DAS)]	Poor couple's relationship (DAS < 101)	2.347	1.769	3.114	<.000
Father-in-law conflict [The Stryker Adjustment Checklist (SAC)]	Poor father-in-law' s relationship (SAC ≥ 9)	1.206	.910	1.599	.192
Mother-in-law conflict [The Stryker Adjustment Checklist (SAC)]	Poor mother-in-law's relationship (SAC ≥ 9)	1.399	1.056	1.854	.019

aOR = Adjusted Odd Ratio
EPDS = Edinburgh Postnatal Depression Scale
Values in boldface indicated *p* value < .05

Significant variables related to antenatal depressive symptoms

Table 2 shows that women with a shorter marital duration (aOR = 1.338; CI: 1.014 – 1.765), having a single source of financial support (aOR = 1.407; 1.099 – 1.800), a poor marital relationship (aOR = 2.347; 1.769 – 3.114), a poor mother-in-law relationship (aOR = 1.399; 1.056 – 1.854) were more likely to have mild to severe depressive symptoms ($p < 0.05$).

Discussion

As shown above, the prevalence of mild to severe antenatal depressive symptoms was 35.9%. These results are similar to those found in previous studies in other countries (13). Empirical evidence shows that western women express their depressive symptoms overtly but Chinese women tend to manifest them through somatic complaints (56). Therefore, the actual prevalence of depressive symptomatology among Chengdu women may be much higher.

Demo-socio-economic factors influencing antenatal depressive symptoms

This study shows, for the first time, that pregnant women living in Chengdu who had been married for less than a year was more likely to experience mild to severe depressive symptoms. In the same vein, another study has showed that the transition to parenthood hastens the typical linear decline in marital satisfaction over the early years of marriage (57) and additional psychological distress results from women's role adjustment with the advent of a baby shortly after marriage (58).

Women in solo-earner couples will have comparatively poor financial resources compared with dual-earner families. As a result, women in this position showed antenatal depressive symptoms, consistent with the findings of western studies (19). Women whose finances are constrained generally suffer from hardship and financial stress that potentially spills over into other areas of emotional wellbeing. This is consistent with a Chinese saying, "destitute couples are sad over a hundred things" (pin jian fu qi bai shi ai) (59).

Consistent with previous western studies (32, 60) as well as a study conducted in Hong Kong (33), our results also show that marital conflict is a significant factor associated with antenatal depressive symptoms. In the traditional Chinese family, patriarchal and Confucian cultures strictly define circumscribed gender roles in which wives are responsible for caretaking and household chores and men tend to place greater emphasis on their work role (26). China's "open-door" policy and its increasing interactions with foreign cultures make cultural learning and change a reality for today's society (61). However, it is also widely recognized that Chinese society is in a transition phase between urbanization and industrialization and is struggling to keep traditional values intact. In a context of rising women's aspirations and economic power, women would have an incentive to, or may be compelled to, devote more effort to their work and less to their families (62). However, the patriarchal ideology persists in Chinese families, especially in men (26) and this discrepancy may precipitate marital conflict. Moreover, Chinese women experience role overload related to work, childcare, and housework even when they are gainfully employed in the workforce, as their husbands' participation in childcare and household chores is limited (63). As a result, depressive symptoms during pregnancy are not surprising.

Empirical studies show a drop in marital satisfaction once a woman has conceived (30, 57). This is because embarking on parenthood heralds a transitional stage in the relationship, and the baby's arrival may produce temporary changes in the quality of the marital relationship as the couple adapt to these new challenges. One study shows that Chinese wives are usually less satisfied than their husbands with their marriage (62). However, it is not infrequent for Chinese women to sacrifice themselves and suppress their feelings in order to maintain harmonious relationships with significant others, particularly spouses and family members (26). Thus, marital conflict leads to self-silencing which leads to depressive symptoms (64).

However, some researchers have discussed the possibility that depression in women is more likely to predate marital conflict (65). According to this perspective, the behaviors of depressed women are aversive to others, including significant others (66) and are also guilt inducing and inhibiting. In this perspective, members of the social networks of depressed women are likely to try to inhibit their negative responses to them, but because this strategy is typically ineffective, these responses are likely to slip through and be perceived by the depressed women. Accordingly, the responses of others serve to reinforce depressive symptoms. A related perspective, that depressive symptoms relate to marital conflict, has been advanced by Bulloch and colleagues who suggest that the relationship between the two is bidirectional (67). However, this relationship is a very complicated matter and there is a long-standing recognition that depression and marital conflict are likely to occur simultaneously (66). The true relationship between depressive symptoms during pregnancy and marital conflict may need to be tested by a longitudinal study.

Mother-in-law conflict and antenatal depressive symptoms

Our findings show that women who experienced more conflict with their mother-in-law were more likely to have antenatal depressive symptoms, which is consistent with previous research (33). Chinese only children will have grown up within the 4-2-1 (four grandparents, two parents, and one child) family structure that has emerged as the new dominant form in mainland society (68). Therefore, each child will have increasingly become the center of attention in the household and become more precious than ever to her parents. Rapid social changes in China, such as the dramatic increase in women's participation in the labor market, mean that Chinese grandmothers are actively engaged in child care (37, 69). An older generation mother-in-law will tend to hold traditional beliefs about antenatal care (an tai or tai jiao) or observe certain restrictions on diet, environment, and activities (33, 41) that may be different from the views held by her daughter-in-law. The excessive attention paid by adults to the only baby in the family will engage this intergenerational conflict, which may be experienced as tension and depressive mood by modern women (70).

Although traditionally the mother-in-law has exercised significant power in the Chinese household, one should expect traditional patriarchalism to be fading away with the dramatic social changes in the past half century (71). Anecdotal evidence seems to suggest that daughters-in-law have been gaining greater decision-making power in households in recent years (27). This can create conflict in intergenerational values because daughters-in-laws may want to adopt modern flexible gender roles, whereas mothers-in-law might resist change and find it difficult to accept a new role (41). Hence, women may struggle to cope in their relationships with their mothers-in-law and experience feelings of depression as a consequence.

To the best of our knowledge, the present study is the first to provide evidence of the correlates of antenatal depressive symptoms among women living in Chengdu. Our results have important implications for public health and social policies. Healthcare providers need to be aware of the increased risk of pregnancy-related depression in these women in order to provide more effective prenatal screening and, eventually, optimal management for this population. This study has identified risk factors for antenatal depressive symptoms in women living in Chengdu so as to optimize prevention on a macro level. This can be delivered by public health education through the mass media, and also in healthcare and community settings. Moreover, the findings may alert policymakers to ensure adequate healthcare resources are available to solve the problem of antenatal depression. Pregnancy requires regular contact with healthcare services. The identification of mothers at risk of antenatal depression is essential for the development of interventions that can prevent or at least alleviate its negative consequences. Early detection limits the direct negative effects of depression on pregnant women and fetuses. The early detection of depressive symptoms during the antenatal period is also important to prevent women from developing postnatal depression. Healthcare professionals who work in maternal and child care are in a key position to assist with the identification, intervention, support, and referral of women who are depressed. This study provides an introductory analysis of antenatal depression in the hopes of inspiring further study in the field.

Despite the contribution that it makes to the literature, this study has several limitations. Firstly, although it examines the correlates of antenatal depressive symptoms, it may have overlooked a number of other variables, such as psychological factors of personality and social networks. Hence, further studies are warranted. Secondly, the use of a cross-sectional survey means that causal factors are undetermined and should be further investigated in a longitudinal study. Thirdly, depressive symptoms were self-reported and not verified with a clinical interview. Finally, family conflict between partners or a parent-in-law is always co-constructed, but this study only considers the woman's contribution. It does not address information about partners and other family members. Hence, the dynamics and dimensions of partners and parents-in-law in familial relationships are undetermined and further study is needed to explore these.

Acknowledgments

This research was substantially supported by a grant from the Macao Polytechnic Institute (research project number P024/DECP/2007; number of the approved proposal, RP/ESS-1/2007). We are grateful for the generous participation of the women in this study, without whom this work would not have been possible.

References

[1] Dossett EC. Perinatal depression. Obstet Gynecol Clin North Am 2008;35:419-34.

[2] Field T, Diego M, Hernandez-Reif M, et al. Depressed pregnant black women have a greater incidence of prematurity and low birth weight outcomes. Infant Behav Dev 2009;32:10-6.

[3] Brandon AR, Trivedi MH, Hynan LS, et al. Prenatal depression in women hospitalized for obstetric risk. J Clin Psychiatr 2008;69:635-643.

[4] Diego MA, Field T, Hernandez-Reif M, et al. Prenatal depression restricts fetal growth. Early Hum Dev 2009;85:65-70.

[5] Dietz PM, Williams SB, Callaghan WM, et al. Clinically identified maternal depression before, during, and after pregnancies ending in live births. Am J Psychiatry 2007;164:1515-20.

[6] Mattes E, McCarthy S, Gong G, et al. Maternal mood scores in mid-pregnancy are related to aspects of neonatal immune function. Brain Behav Immunity 2009;23:380-8.
[7] Alder J, Fink N, Bitzer J, Hosli I, Holzgreve W. Depression and anxiety during pregnancy: a risk factor for obstetric, fetal and neonatal outcome? A critical review of the literature. J Matern Fetal Neonat Med 2007;20:189-209.
[8] Deave T, Heron J, Evans J, Emond A. The impact of maternal depression in pregnancy on early child development. BJOG 2008;115:1043-51.
[9] Pawlby S, Hay DF, Sharp D, Waters CS, O'Keane V. Antenatal depression predicts depression in adolescent offspring: prospective longitudinal community-based study. J Affect Disord 2009;113:236-43.
[10] Gausia K, Fisher C, Ali M, Oosthuizen J. Antenatal depression and suicidal ideation among rural Bangladeshi women: a community-based study. Arch Women Ment Hlth 2009;12:1435 -1102.
[11] Freeman MP. Managing depression during pregnancy. J Clin Psychiatr 2009;70:e25.
[12] Oates MR. Perinatal psychiatric syndromes: clinical features. Psychiatr 2009;8:1-6.
[13] Leung BM, Kaplan BJ. Perinatal depression: prevalence, risks, and the nutrition link--a review of the literature. J Am Diet Ass 2009;109:1566-1575.
[14] Sawyer A, Ayers S, Smith H. Pre- and postnatal psychological wellbeing in Africa: A systematic review. J Affect Disord 2010;123:17-29.
[15] Pottinger AM, Trotman-Edwards H, Younger N. Detecting depression during pregnancy and associated lifestyle practices and concerns among women in a hospital-based obstetric clinic in Jamaica. Gen Hosp Psychiatr 2009;31:254-61.
[16] Bunevicius R, Kusminskas L, Bunevicius A, et al. Psychosocial risk factors for depression during pregnancy. Acta Obstet Gyn Scand 2009;88:599-605.
[17] Gagnon AJ, Zimbeck M, Zeitlin J, et al. Migration to western industrialized countries and perinatal health: a systematic review. Soc Sci Med 2009;69:934-46.
[18] Lara-Cinisomo S, Griffin BA, Daugherty L. Disparities in detection and treatment history among mothers with major depression in Los Angeles. Womens Hlth Iss 2009;19:232-42.
[19] Leigh B, Milgrom J. Risk factors for antenatal depression, postnatal depression and parenting stress. BMC Psychiatry 2008;8:1-11.
[20] Kitamura T, Yoshida K, Okano T, et al. Multicentre prospective study of perinatal depression in Japan: incidence and correlates of antenatal and postnatal depression. Arch Women Ment Hlth 2006;9:121-30.
[21] Karmaliani R, Asad N, Bann CM, et al. Prevalence of anxiety, depression and associated factors among pregnant women of Hyderabad, Pakistan. Int J Soc Psychiatr 2009;55:414-24.
[22] Records K, Rice M. Psychosocial correlates of depression symptoms during the third trimester of pregnancy. JOGNN 2007;36:231-42.
[23] Dhillon N, MacArthur C. Antenatal depression and male gender preference in Asian women in the UK. Midwifery 2010; 26:286-93.
[24] Kim HG, Mandell M, Crandall C, et al. Antenatal psychiatric illness and adequacy of prenatal care in an ethnically diverse inner-city obstetric population. Arch Women Ment Hlth 2006;9:103-7.
[25] Cheung F, Tang C. Women's lives in contemporary Chinese societies. In: Gielen UP, Gibbons JL eds, Women around the world: Psychosocial perspectives. Greenwich, CT: Information Age Publ, 2008.
[26] Tang CSK, Lai BPY. A review of empirical literature on the prevalence and risk markers of male-on-female intimate partner violence in contemporary China, 1987 - 2006. Aggress Violent Behav 2008;13:10 – 28.
[27] Yi Q, Chen Y. The family status of Chinese women: Taiwan, Tianjin, Shanghai and Hong Kong compared (in Chinese). Beijing: Soc Sci Acad Press (China), 2006.
[28] Murphy R, Johnson D. Education and development in China - institutions, curriculum and society. IntEducDev 2009;29:447-53.
[29] Meleis A. Theoretical nursing: development and progress. Philadelphia, PA: Lippincott-Raven, 2007.
[30] Medina AM, Lederhos CL, Lillis TA. Sleep disruption and decline in marital satisfaction across the transition to parenthood. Fam Syst Hlth 2009;27:153-60.

[31] Lawrence E, Nylen K, Cobb RJ. Prenatal expectations and marital satisfaction over the transition to parenthood. J Fam Psychol 2007;21:155-64.
[32] Lancaster CA, Gold KJ, Flynn HA, et al. Risk factors for depressive symptoms during pregnancy: a systematic review. Am J Obstet Gynecol 2010, in press.
[33] Lau Y, Wong FWD. Correlates of depressive symptomatology during the second trimester of pregnancy among Hong Kong Chinese. Soc Sci Med 2007;64:1802-11.
[34] Brock GW, Barnard CP. Procedures in marriage and family therapy. 4th ed. Boston: Pearson/Allyn and Bacon; 2009:xvi, 204.
[35] Chen XP, Chen CC. On the Intricacies of the Chinese Guanxi: a process model of Guanxi development. Asia Pac J Manage 2004;21:305-24.
[36] Chen F. The division of labor between generations of women in rural China.Soc Sci Res 2004;33:557-80.
[37] Goh ECL. Grandparents as childcare providers: an in-depth analysis of the case of Xiamen, China. J Aging Stud 2009;23:60-8.
[38] Masvie H. The role of Tamang mothers-in-law in promoting breast feeding in Makwanpur District, Nepal. Midwifery 2006;22:23-31.
[39] Geckil E, Sahin T, Ege E. Traditional postpartum practices of women and infants and the factors influencing such practices in South Eastern Turkey. Midwifery 2009;25:62-71.
[40] Ozsoy SA, Katabi V. A comparison of traditional practices used in pregnancy, labour and the postpartum period among women in Turkey and Iran. Midwifery 2008;24:291-300.
[41] Lee DT, Ngai IS, Ng MM, et al. Antenatal taboos among Chinese women in Hong Kong. Midwifery 2009;25:104-13.
[42] Zheng YP, Lin KM. A nationwide study of stressful life events in Mainland China. Psychosom Med 1994;56:296-305.
[43] Pearson V, Philips M, He F, Ji H. Attempted suicide among young rural women in the People's Republic of China: possibilities for prevention. Suicide Life Threat Behav 2002;32:359-69.
[44] Cox JL, Holden JM, Sagovsky R. Detection of postnatal depression: development of the 10-item Edinburgh postnatal depression scale. Br J Psychiat 1987;150:782-6.
[45] Spanier GB. Measuring dyadic adjustment: new scales for assessing quality of marriage and other dyads. J Marriage Fam 1976;38:15-28.
[46] Stryker S. The adjustment of married offspring to their parents. Am SociolRev1955;20:149-54.
[47] Felice E, Saliba J, Grech V, Cox J. Validation of the Maltese version of the Edinburgh Postnatal Depression Scale. Arch Women Ment Hlth 2006;9:75-80.
[48] Lee DTS, Yip SK, Chiu HFK, et al. Detecting postnatal depression in Chinese women: validation of the Chinese version of the Edinburgh Postnatal Depression Scale. Br J Psychiat 1998;172:433-7.
[49] Lee DT, Chan SSM, Sahota DS, et al. A prevalence study of antenatal depression among Chinese women. J Affect Disord 2004;82:93-9.
[50] Shek DTL. Chinese version of Dyadic Adjustment Scale (C DAC). Psychologia 1994;37:7-17.
[51] Young K. Marriages under stress: a report on marriage counselling cases at the Hong Kong Family Welfare Society and the Hong Kong Catholic Marriage Advisory Council. Hong Kong: Dept Soc Work, Univ Hong Kong, 1993.
[52] Chu ML. The mother-in-law and daughter-in-law relationships during the tradition to parenthood. Hong Kong: Soc Work Soc Adm, Univ Hong Kong, 1992.
[53] Farrington DP, Loeber R. Some benefits of dichotomization in psychiatric and criminological research. Crim Behav Ment Hlth 2000; 10:100-22.
[54] Hair JF. Multivariate data analysis, 5th ed. Upper Saddle River, NJ: Prentice Hall, 1998:xx, 730, I712.
[55] Hosmer Jr DW, Lemershow S. Applied logistic regression. Wiley: New York, 2000.
[56] Klainin P, Arthur DG. Postpartum depression in Asian cultures: a literature review. Int J Nurs Stud 2009;46:1355-73.
[57] Lawrence E, Rothman AD, Cobb RJ, Rothman MT, Bradbury TN. Marital satisfaction across the transition to parenthood. J Fam Psychol 2008;22:41-50.
[58] Lavender V ed. Body image: Change, dissatisfaction and disturbance. Edinburgh: Churchill Livingstone, 2007.

[59] Luk W, Wong KM, Yuet SYL, Cheng SK. Marital intimacy and satisfaction among Chinese couples in Hong Kong. Hong Kong: City Univ Hong Kong, Div Soc Stud, Hong Kong Catholic Marriage Adv Council, 2001.

[60] Karacam Z, Ancel G. Depression, anxiety and influencing factors in pregnancy: a study in a Turkish population. Midwifery 2009;25:344-56.

[61] Quach AS, Anderson EA. Implications of China's open-door policy for families. J Fam Issues 2008;29:1089-1103.

[62] Liu X. Material vs. spiritual - a novel economics perspective on marriage and divorce. J Socio Econ 2008;37:2330-9.

[63] Zhang Y, Hannum E, Wang M. Gender-based employment and income differences in urban China: Considering the contributions of marriage and parenthood. SocForces 2008;86:1529-60.

[64] Whiffen VE, Foot ML, Thompson JM. Self-silencing mediates the link between marial conflcit and depression. J Soc Pers Relat 2007;24:993-1006.

[65] Hammen C, Brennan PA. Interpersonal dysfunction in depressed women: impairments independent of depressive symptoms. J Affect Disord 2002;72:145-56.

[66] Beach SRH. Marital and family process in depression: A scientific foundation for clinical practice. Washington, DC: Am Psychol Assoc, 2001.

[67] Bulloch AG, Williams JV, Lavorato DH, Patten SB. The relationship between major depression and marital disruption is bidirectional. Depress Anxiety 2009;26:1172-7.

[68] Wang Y, Fong VL. Little emperors and 4:2:1 generation: China's singletons. J Am Acad Child Adolesc Psychiatr 2009;48(12):1137-9.

[69] Li L, Liang J, Toler A, Gu S. Widowhood and depressive symptoms among older Chinese: Do gender and source of support make a difference? Soc Sci Med 2005;60:637-47.

[70] Wong J, Fisher J. The role of traditional confinement practices in determining postpartum depression in women in Chinese cultures: a systematic review of the English language evidence. J Affect Disord 2009;116:161-9.

[71] Dong X, Beck T, Simon MA. The associations of gender, depression and elder mistreatment in a community-dwelling Chinese populations: The modifying effect of social support. Arch Gerontol Geriat 2010;50:202-8.

In: Mental Health from an International Perspective
Editors: J. Merrick, S. Aspler and M. Morad

ISBN: 978-1-62948-519-5

Chapter 5

Self-reported mood sensitivity to pollen, seasonality of mood and depressive symptoms in a college sample

Alice Kosak, BA[1], Kelly J Rohan, PhD[*1], Yael I Nillni, BA[1] and Teodor T Postolache, MD[2]

[1]Department of Psychology, University of Vermont, Burlington, Vermont
[2]Department of Psychiatry, University of Maryland School of Medicine, Mood and Anxiety Program, Baltimore, Maryland, United States of America

This chapter is in part a replication of a prior study by Guzman and colleagues that examined mood sensitivity to pollen and seasonality of mood in a convenience sample of African and African American college students in Maryland. The current study used a sample of primarily Caucasian students (n = 444) at a northeastern college. Participants completed a battery of questionnaires including the Seasonal Pattern Assessment Questionnaire (SPAQ) from which the Global Seasonality Score (GSS) was calculated, diagnosis of Seasonal Affective Disorder (SAD) or sub-syndromal SAD (S-SAD) was derived, a seasonal pattern (high pollen vs. no pollen) identified, and self-reported mood changes during high pollen counts obtained. Unique to this study, participants completed two questionnaire measures of current depressive symptoms, the Structured Interview Guide for the Hamilton Depression Rating Scale, Seasonal Affective Disorder, Self Rating Version (SIGH-SAD-SR) and the Center for Epidemiological Studies-Depression Scale (CES-D), and the month of assessment was recorded. Contrary to expectation, seasonality of mood was not different between participants who endorsed mood sensitivity to pollen and those who did not. In addition, mood sensitivity to pollen was not significantly related to SAD/S-SAD high pollen pattern status vs. no diagnosis. In participants with mood sensitivity to pollen there was no difference in depression scores on the SIGH-SAD-SR and CES-D when assessed during months when atmospheric

[*] Correspondence: Kelly J Rohan, Department of Psychology, University of Vermont, John Dewey Hall, 2 Colchester Ave., Burlington, VT, 05405 United States. E-mail: krohan@uvm.edu

pollen is undetectable vs. months with detectable atmospheric pollen counts. Ethnic differences, latitude, statistical error, or unmeasured variables may explain differences between Guzman et al.'s study and this negative report.

Introduction

Major Depressive Disorder is characterized by depressed mood and/or anhedonia (i.e., loss of interest/pleasure in normally enjoyed activities) and a combination of either significant appetite or weight change (increase or decrease), significant sleep change (hypersomnia or insomnia), psychomotor agitation or retardation, loss of energy, worthlessness or guilt, decreased concentration or indecision, and/or suicidal ideation, which causes functional impairment in interpersonal and/or occupational functioning (1). The majority (>80%) of individuals who develop a major depressive episode will experience at least one recurrence (2). The highly recurrent course of major depression emphasizes the need for identifying risk factors and developing effective and durable prevention and treatment interventions to keep people who are vulnerable to depression well over time.

Allergic rhinitis (i.e., an inflammation of the nasal passages caused by exposure to aeroallergens in previously sensitized individuals) may affect more than 20% of the general United States population (3). Several studies suggest that allergy patients frequently report depressive symptoms, including depressed mood and fatigue. Marshall, O'Hara and Steinberg (4) prospectively examined the effect of symptomatic allergic reactions on affect and fatigue levels in patients with allergic rhinitis. Allergic patients showed a change from high energy and positive mood in the winter, when pollen is virtually absent, to lethargy and sadness in ragweed seasons (4). Patients also reported a decline in alertness and attentiveness and more mental fatigue in ragweed seasons (4). Kovacs, Stauder and Szedmak (5) compared participants with different allergic complaints, including asthma, allergic rhinitis, and skin allergies, to a control group from the general population on Beck Depression Inventory (BDI) scores. Allergic patients had an increased risk of high depression scores, defined as BDI = 10, compared to the control group (32.2% vs. 22.4%) (5). BDI scores also increased with age and with the severity of allergic complaints (5). Using a direct measurement of tree pollen and a serological marker of allergy to tree pollen (tree pollen specific IgE), found a positive correlation between changes in allergy scores and changes in depression scores in patients with recurrent mood disorders evaluated twice, once when tree pollen counts were low and once when the counts were high (6).

The association between allergies and depression may extend to suicide (7). Specifically, tree pollen may act as an environmental trigger for suicide in vulnerable individuals. Postolache and colleagues reported (8) an increase in the frequency of nonviolent suicides in women in the U.S. between 1995 and 1998 during periods of high tree pollen as compared to control periods before and after the pollen peak. There was a two-fold increase in the rate of nonviolent suicides among younger females in the peak-pollen period compared with the control period before the peak (8). Tree pollen peaks in spring coincide with the highly replicated spring peak of suicide across the world (9). Cytokines produced during allergic reactions may mediate the behavioral effects of allergic sensitization and exposure (10). Moreover, the genes for allergy related cytokines have a greater expression in the orbitofrontal cortex (i.e., region of the brain involved in mood and behavioral regulation) in suicide victims as compared to controls who died from other causes (11).

Although the majority of prior work has focused on photoperiod (day length) as a trigger of seasonal deterioration in mood, pollen, the most prevalent seasonal aeroallergen, may also represent a cyclical environmental stressor that increases vulnerability to depression at particular times of year. In certain populations, mood sensitivity to pollen (i.e., mood worsening during periods of high pollen count) may coincide with seasonality of mood, which is defined as the degree of seasonal fluctuation in mood, energy level, sleep length, weight, appetite, and social activities. Depending on the severity of symptoms, marked seasonality of mood can be classified as seasonal affective disorder (SAD), which is a regular pattern of major depressive episode onset and remission associated with particular seasons. A winter-type SAD is characterized by depressive episodes during the winter months that remit in the spring and summer (12). Although less well established, a non-winter type SAD is characterized by a regular pattern of depressive episodes in any one or more non-winter month i.e., March through November (13). Although Guzman et al. (13) adopted the term "non-winter SAD," they intended to capture meeting SAD criteria during those months when pollen is present.

To examine the association between mood sensitivity to pollen and seasonality, Guzman et al. (13) assessed these variables in a convenience sample of 845 African and African American college students in Maryland. Using the Seasonal Pattern Assessment Questionnaire (SPAQ) (14), a Global Seasonality Score (GSS) was calculated for each participant to quantify their degree of seasonality of mood and accepted SPAQ criteria were applied to classify those participants with winter and non-winter type SAD and subsyndromal SAD (S-SAD) (13). Mood sensitivity to pollen was measured by an item on the SPAQ asking participants to indicate how high pollen conditions make them feel. This was evaluated on a Likert scale ranging from -3 "in very low spirits or markedly slow down" to 3 "markedly improves your mood or energy level", with 0 referring to no effect. Participants who reported mood worsening with high pollen counts had significantly higher GSS totals compared to those who did not report mood worsening with high pollen counts. In addition, they found that mood sensitivity to pollen predicted meeting criteria for non-winter type SAD or S-SAD but did not predict meeting criteria for winter-type SAD or S-SAD. Therefore, mood sensitivity to pollen was associated with a pattern of SAD during months when pollen was present in Maryland (March-November), but was not associated with a pattern of SAD when pollen was virtually absent (i.e., the winter months of December-February). Contrary to their hypothesis for a stronger association among females, the relationship between non-winter SAD/S SAD and mood sensitivity to pollen did not differ between female and male participants.

The current study examined 444 students at a northeastern university over an academic year to examine the relationship between mood sensitivity to high pollen counts and 1) seasonality of mood, 2) a pattern of meeting SAD or S-SAD criteria during the months when atmospheric pollen is detectable vs. undetectable and 3) depressive symptom severity in the pollen present vs. pollen absent months. This study provides information about the generalizeablity of Guzman et al.'s (13) results to: 1) a primarily Caucasian sample (91.2%) and 2) a more northern location with different pollen and weather patterns. Additionally, this study includes two measures of current depressive symptoms and will consider the specific month of assessment in examining whether month of assessment (and thus, presence or absence of detectable atmospheric pollen) relates to current depression scores among those who endorse mood sensitivity to pollen.

In this study, Guzman et al.'s (13) labels of winter-type SAD/S-SAD and non-winter type SAD/S-SAD and the monthly criteria for defining each pattern have been changed to "SAD/S-SAD no pollen pattern (SAD_NPP)," which includes the pollen-absent months in Vermont: November through February, and to "SAD/S-SAD high pollen pattern (SAD_HPP)," which includes pollen-present months in Vermont: March through October. This was necessary because pollen may still be present in Maryland in November, but is virtually absent in Vermont by then.

In this chapter we aim to: 1) examine whether mood sensitivity to pollen is related to greater seasonality of mood, 2) explore whether mood sensitivity to pollen is more frequently related to SAD and S-SAD no pollen pattern or to SAD and S-SAD high pollen pattern, and 3) compare current depressive symptom severity when assessed in pollen-absent versus pollen-present months in participants with mood sensitivity to pollen. It was hypothesized that mood sensitivity to pollen will: 1) be related to greater seasonality of mood, 2) predict meeting criteria for SAD_HPP vs. no SPAQ diagnosis, but not SAD_NPP vs. no SPAQ diagnosis, and 3) participants with mood sensitivity to pollen who were assessed in September, October, March, or April will report greater depressive symptoms than those who were assessed in November, December, January, or February.

Our sample

Participants were 444 undergraduate students enrolled at The University of Vermont (28.2% male, 71.8% female). Participants were primarily Caucasian (91.2% Caucasian, 0.9 % Black, 2.7% Asian, 0.9 % Native American, 0.9% Latino, 0.2 % International, 2.9% other). For the purpose of analysis, ethnicity was categorized as white (90.7%) versus non-white (8.3%). The age of participants ranged from 17 to 32 (M =18.9, SD = 1.3).

Procedures

The data for this study come from a larger study conducted by Dr. Kelly Rohan during the 2005-2006 school year. Participants were recruited from undergraduate psychology courses in response to ads about an "online questionnaire study about mood and thinking" and received extra credit for their involvement in the study. Participants completed a battery of surveys, via a secure website, which included questionnaires addressing seasonality, seasonal attitudes, cognitive style, and depressive symptoms and thoughts.

Measures

Seasonal Pattern Assessment Questionnaire (SPAQ). The SPAQ (14) assesses changes in behavior and mood throughout the seasons. Six items measuring seasonal variations in mood, appetite, weight, sleep, energy, and socializing are rated using a Likert scale ranging from 0 "no change" to 4 "extremely marked change". The sum of these items is the Global Seasonality Score (GSS), which can range from 0 to 24. The SPAQ also assesses whether or not the reported seasonal changes present a problem (and to what degree: mild, moderate, marked, severe, disabling) and in which month(s) of the year the respondent "feels worst."

The combination of the GSS, severity of problem associated with changes, and month(s) feeling worst can be used to estimate seasonal affective disorder (SAD) or sub-syndromal seasonal affective disorder (S-SAD) status. The SPAQ criteria for SAD are a) a GSS of 11 or above, and b) reporting a problem with seasonal mood changes, rated as at least moderate in degree (15). S-SAD criteria are a) a GSS of 11 or more with problem severity rating of none or only mild or b) a GSS of 9 or 10 with a problem severity rating of at least mild (15). For this study, a "cumulative SAD" category was used for those meeting the criteria for either SAD or S-SAD as in Guzman et al. (13). To qualify the pattern of SAD/S-SAD as it applies to pollen patterns in Vermont, a no pollen pattern of SAD/S-SAD (SAD_NPP) was defined as feeling worst during one or more of the four months when atmospheric pollen is virtually absent and undetectable in Vermont (i.e., November, December, January, and February) with or without other months excluding July or August. A high pollen pattern of SAD/S-SAD (SAD_NP) was defined as feeling worst during any one or more of the months when atmospheric pollen is present and detectable in Vermont (i.e., March through October) excluding November, December, January, and February (16) .

The GSS scale of the SPAQ has shown high internal reliability (Cronbach's a = 0.8) and test-retest reliability (r = 0.76) (17). The SPAQ discriminates well between individuals who do vs. do not have a clinically significant seasonal mood problem; however, it does not discriminate well between individuals who have SAD vs. S-SAD on the basis of a clinical interview (18-22), which is our rationale for merging SAD and S-SAD on the basis of the SPAQ into a combined SAD category.

Mood sensitivity to pollen was measured from the SPAQ section on sensitivity of mood to different environmental variables and weather changes, specifically using the item "high pollen count." The respondent is instructed to indicate how each variable makes him or her feel on a Likert scale ranging from -3 "in very low spirits or markedly slowed down" to +3 "markedly improves your mood or energy level," with 0 as "no effect." Consistent with Guzman et al. (13) mood sensitivity to pollen was defined as a score of-1, -2, or -3 on this SPAQ question concerning sensitivity of mood to high pollen count, and no mood sensitivity to pollen was defined as a score of 0, +1, +2, or +3. Respondents who selected "don't know" were not included in the analyses.

Structured Interview Guide for the Hamilton Depression Rating Scale, Seasonal Affective Disorder, Self Rating Version (SIGH-SAD-SR). The SIGH-SAD-SR (23) is a self-rating form of the Structured Interview Guide for the Hamilton Rating Scale for Depression- SAD Version (23), which includes the 21-item Hamilton Rating Scale for Depression (HAM-D) (24) and an 8-item supplemental scale to measure atypical depressive symptoms common in SAD. Respondents are instructed to rate the severity of each of the 29 included symptoms over the past week, and total scores can range from 0 to 83. The HAM-D is the most commonly used measure of depression in research studies (25). Many of the psychometric properties of the HAM-D, including internal consistency, test-retest reliability, and convergent and predictive validity, have been shown to be adequate (25).

Center for Epidemiological Studies-Depression Scale (CES-D). The CES-D (26) is a self-report depression scale that includes 20 items corresponding to specific symptoms experienced over the past week. The Likert scale ranges from 0 "rarely or not at all-less than 1 day" to 3 "most or all of the time." Scores range from 0-60 with a rating of 22 or higher indicating a probable major depressive episode and a score of 16 or higher suggesting clinically significant symptoms of depression (26). The CES-D demonstrates high internal consistency (ranging from .85 to .90) and moderate test-retest reliability (ranging from .32 to .67) for 3 different population samples (26).

Findings

Prevalence of mood sensitivity to pollen and of SAD high pollen pattern and SAD no pollen pattern

35.1% of participants (n = 156) reported mood sensitivity to pollen on the SPAQ. Of participants with mood sensitivity to pollen, 71.2% (n = 111) were assessed during months when atmospheric pollen is detectable, and 28.8% (n = 45) were assessed during months when pollen is undetectable in Vermont. This reflects the general distribution of the overall sample in timing of assessment: 68.0% of participants (n = 302) were assessed during months when pollen is detectable (i.e., March-October), and 32.0% (n = 142) were assessed during months when pollen is undetectable (i.e., November-February).

Of the total sample, 3.6% (n = 16) of participants met criteria for cumulative SAD/S-SAD high pollen pattern (SAD_HPP; i.e., either SAD or subsyndromal SAD), 24.1% (n = 107) met criteria for cumulative SAD/S-SAD no pollen pattern (SAD_NPP), and 72.3% (n = 321) had no diagnosis on the SPAQ.

Relation of mood sensitivity to pollen to seasonality of mood and to high pollen pattern and no pollen pattern SAD/S-SAD

A one-way ANOVA tested differences between participants with and without mood sensitivity to pollen on SPAQ Global Seasonality Scores. Contrary to our hypothesis, participants with a mood sensitivity to pollen ($M = 9.03$, $SD = 4.64$) did not differ from participants without a mood sensitivity to pollen ($M = 8.64$, $SD = 4.79$) on GSS, $F(1, 442) = 0.696$, $p = .404$, $d = 0.083$.

To explore whether mood sensitivity to pollen is more frequently related to SAD_NPP or SAD_HPP, a series of hierarchical logistic regressions were conducted with the following dependent variables: (1) SAD_HPP vs. no diagnosis on the SPAQ and (2) SAD_NPP vs. no diagnosis on the SPAQ. Ethnicity, gender, and age were entered on Step 1, mood sensitivity to pollen status was entered on Step 2, and the interaction between mood sensitivity to pollen and sex was entered on Step 3. The regression was then repeated twice for each dependent variable, once with the interaction of mood sensitivity to pollen and age and once with the interaction of mood sensitivity to pollen and ethnicity entered on Step 3. To reduce multicollinearity and maximize interpretability, the predictors used in each interaction were mean centered prior to running the analysis using the procedures outlined by Aiken and West (27). Even though the cell sizes for the different groups are quite different (n = 16 with

SAD_HPP vs. n = 321 with no diagnosis and n = 107 with SAD_NPP vs. n = 321 with no diagnosis), Monte Carlo studies have found logistic regression to be appropriate with very discrepant cell sizes (28).

Contrary to expectation, mood sensitivity to pollen did not significantly predict SAD_HPP vs. no diagnosis after controlling for sex, age, and race. In addition, but as expected, mood sensitivity to pollen did not predict SAD_NPP vs. no diagnosis, after controlling for demographic characteristics. In the series of regressions, only one statistically significant interaction was revealed: a significant age × mood sensitivity to pollen interaction in predicting SAD_NPP vs. no diagnosis, B = -0.535, SE = 0.242, Wald (df = 1) = 4.891, p = .027. This suggests that the effect of age on diagnostic status (SAD_NPP vs. no diagnosis on the SPAQ) depended upon mood sensitivity to pollen status. Specifically, participants who met criteria for SAD_NPP and were not mood sensitive to pollen were generally older than participants who met SAD_NPP criteria and were mood sensitive to pollen. Participants with no diagnosis and who were mood sensitive to pollen tended to be older than participants with no diagnosis who were not mood sensitive to pollen (see figure 1). The age × mood sensitivity to pollen interaction approached significance in predicting SAD_HPP vs. no diagnosis, B = 1.149, SE = 0.595, Wald (df = 1) = 3.734, p = .053. Visual inspection of the means suggested that the trend was in the same direction as it was for the SAD_NPP vs. no diagnosis outcome.

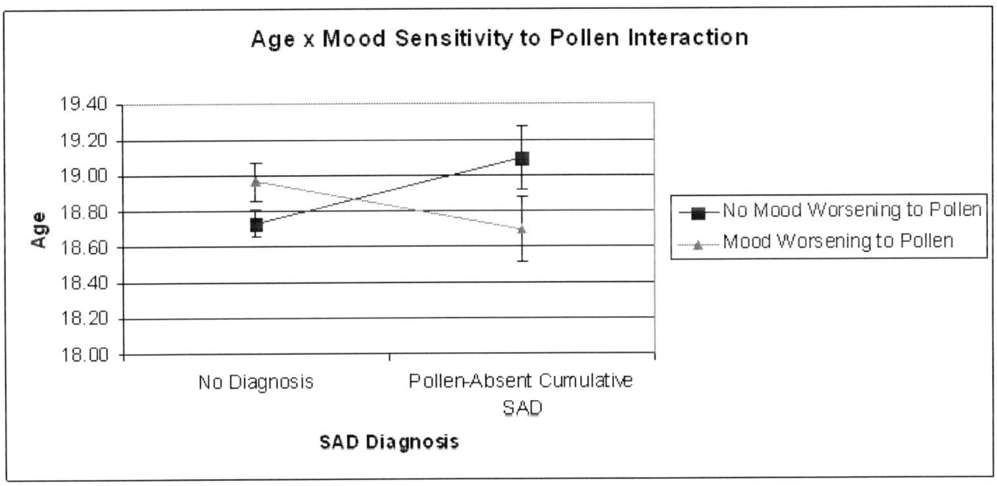

Figure 1. Age × mood sensitivity to pollen interaction.

Depressive symptom severity during pollen-present versus pollen-absent months of assessment

To compare current depressive symptom severity when assessed in months when atmospheric pollen is detectable versus undetectable in participants with mood sensitivity to pollen, a one-way ANOVA tested differences on SIGH-SAD-SR scores between participants with mood sensitivity to pollen assessed in pollen-present months (i.e., March-October) versus participants with mood sensitivity to pollen assessed in pollen-absent months (i.e.,

November-February). Contrary to the hypothesis, participants with mood sensitivity to pollen assessed in pollen-present months (M = 14.37, SD = 9.51) did not differ from participants assessed in pollen-absent months (M = 13.09, SD = 9.92) on SIGH-SAD-SR scores, F (1, 154) = 0.566, p = .453, d = 0.133. Although not a statistically significant difference, the effect size for this difference (Cohen's d) was small and may be clinically meaningful.

A one-way ANOVA tested differences on CES-D scores between participants with mood sensitivity to pollen assessed in pollen-present months (i.e., March-October) versus participants with mood sensitivity to pollen assessed in pollen-absent months (i.e., November-February). Participants with mood sensitivity to pollen assessed in pollen-present months (M = 17.14, SD = 10.36) did not differ from participants assessed in pollen-absent months (M = 15.38, SD = 10.67) on CES-D scores, F (1, 154) = 0.906, p = .343, d = 0.168. The effect size for this difference was small and, therefore, may be clinically meaningful.

Discussion

The aim of this study was to explore the association between mood sensitivity to pollen and seasonal fluctuation of mood in a college student sample. Contrary to expectations, participants with and without a mood sensitivity to pollen did not differ on their overall degree of self-reported seasonal fluctuations in mood and behavior. Moreover, participants with a mood sensitivity to pollen did not report significantly more depressive symptoms if assessed during a month when pollen is detectable than if assessed during a month when pollen is undetectable. Although the differences in current depressive symptom severity during pollen-present vs. pollen-absent months were not statistically significant, small effect sizes indicate that the observed differences may be clinically meaningful. Also contrary to expectation, mood sensitivity to pollen was not significantly associated with meeting criteria for SAD high pollen pattern (SAD_HPP), defined as meeting SAD or S-SAD criteria during the pollen-present months, vs. no diagnosis.

This study, in part, replicated a prior study (13) to evaluate whether previous results are generalizeable across populations. Guzman et al.'s sample (13) of African and African American college students in Maryland found that participants with a mood sensitivity to pollen endorsed greater seasonality of mood than participants without a mood sensitivity to pollen and that mood sensitivity to pollen predicted SAD_HPP status, but did not predict SAD/S-SAD no pollen pattern status (SAD_NPP). Therefore, Guzman's et al.'s (13) results did not generalize to this sample of predominantly Caucasian college students in Vermont. This difference may be explained by the varying base rates between the studies. Guzman et al. (13) reported that more than two-thirds (68.3%) of respondents endorsed mood sensitivity to pollen, 26.5% of participants met criteria for SAD_HPP, and 15.3% of respondents met criteria for SAD_NPP. These rates are substantially different than those found in the current sample: 35.1% endorsed mood sensitivity to pollen, 3.6% met criteria for SAD_HPP, and 24.1% met criteria for SAD_NPP. The difference in rates of SAD_NPP was expected, given that this category encompasses a pattern of feeling worse during the winter months and that winter-type SAD prevalence increases with latitude in the United States (29). Differences in observed rates between the current study and Guzman et al. (13) cannot be explained by differences in measurement because both studies used the same measure of seasonality of mood (i.e., the global seasonality score; GSS) and the same definition of mood sensitivity to pollen, and both studies adopted accepted criteria for SAD and S-SAD to reflect the pollen patterns of the geographic location.

Whereas the reported rates of mood sensitivity to pollen and diagnosis of SAD_HPP and SAD_NPP were different between studies, the degree of seasonality in this study's participants with mood sensitivity to pollen (GSS Mdn = 9) was similar to Guzman et al.'s (13) participants with mood sensitivity to pollen (GSS Mdn = 9). The degree of seasonality for those without mood sensitivity to pollen was also very similar (current study GSS Mdn = 8; Guzman et al. GSS Mdn = 6.5). The similarity on these measures, but the differences in overall rates of mood sensitivity to pollen and diagnosis of SAD_HPP, may reflect that there is a higher prevalence of allergies, specifically asthma, in non-whites than in whites (30).

The limitations of this study include the cross-sectional design and reliance on a self-report measure of mood sensitivity to pollen. Our definition of this construct was consistent with Guzman et al. (13); however, this measure has not been validated. This study also relied on a self-report measure of seasonality, the Seasonal Pattern Assessment Questionnaire, as opposed to a structured clinical interview to classify participants into SAD, S-SAD, or no diagnosis groups. Another limitation is that our study took place over an academic year and, therefore, did not capture the summer months of the allergy season. The summer is the season when grass pollination (early summer) and weed pollination (late summer) are at their peak.

African Americans have a greater prevalence and severity of allergic asthma (31). Moreover, African immigrants have arrived new in an environment with different aeroallergens as compared with their country of origin- and there is literature to support more severe sensitization and clinical consequence of exposure to aeroallergens in those newly exposed to pollen (32).

In addition, unmeasured seasonal confounders (e.g., seasonal academic demands, climatic differences, other socioeconomical factors) may have created a spurious relationship in Guzman et al.'s study (13) or alternatively may have obscured a true association in the current study. Moreover, the degree of clinical manifestations and treatment of allergy may have also differed between VT and DC. Specifically, 1) the incidence of asthmatic reaction and its treatment (33) and 2) differences in the threshold for treatment of allergic rhinitis (e.g., using intranasal corticosteroids, which reduce cytokine production in nasal cavities, as opposed to antihistamines or decongestants, which act mainly symptomatically). Finally, the specific years in which each of the studies took place may have also contributed to differences in results.

Despite this study's negative results, more research is needed on the topic of mood sensitivity to pollen, the most prevalent outdoor aeroallergen, as well as indoor perennial aeroallergens, dust mite feces, which are potentially the most important and controllable aeroallergens, given that there is a demonstrated relationship between allergies and elevated depression symptoms (4, 5). In future studies, a prospective longitudinal assessment of the same participants over time (during pollen-present and pollen-absent months) would be beneficial. Also, in future studies, measures of allergies, asthma, allergic rhinitis, and of actual pollen counts would aid in elucidating the relationship between mood sensitivity to pollen and depression. In addition, these studies should use more accurate and largely used measures of the mood sensitivity to pollen such as skin prick tests or measurements of allergen specific IgEs (such as in Postolache et al. (6, 7)).

References

[1] American Psychiatric Association. Diagnostic and statistical manual of mental disorders: DSM-IV-TR, 4th ed, text rev. Washington, DC: APA, 2000.

[2] Bouland RJ, Keller MB. Course and outcome of depression. In: Gotlib IH, Hammen CL. Handbook of depression. New York: Guilford, 2002:43-60.

[3] Weeke ER. Epidemiology of hay fever and perennial allergic rhinitis. Monogr Allergy 1987;21:1-20.

[4] Marshall SP, O'Hara C, Steinberg P. Effects of seasonal allergic rhinitis on fatigue levels and mood. Psychosom Med 2002;64: 684-91.

[5] Kovacs M, Stauder A, Szedmak S. Severity of allergic complaints: The important of depressed mood. J Psychosom Res 2003;54:549-57.

[6] Postolache TT, Lapidus M, Sander ER, Langenberg P, Hamilton RG, Soriano JJ, et al. Changes in allergy symptoms and depression scores are positively correlated in in patients with recurrent mood disorders exposed to seasonal peaks in aeroallergens. Scientific World Journal 2007;7:1968-77.

[7] Postolache TT, Komarow H, Tonelli LH. Allergy: A risk factor for suicide? Curr Treat Options Neurol 2008;10:363-76.

[8] Postolache TT, Stiller JW, Herrell R, Goldstein MA, Shreeram SS, Zebrak R, et al. Tree pollen peaks are associated with increased nonviolent suicide in women. Mol Psychiatry 2005;10:232-8.

[9] Postolache TT, Mortensen PB, Tonelli LH, Jiao X, Frangakis C, Soriano JJ, Qin P. Seasonal spring peaks of suicide in victims with and without prior history of mood disorders. J Affect Disord, in press.

[10] Tonelli LH, Katz M, Kovacsics CE, Gould TD, Joppy B, Hoshino A, et al. Allergic rhinitis induces anxiety-like behavior and altered social interaction in rodents. Brain Behav Immun, in press.

[11] Tonelli LH, Stiller J, Rujescu D, Giegling I, Schneider B, Maurer K, et al. Elevated cytokine expression in the orbitofrontal cortex of victims of suicide. Acta Psychiatr Scand 2008;117:198-206.

[12] Rosenthal NE, Sack DA, Gillin JC, Lewy AJ, Goodwin FK, Davenport Y, et al. Seasonal affective disorder. A description of the syndrome and preliminary findings with light therapy. Arch Gen Psychiatry 1984;41:72-80.

[13] Guzman A, Tonelli LH, Roberts D, Stiller JW, Jackson MA, Soriano JJ, et al. Mood-worsening with high-pollen-counts and seasonality: A preliminary report. J Affect Disord 2007;101:269-74.

[14] Rosenthal NE, Bradt GH, Wehr TA. Seasonal Pattern Assessment Questionnaire. Bethesda, MD: Natl Inst Ment Health, 1987.

[15] Kasper S, Rogers SL, Yancey A, Schulz PM, Skwerer RG, Rosenthal NE. Phototherapy in individuals with and without subsyndromal seasonal affective disorder. Arch Gen Psychiatry 1989;46:837-44.

[16] American Academy of Allergy, Asthma and Immunology. National Allergy Bureau pollen and mold counts from stations across the United States. Accessed 2009 Oct 19. URL: http://www.aaaai.org/nab/index.cfm?p=pollen

[17] Young MA, Blodgett C, Reardon A. Measuring seasonality: Psychometric properties of the seasonal pattern assessment questionnaire and the inventory for seasonal variation. Psychiatry Res 2003;117:75-83.

[18] Hardin TA, Wehr TA, Brewerton T, Kasper S, Berrettini W, Rabkin J, Rosenthal NE. Evaluation of seasonality in six clinical and two normal populations. J Psychiatr Res 1991;25:75-87.

[19] Magnusson A. Validation of the seasonal pattern assessment questionnaire (SPAQ). J Affect Disord 1996;40:121-9.

[20] Magnusson A, Friis S, Opjordsmoen S. Internal consistency of the seasonal pattern assessment questionnaire (SPAQ). J Affect Disord 1997;42:113-6.

[21] Raheja SK, King EA, Thompson C. The seasonal pattern assessment questionnaire for identifying seasonal affective disorders. J Affect Disord 1996;41:193-9.

[22] Thompson C, Stinson D, Fernandez M, Fine J, Isaacs G. A comparison of normal, bipolar, and seasonal affective disorder subjects using the seasonal pattern assessment questionnaire. J Affect Disord 1988;14:257-64.

[23] Williams JBW, Link MJ, Rosenthal NE, Amira L, Terman M. Structured Interview Guide for the Hamilton Rating Scale-Seasonal Affective Disorder Version (SIGH-SAD; SIGH-SAD-SR, Self-Rating Version). New York: New York State Psychiatric Institute, 1992.

[24] Hamilton M. A rating scale for depression. J Neurol Neurosurg Psychiatry 1960;23:56–62.

[25] Bagby RM, Ryder AG, Schuller DR, Marshall MB. The Hamilton depression rating scale: Has the gold standard become a lead weight? Am J Psychiatry 2004;161:2163-77.

[26] Radloff LS. The CES-D scale: A self report depression scale for research in the general population. Appl Psychol Measurement 1977;1:385-401.

[27] Aiken LS, West SG. Multiple Regression: Testing and interpreting interactions. Newbury Park, CA: Sage, 1991.

[28] Fan X, Wang L. Comparing Linear discriminant function with logistic regression for the two-group classification problem. J Exp Educ 1999;67:265-86.

[29] Rosen L, Targum SD, Terman M, Bryant MJ, Hoffmann H, Kasper S, Hamovit JR, Docherty JP, Welch B, Rosenthal NE. Prevalence of seasonal affective disorder at four latitudes. Psychiatry Res 1990;31:131-44.

[30] Skoner D. Allergic rhinitis: Definition, epidemiology, pathophysiology, detection, and diagnosis. J Allergy Clin Immunol 2001;108:S2-8.

[31] Fagan JK, Scheff PA, Hryhorczuk D, Ramakrishnan V, Ross M, Persky V. Prevalence of asthma and other allergic diseases in an adolescent population: association with gender and race. Ann Allergy Asthma Immunol 2001;86:177-84.

[32] Geller-Bernstein C, Kennet R. Allergies in immigrants. Allerg Immunol 2004;36:313-6.

[33] Kewalramani A, Bollinger ME, Postolache TT. Asthma and mood disorders. Int J Child Health Hum Dev 2008;1:115-23.

In: Mental Health from an International Perspective
Editors: J. Merrick, S. Aspler and M. Morad
ISBN: 978-1-62948-519-5

Chapter 6

Mood improvement with one hour of light treatment in patients with seasonal affective disorder

Gloria M Reeves, MD*[*1,2], Johanna Cabassa[2], Mei Kwan[2], Manana Lapidus[2], Debra Scrandis[2], Gagan Virk[2,3], Alvaro Guzman[2,4] and Teodor T Postolache, MD[2,3,4]
[1]Child and Adolescent Psychiatry Division, Department of Psychiatry
[2]Mood and Anxiety Program, Department of Psychiatry, University of Maryland School of Medicine, Baltimore, Maryland
[3]St Elizabeths Hospital, Psychiatry Residency Program, Washington DC
[4]National Center for the Treatment of Phobias, Anxiety and Depression, Washington DC, United States of America

A course of daily light treatment is an effective intervention for seasonal affective disorder (SAD). There is preliminary evidence to support that light may have some mood elevating effects after one treatment, but this rapid response has not been tested in a clinical population using a placebo controlled study design. Methods: Nine participants with SAD received one hour of bright light and one hour of placebo, dim red light, in a randomized crossover design with a 30 minute washout. Mood ratings were conducted at baseline and after each hour of light. Results: The Friedman ANOVA for total scores on the Profile of Mood State Depression-Dejection plus anxiety-tension subscales (POMS dep-anx) after red light, and after bright light treatment, adjusted for order, showed a significant effect for the conditions (Friedman test statistic = 9.176, df =2, p=0.010). With a Wilcoxon test, POMS dep-anx scores were significantly lower after bright light treatment than after red light (Z= 2.018, p=.044). Conclusions: This preliminary data confirms (for the first time in placebo controlled randomized design in clinically depressed SAD patients) previous evidence that light therapy improves mood after one single hour of treatment. Possible underlying mechanisms of rapid response are

* Correspondence: Gloria M Reeves, MD, University of Maryland School of Medicine, 701 W Pratt Street, Baltimore, MD 21201, United States. E-mail: greeves@psych.umaryland.edu.

discussed. Rapid improvement after initial treatment may provide some symptomatic relief, and patient feedback on positive response may support light therapy adherence.

Introduction

Patients with seasonal affective disorder (SAD) experience significant changes in mood and activity over the fall/winter months with spontaneous remission in the spring/summer. Common presenting symptoms of SAD include depressed mood, intense carbohydrate cravings, weight gain, hypersomnia, anhedonia, and low energy. Light therapy is an effective treatment for SAD (1, 2), with effect sizes comparable to antidepressant medication trials (3). In a double blind, randomized, controlled study comparing light therapy to fluoxetine for treatment of SAD, there were no significant differences in response (67% for both treatments) and remission rate (50% for light and 54% for fluoxetine) at eight weeks (4). Symptom improvement, however, was greater for light therapy after the first week of treatment, suggesting that light therapy may induce a more rapid response than antidepressant medication. There is evidence to suggest that individuals may experience an initial antidepressant response to light after even the first treatment. For instance, Sher et al. (5) reported an improvement on scores on the Seasonal Affective Disorder Version of the Hamilton Depression rating Scale (SIGH SAD) after one hour light therapy in SAD patients, an early improvement that predicted response at two weeks. However, this study was conducted a in an artificial setting (PET scanner) and did not have a placebo control group. In a study of mildly depressed and non-depressed adults, significant mood improvement was detected in both groups after 30 minutes of light treatment in comparison to a low density negative ion placebo (6). In this study, we investigate if rapid mood improvement can be detected in patients with clinically diagnosed SAD after one hour of bright light treatment as compared to a dim red placebo light.

Our sample

Participants were recruited through local advertisement. Inclusion criteria were age 18-65 years, current Major Depressive Disorder with seasonal specifier, and SIGH SAD score of 21 or greater. We excluded individuals with a psychotic or bipolar I disorder, current suicidality, vision problems not correctable by glasses, somatic conditions that had increased sensitivity to light, work schedule that included an overnight shift, illicit substance use or alcohol abuse in the past year, and treatment with an antidepressant, mood stabilizer, or antipsychotic medication in the past 30 days. This study was conducted with IRB approval at University of Maryland.

Diagnosis of SAD was confirmed by (1) diagnosis of Major Depressive Episode with seasonal specifier on SCID ; and (2) SIGH SAD score of 21 or greater. Interviews were conducted by trained research staff who were physician or nurse clinicians.

The initial light treatment session was administered under observation at a research center. Each participant received two hours of light this first session. The two hours of light included one hour of bright white light and one hour of dim red placebo light administered in randomized order. We used a standard light therapy unit Brite Light III light box (Apollo, Salt Lake City, Utah, dimensions = 12"x 22" x 4.5") that emits 10,000 lux of light to the eye when the user is within 24 inches The placebo light consisted of an identical structure with a red screen which will produce a dim red luminance of 50 lux at the level of the eye. The dim red light placebo had an identical appearance except a red screen on top of the diffuser, which will deliver a red light with maximum 50 lux at 24 inches. A light meter was used to confirm luminosity at the level of the eye for each participant. An photometric analysis of the two light boxes confirmed the bright light had a total illuminance 10,050 lux at 24 inches, peak wavelength 545 nm (but with several peaks across spectrum), and total irradiance 3,386 μW/cm2. The placebo red light total illuminance was 42 lux, with peak wavelength 612 nm, and total irradiance of 32 μW/cm2. A treatment expectation survey was completed after five minutes of each light condition. This survey asked individuals to rate on a scale of 1 -10 how effective they believed this light would be for their symptoms of seasonal depression.

Three mood ratings will be completed at baseline and after each light session using the SIGH SAD (7); BDI II (8); and Profile of Mood States Depression-Dejection and Tension-Anxiety scales (9). The SIGH SAD is a semi structured interview with 29 items, including the 21 item Hamilton depression scale plus an 8 items to assess atypical symptom. The BDI II is a self report measure which consists of 21 items which individuals respond on a scale of 0 to 3. The POMS is a 24 item, self report measure in which individuals respond on a likert scale of 0 ("not at all") to 4 ("extremely") how much they are experiencing a specific feeling. Depression/dejection items include "unhappy," "sorry for things done", "unworthy"; and anxiety-tension items include "tense", "shaky", and "on edge". The POMS was developed as a measure of transient, fluctuating affective states.

Primary statistical analysis included a Friedman ANOVA to test for differences between baseline, active bright light, and placebo red light, with Wilcoxon Signed Ranks pairwise test. We also tested interactions between the order of treatments and the changes in mood, using a repeated measure ANOVA with order as a factor.

Findings

Nine individuals participated in the two hour light session. The participants were two Caucasian males, two African American males, three African American women and two Caucasian women. Age of participants ranged from 35 to 62 years old, with a mean age of 47.1 with standard deviation 7.5 years. All of the participants were treatment naïve to light therapy at the time of starting the study. Although not an exclusion criteria, none of the participants were receiving psychotherapy treatment during the course of the study. Five participants were randomized to bright light therapy first, and the remaining four received the placebo light first.

On the treatment expectation survey, two participants expected no difference between red and white light, four expected red light to have a superior effect to bright light and three expected bright light to have a superior effect to red light. There were no statistical differences in expectation between the two treatments

Five patients started with the bright light first, and four with the dim red light first. There was no significant interaction between response to the red dim vs. white light and the order of the administration ($F(2,14)= 0.732$, $p= 0.499$)

The Friedman ANOVA for total scores on the POMS dep-anx scale at baseline, after red light, and after bright light treatment showed a significant effect for the different conditions (Friedman test statistic = 9.176, df =2, $p=0.010$). With a Wilcoxon test, POMS dep-anx scores were significantly lower after bright light treatment than after red light ($Z= 2.018$, $p=.044$). The direct comparison of changes from baseline POMS dep-anx scores between dim red and bright light are presented in figure 1.

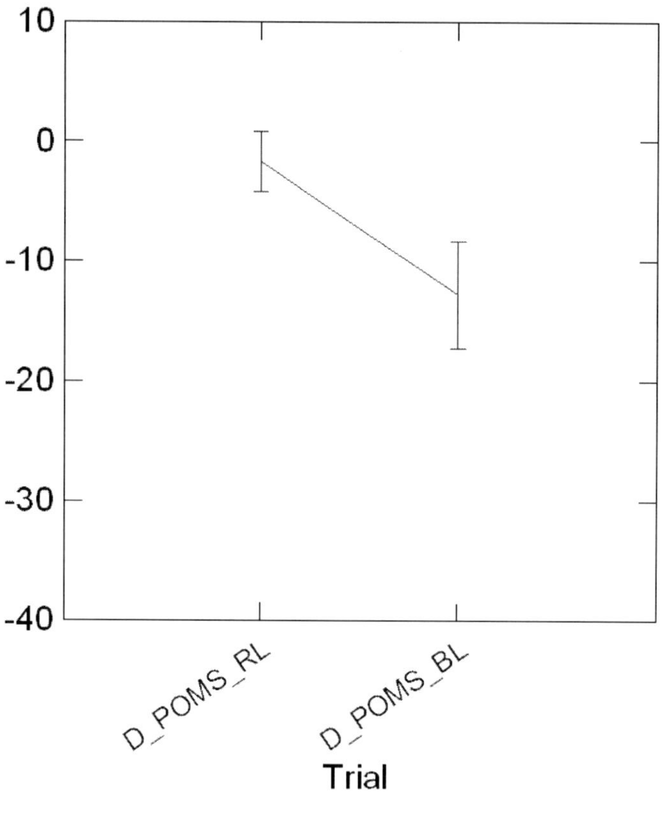

Figure 1. Decrease in POMS dep-anx after treatment with placebo red light (D-POMS-RL) and after treatment with bright light (D-POMS-BL). Improvement after bright light is significantly greater than with dim red light ($p<0.05$).

Analysis of SIGH SAD ($Z=1.544$, $p=0.123$) and BDI ($Z= 0.986$, $p= 0.324$) scores did not yield significant differences.

Discussion

To our knowledge, this is the first placebo controlled study to demonstrate significant improvement in mood rating after one hour of light bright light treatment in patients with

SAD. It is consistent with the results by both Sher et al. (5) and Goel & Etwaroo (6) that mood elevating effect can be detected after only one light treatment.

What are the possible underlying mechanisms of light therapy that promote rapid response? Early effects of light may be mediated at least in part by the serotonin system. For instance, Lambert et al. (10) demonstrated in healthy adult males that serotonin turnover, measured invasively, was directly related to the luminosity of day of the test rather than lagged luminosity or averages of previous weeks. In a study of non-depressed women with mild seasonal changes in mood symptoms, rapid tryptophan depletion was associated with mood worsening under dim light conditions, but not under bright light conditions (11). Thus, bright light appeared to counter the mood depressing effect of depleting precursor of serotonin. Rapid antidepressant effects of light may also be mediated by a specialized group of photoreceptors in the mammalian retina. The recently discovered melanopsin cells are specialized for detection of bright light (12, 13). Melanopsin ganglion cells project to the suprachiasmatic nuclei and other nonvisual centers in the brain, thus effecting centers that regulate circadian rhythm and mood. In a study of 130 individuals with SAD compared to 90 healthy adults, a missense variant of the melanopsin gene was 5.6 times more likely to be in the SAD group than the control group (14).

This study is consistent with growing evidence from randomized controlled trials that early antidepressant effects are not solely attributable to placebo response, and that mood improvement can be detected earlier than the 2-3 week timeframe previously thought to be necessary for response to biologic treatments. Meta-analysis of placebo controlled randomized trials indicate that patients who receive antidepressant medication are more likely to have a significant improvement after one week than those who receive placebo (15). A methodology limitation in previous depression treatment trials is the exclusive use of measures which assess mood symptoms over a period of 1-2 weeks, rather than also utilizing measures more able to detect rapid changes over hours or days (16). There have been efforts to expand biologic treatments for depression beyond antidepressant medication to increase speed of response. A sample of 49 patients with bipolar depression were randomized to either medication treatment only or medication treatment plus circadian-related interventions (sleep deprivation, bright light, sleep phase advance). Improvement in mood ratings at 48 hours were superior in the treatment augmentation group compared to medication only, and improvement was sustained over a seven week period (17). Ketamine, a NMDA antagonist, has also been demonstrated to have early and rapid antidepressant response, with detectable response within 2 hours in individuals with treatment refractory depression (18). In summary, there are an array of biologic interventions which may have a more rapid onset than traditional antidepressant medication treatment and that early antidepressant response has been demonstrated to be evident compared to placebo in controlled trials.

A consideration in assessing immediate response to light or other treatments is whether early response is more specifically due to an anxiolytic response. The POMS measure that detected significant improvement measures both depression-dejection as well as anxiety-tension. In an open label study of health adults, a modest but significant decrease in Spielberger State Anxiety ratings occurred 20 minutes after 3 hour exposure to 3000 lux (19). This result is not consistent with the prior finding that the anxiety – tension subscale of the POMS did not improve significantly after one hour in patients with mild depression (6).

This study reported on preliminary data from the first year of a three year study. The sample size was small, especially for scales like SIGH SAD or BDI that are probably not as sensitive to change as POMS dep-anx. Analysis of larger samples should follow. The results of the study may not generalize to individuals with more severe depression since we excluded individuals with suicidality, bipolar I depression, comorbid substance abuse, or patients currently treated with mood medication.

Conclusion

The first placebo controlled study on improvement in mood after one hour of light treatment in a clinical population is a promising result on a small sample to be confirmed in larger samples. In itself, having a depressed patient feel better (even if not close to remission) after the first session of an antidepressant intervention has an important clinical value. This may reduce feelings of hopelessness as well as improve treatment adherence. Future studies are needed to investigate if early response predicts remission of SAD after a full course of treatment, to assess differences in early response among subgroups of patients with different symptom profiles or demographic variables. Further, associations between biomarkers and early response are needed to study possible mechanisms of early antidepressant response.

Acknowledgments

This study was funded by NIMH 1R34MH073797-01A2 (PI Postolache), with additional support by the University of Maryland GCRC 5M01RR016500-08, NIH 1K12RR023250-01 (supporting Dr. Reeves) and the St. Elizabeths Residency Training Program (Drs. Virk and Postolache).

References

[1] Terman M, Terman JS, Ross DC. A controlled trial of timed bright light and negative air ionization for treatment of winter depression. Arch Gen Psychiatry 1998;55:875-82.

[2] Eastman CI, Young MA, Fogg LF, Liu L, Meaden PM. Bright light treatment of winter depression: a placebo controlled trial. Arch Gen Psychiatry 1998;55:883-9.

[3] Golden RN, Gaynes BN, Ekstrom RD, Hamer RM, Jacobsen FM, Suppes T, Wisner KL, Nemeroff CB. The efficacy of light therapy in the treatment of mood disorders: a review and meta-analysis of the evidence. Am J Psychiatry 2005;162(4):656-62.

[4] Lam RW, Levitt AJ, Levitan RD, Enns MW, Morehouse R, Michalak EE, Tam EM. The Can-SAD study: a randomized controlled trials of the effectiveness of light therapy and fluoxetine in patients with winter seasonal affective disorder. Am J Psychiatry 2006;163(5):805-12.

[5] Sher L, Matthews JR, Turner EH, Postolache TT, Katz KS, Rosenthal NE. Early response to light therapy partially predicts long-term antidepressant effects in patients with seasonal affective disorder. J Psychiatry Neurosci 2001;26(4):336-8.

[6] Goel N, Etwaroo GR. Bright light, negative ions, and auditory stimuli produce rapid mood changes in a student population: a placebo-controlled study. Psychol Med 2006;26(4):1253-63.

[7] Williams JBW, Link MJ, Rosenthal NE, Amira L, Terman M. Structured Interview Guide for the Hamilton Depression Rating Scale, Seasonal Affective Disorders Version (SIGH SAD), revised ed. New York, New York State Psychiatr Inst, 1994.

[8] Beck A, Steer R, Brown G, eds. BDI-II: The Beck Depression Inventory. San Antonio, Texas The Psychological Corporation 1996.

[9] McNair DM, Lorr M, Droppleman LF. Profile of mood states. San Diego, CA: Educ Industr Testing Serv, 1971.

[10] Lambert GW, Reid C, Kaye DM, Jennings GL, Esler MD. Effect of sunlight and season on serotonin turnover in the brain. Lancet 2002;360(9348):1840-2.

[11] aan het Rot M, Benkelfat C, Boivin D, Young S. Bright light exposure during acute tryptophan depletion prevents a lowering of mood in mildly seasonal women. Eur Neuropsychopharmacol 2008;18(1):14-23.

[12] Hattar S, Liao HW, Takao M, Berson DM, Yau KW. Melanopsin containing retinal ganglion cells: architecture, projections, and intrinsic photosensitivity. Science 2002;295(5557):1065-70.

[13] Berson DM, Dunn FA, Takao M. Phototransduction by retinal ganglion cells that set the circadian clock. Science 2002; 295(5557):1070-3.

[14] Roecklein KA, Rohan KJ, Duncan WC, Rollaq MD, Rosenthal NE, Lipsky RH, Provencio I. A missense variant (P10L) of the melanopsin (OPN4) gene in seasonal affective disorder. J Affect Disord 2009;114(1-3):279-85.

[15] Taylor MJ. Rapid onset of true antidepressant action. Curr Psychiatry Rep 2007;9(6):475-9.

[16] Machado-Vieira R, Salvadore G, Luckenbaugh DA, Manji HK, Zarate CA Jr. Rapid onset of antidepressant action: a new paradigm in the research and treatment of major depressive disorder. J Clin Psychiatry 2008;69(6):946-58.

[17] Wu JC, Kelsoe JR, Schachat C, Bunney BG, Demodena A, Golshan S, Gillin JC, Potkin SG, Bunney WE. Rapid and sustained antidepressant response with sleep deprivation and chronotherapy in bipolar disorder. Biol Psychiatry, in press.

[18] Machado-Vieira R, Salvadore G, Diazgranados N, Zarate CA Jr. Ketamine and the next generation of antidepressants with a rapid onset of act ion. Pharacol Ther, in press.

[19] Youngstedt SD, Kripke DF. Does bright light have an anxiolytic effect? BMC Psychiatry 2007;7:62:1-5.

In: Mental Health from an International Perspective
Editors: J. Merrick, S. Aspler and M. Morad

ISBN: 978-1-62948-519-5

Chapter 7

Challenging behavior and people with an intellectual disability

Amanda Sinai, MB ChB (Honors), MRCPsych, MSc[1], Ariel Tenenbaum, MD[1,2], Shoshana Aspler, RN, MSci[1], Meir Lotan, BPT, MScPT, PhD[1,3], Mohammed Morad, MD, FRCP (Edin), MRCPS(Glasg)[1,4,5] and Joav Merrick, MD, MMedSci, DMSc[1,2,5]*

[1]National Institute of Child Health and Human Development, Office of the Medical Director, Health Services, Division for Intellectual and Developmental Disabilities, Ministry of Social Affairs and Social Services, Jerusalem
[2]Division of Pediatrics, Hadassah Hebrew University Medical Center, Mount Scopus Campus, Jerusalem
[3]Department of Physical Therapy, Ariel University of Samaria, Ariel
[4]Yaski Community Medical Center, Ben Gurion University of the Negev and Clalit Health Services, Beer-Sheva, Israel
[5]Kentucky Children's Hospital, University of Kentucky, Lexington, United States of America

Abstract

People with intellectual disabilities have higher rates of mental ill-health and problem behaviors than the general population. In this chapter, we present data on trends in challenging behavior in residential care centers in Israel from 1998-2008 and further data on trends in employment of psychiatrists from 1998-2009 and psychotropic

* *Correspondence:* Professor Joav Merrick, MD, MMedSci, DMSc, Medical Director, Health Services, Division for Intellectual and Developmental Disabilities, Ministry of Social Affairs and Social Services, POBox 1260, IL-91012 Jerusalem, Israel. E-mail: jmerrick@zahav.net.il.

medication use from 1998–2008. Data was collected from annual questionnaires sent out to all residential care centres in Israel, from the Office of the Medical Director, Division for Intellectual and Developmental Disabilities, Ministry of Social Affairs and Social Services. Rates of challenging behaviors in people with intellectual disabilities living in residential care centres in Israel continues to rise. Alongside this, trends in regular psychotropic medication use also continues to increase. Consideration of biological, psychological, social and environmental factors in the assessment and management of people with challenging behaviors is important. This is best conducted using a multidisciplinary approach. This may include psychiatric assessment and consideration of medication, although non-pharmacological interventions should always be considered either alongside, or instead of medication.

Introduction

In Israel, support services for people with intellectual disability are provided by the Ministry of Social Affairs and Social Services. Approximately 10,000 people out of a total of 35,000 registered people with intellectual disabilities in Israel live in residential care (1). Residential or supported care accommodation can vary from larger centers, which house up to 300 residents, to smaller, community based accommodation (in 2009 mean 112.17 (range 21-324) per residential care center).

It is well known that people with intellectual disabilities have higher rates of mental ill-health and problem behaviors (2). It is therefore important that this population receive appropriate mental health care, although each individual may need adjustments to the standard treatment plan in order to tailor treatment according to their needs. Although people with intellectual disabilities living in residential centers in Israel are entitled to use general mental health services, in reality this is difficult to access and residential centers often choose to employ psychiatrists on a private basis to review the mental health of their residents.

Challenging behaviour can be defined as behaviour "of such an intensity, frequency or duration as to threaten the quality of life and/or the physical safety of the individual or others and is likely to lead to responses that are restrictive, aversive or result in exclusion" (3). Behaviors that could be described as challenging can include shouting, self injurious behavior and verbal and physical aggression directed at others. These behaviors may influence the decision regarding accommodation for an individual with intellectual disabilities and may therefore play an important role in determining whether a person lives in residential care.

Challenging behavior is not a diagnosis in itself, and can be due to a number of different reasons, including environmental, social or psychological factors, sensory impairments, communication difficulties and/or physical or mental health problems. Amongst other professionals, psychiatrists are often asked to assess people with challenging behavior and can play an important role in assessment and management. Psychotropic medications are not generally used for challenging behavior in people with intellectual disabilities (unless the cause is related to mental illness) but are sometimes considered on a case-by-case basis. Psychotropic medications have a number of side effects, and the risks and benefits of prescribing these medications should be carefully considered. Efficacy of psychotropic medication for people with challenging behaviors remains uncertain. Tyrer et al. (4) found that although agression in people with intellectual disability decreased over four weeks with haloperidol, risperidone or placebo, it was the group on placebo who showed the greatest reduction in agression. However, a number of people with intellectual disabilities and challenging behavior remain on psychotropic medication, due to a variety of reasons, including worsening of challenging behaviour when medication is reduced.

Although trends in physical and mental health problems in people with intellectual disabilities living in residential care centres in Israel have been reported, including data on medication use (5) and employment of psychiatrists (6), as far as the authors are aware, trends in challenging behaviour of people with intellectual disabilities living in residential care centers in Israel have not been previously reported in the literature.

Our sample

In this study, we present data on trends in challenging behavior in residential care centers in Israel from 1998-2008 and further data on trends in employment of psychiatrists from 1998-2009 and psychotropic medication use from 1998–2008.

Data regarding trends in challenging behavior, the employment of psychiatrists and psychotropic medication use in people with intellectual disability living in residential care in Israel were examined in this study. Data was collected from annual questionnaires (7) sent out to all residential care centres in Israel, from the Office of the Medical Director, Division for Intellectual and Developmental Disabilities, Ministry of Social Affairs and Social Services.

This questionnaire collects information on health and health-related factors of residents living in residential care centers, including demagraphic information such as age, gender and level of intellectual disability of the residents. Amongst other things, it also collects information on mental health factors including number of residents with challenging behaviour, number of residents on medication (including psychotropic medication) and whether a psychiatrist is employed by the residential care center.

Questionnaires were completed by staff at the residential care centers. Data was given as total numbers from each residential care centre and therefore individual residents were anonymised. Residential care centers were anonymised before data entry.

Data from the questionnaire responses was entered on a database and was then compiled into tables. As data is grouped and anonymous, we were unable to analyse any associations between the trends.

Findings

Table 1 shows the trends in the number of cases of challenging behavior for people in residential care during 1998-2008 together with the total number of residents for each year, the number of people getting chronic medication every day, number of people getting anti-epiletic treatment, psychotropic medication and the total number of emergency or SOS medication for aggressive behavior.

In table 2 the number of residentail care centers that employed a consultant psychiatrist over the 1998-2008 time span. The amount of hours employed is also translated into equivalent full time positions.

Table 1. Trends in challenging behavior and medication for people with intellectual disability

Year	Total residents (number of centers)	Challenging behavior (%)	Number of residents receiving long-term medication (%)	Number of residents receiving anti-epileptic medication (%)	Number of residents receiving psychotropic medication (%)	Total numbers of SOS (as required) medications given
1998	6,022 (53)	1,599 (26.55)	3,922 (65.13)	1,730 (28.73)	2,741 (45.52)	1,573
1999	6,122 (53)	1,774 (28.98)	4,330 (71.44)	1,816 (29.66)	2,929 (47.84)	5,343
2000	6,213 (53)	1,959 (31.53)	4,785 (77.02)	1,835 (29.53)	2,848 (45.84)	4,735
2001	6,370 (54)	2,184 (34.29)	4,976 (78.12)	1,873 (29.40)	3,240 (50.86)	6,128
2002	6,352 (57)	2,250 (35.42)	5,098 (80.26)	1,967 (30.97)	3,225 (50.77)	6,814
2003	6,500 (57)	2,250 (34.62)	5,233 (80.51)	2,016 (31.02)	3,162 (48.65)	5,632
2004	6,610 (58)	2,487 (37.62)	5,483 (82.95)	2,127 (32.18)	3,473 (52.54)	6,474
2005	6,749 (58)	2,344 (34.73)	5,548 (82.20)	2,043 (30.27)	3,440 (50.97)	6,739
2006	6,840 (59)	2,488 (36.37)	5,890 (86.11)	2,287 (33.44)	3,515 (51.39)	6,297
2007	6,872 (59)	2,729 (39.71)	5,886 (85.65)	2,306 (33.56)	3,515 (51.15)	5,864
2008	6,988 (63)	2,906 (41.59)	6,082 (87.03)	2,295 (32.84)	3,828 (54.78)	6,355

Table 2. Trends in the number of psychiatrists employed by residential care centres in Israel for people with intellectual disability

Year	Total residents (number of centers)	Number of centers with psychiatrists	Rate per 1,000 Pop	Percent	Equivalent to full time positions	Rate per 1,000 pop
1998	6,022(53)	16	2.66	30.19	6.49	1.08
1999	6,122(53)	44	7.19	83.02	11.96	1.95
2000	6,213(53)	42	6.76	79.25	11.55	1.86
2001	6,370(54)	44	6.91	81.48	11.77	1.85
2002	6,352(57)	45	7.08	78.95	14.05	2.21
2003	6,500(57)	47	7.23	82.46	14.48	2.23
2004	6,610(58)	50	7.56	86.21	17.53	2.65
2005	6,749(58)	52	7.70	89.66	18.83	2.79
2006	6,840(59)	53	7.75	89.83	18.07	2.64
2007	6,872 (59)	51	7.42	86.44	18.10	2.63
2008	6,988(63)	53	7.58	84.13	20.89	2.99
2009	7,067(63)	56	7.92	88.89	23.96	3.39

Discussion

As shown in table 1, the number of people with challenging behavior living in residential care centers in Israel has increased from just under 27% in 1998 to just under 42% in 2008. We do not have any further information on type of behavior, cause or management. These results also show an increase in long-term medication use in people with intellectual disabilities living in residental care centers. They also show an increase in the use of regular psychotropic medication and an increase in anti-epileptic medication use. The use of regular and SOS psychotropic medication may be related to the increase in challenging behavior, although the use of SOS medication has fluctuated through the years, whereas the levels of challenging behaviour reported continue to rise.

This increase in challenging behaviour may be explained as it may be that residential care centers are supporting a higher proportion of people with challenging behaviors, and those without challenging behaviors are more likely to be living in the community. Alternatively, it may be that residential homes have started identifying behaviors as challenging, whereas, perhaps previously, they were not recognised as challenging behaviour. It is not possible to confirm this without further information.

One interesting finding is that over a similar period of time, the proportion of people with intellectual disability living in residential centers taking regular psychotropic medication has increased. This may be linked to the increase in challenging behaviours in this population, although we do not have information on reasons for prescribing and therefore cannot identify the percentage of people on psychotropic medication specifically for challenging behaviours. As the evidence for use of medication for challenging behavior in adults is equivocal (8), this increase highlights the importance of using a multidisciplinary approach to managing challenging behavior, and considering biological, psychological, social and environmental factors in assessment and management.

Alongside the increase of psychotropic medication use, there was also an increase in the number of psychiatrists employed by the residential centers for consultation from 1998 - 2002. This rate has stabilisedstabilized from 2002. Although our study did not directly look at the link between psychiatrists and psychotropic medication use, this is likey to have an impact on psychotropic medication use, as an increase in psychiatrists is likely to lead to an increase in consultations and subsequently may lead to an increase in prescribing of psychotropic medications. These figures may therefore imply that more psychiatrists are reviewing residents in residential care and are subsequently prescribing psychotropic medication for more people with intellectual disabilities.

Interestingly, previous research has shown that, amongst other factors, challenging behavior and review by a consultant psychiatrist is associated with the use of neuroleptic (antipsychotic) medication in adults with intellectual disability (9). Also, people living in residential campus accommodation in the United Kingdom were found to be significantly more likely to receive regular antipsychotic, antidepressant and/or anti-epileptic medication as well as required (SOS) antipsychotic medication when compared to those living in village communities or dispersed housing (10). This study also drew attention to link between factors relating to challenging behavior and the prescription of antipsychotic or hypnotic/anxiolytic medication (10).

Assessment and management of challenging behavior should consider underlying causes such as physical and mental health problems, sensory and communication issues, and social, environmental and psychological factors, amongst other things. The person with intellectual disability should be at the centre of their management plan. Non-pharmacological interventions, including psychological and behaviouralbehavioral interventions, should always be considered either alongside, or instead of medication (11).

Although psychiatrists are often involved in the assessment and management of people with challenging behavior, it is important to remember that there may be a number of factors contributing to challenging behavior, which, alongside mental health problems, may include physical health problems or environmental factors. The same behavior may pose a challenge for services in one particular environment, but may not be a challenge in another environment. For example, a person who wanders may pose a risk to themselves or others if they live near a busy street, but may not pose a risk if they live in a place with large, open grounds, where people recognize them and can direct them back appropriately.

The Royal College of Psychiatrists, British Psychological Society and Royal College of Speech and Language Therapists guidelines provide a very helpful framework for assessing and managing challenging behavior in people with intellectual disability and highlight the importance of considering the individual, their environment and the interaction between the two (3).

Medication and its side effects should be discussed with the individual, and their family and support workers and medications should be regularly reviewed, and reduced if no benefit is found, or if side effects outweigh the benefits. As people with intellectual disabilities may be more sensitive to medications, it is recommended that psychotropic medications are started at low doses and titrated up slowly, monitoring for side effects. Residential centers should have measures in place to monitor medication use and side effects, including SOS (as required) medication.

Further research into challenging behavior in people with intellectual disabilities living in Israel, including assessment, management, type of behavior and type of environment is required to develop a further understanding of how best to manage this complex area.

Conclusion

Rates of challenging behaviors in people with intellectual disabilities living in residential care centers in Israel continues to rise. Alongside this, trends in regular psychotropic medication use also continues to increase.

Consideration of biological, psychological, social and environmental factors in the assessment and management of people with challenging behaviors is important. This is best conducted using a multidisciplinary approach. This may include psychiatric assessment and consideration of medication, although non-pharmacological interventions should always be considered either alongside, or instead of medication.

Acknowledgments

This chapter is a revised version of an earlier publication: Sinai A, Tenenbaum A, Aspler S, Lotan M, Morad M, Merrick J. Challenging behavior and related factors in people with intellectual disability living in residential care centers in Israel. Front Public Health 2013;1:13. doi:10.3389/fpubh.2013.00013

References

[1] Nissim D, Gorbatov R, Ben Simhon M. People with intellectual disability. In: Sabah Y, ed. Social services. Jerusalem: Ministry Social Affairs, 2011:441-74.

[2] Cooper SA, Smiley E, Morrison J, Williamson A, Allan L. Mental ill-health in adults with intellectual disabilities: prevalence and associated factors. Br J Psychiatry 2007;190:27-35.

[3] Royal College of Psychiatrists, British Psychological Society and Royal College of Speech and Language Therapists. Challenging behaviour; A unified approach. Clinical and service guidelines for supporting people with learning disabilities who are at risk of receiving abusive or restrictive practices. London: Royal College Psychiatrists, 2007.

[4] Tyrer P, Oliver-Africano PC, Ahmed Z, Bouras N, Cooray S et al. Risperidone, haloperidol and placebo in the treatment of aggressive challenging behaviour in patients with intellectual disability: a randomised controlled trial. Lancet 2008;371(9606):57-63.

[5] Merrick J, Kandel I, Lotan M, Aspler S, Fuchs BS, Morad M. National survey 2007 on medical services for persons with intellectual disability in residential care in Israel. Int J Adolesc Med Health 2010;22(4):575-82.

[6] Merrick J, Kandel I, Morad M. Mental health services for people with intellectual disability in residential care in Israel. Trends for 1998-2006. Int J Adolesc Med Health 2009;21(1):127-30.

[7] Merrick J. National survey 1998 on medical services for persons with intellectual disability in residential care in Israel. Int J Disabil Hum Dev 2005;4(2):139-46.

[8] Deb S, Mungar N. Module 9: Use of medication in challenging behaviour. In: Hardy S, Brighton JT, eds. Challenging behaviour – a training pack to develop good practice in working with people with learning disabilities whose behaviour is described as challenging. East Sussex: Pavillion Publishing, 2010.

[9] Molyneux P, Emerson E, Caine A. Prescription of psychotropic medication to people with intellectual disabilities in primary health care settings. J Appl Res Intellect Disabil 1999;12(1):46-57.

[10] Robertson J, Emerson E, Gregory N, Hatton C, Kessissoglou S et al. Receipt of psychotropic medication by people with intellectual disability in residential settings. J Intellect Disabil Res 2000;44(6):666-76.

[11] Deb S. (2009). The role of medication in the management of behaviour problems in people with learning disabilities. Adv Ment Health Learn Disabil 2009;1(2):26-31.

In: Mental Health from an International Perspective
Editors: J. Merrick, S. Aspler and M. Morad
ISBN: 978-1-62948-519-5

Chapter 8

Adult perceptions of youth mental health problems

Amy Metcalfe, PhD[1], Julius Salegio, MSc[2], Nancy Reynolds, BScOT[2] and Suzanne Tough, PhD[*2,3]

[1]University of British Columbia, Department of Obstetrics and Gynaecology, Vancouver, British Columbia, Canada

[2]Alberta Centre for Child Family and Community Research

[3]University of Calgary, Departments of Paediatrics and Community Health Sciences, Calgary, Alberta, Canada

Although 15% of Canadian youth experience mental health problems, barriers to disclosure and treatment exist. In this chapter we assess public opinion about the prevalence of mental illness among youth, treatment for mental illness, and comfort interacting with youth with mental health problems. Study Group: A random sample of adults residing in Alberta Canada. Methods: Chi-square tests and t-tests were used to understand responses by demographics. Logistic regression was used to determine factors predictive of comfort in interacting with youth with moderate mental health problems. Results: Twenty percent were able to correctly identify the prevalence of youth mental health problems. Over 50% stated that they believed that <10% of youth with mental health problems received treatment. Approximately 70% of the sample reported they would be comfortable interacting with youth with moderate mental health problems in work, school, social and community settings. Consistent predictors of comfort interacting with youth with moderate mental health problems included: being between the ages of 18-24, high school completion, Caucasian ethnicity, and annual household income >$40,000/year. Conclusions: There are meaningful gaps in Albertans understanding of the prevalence of youth mental health issues, but the majority of adults would be comfortable interacting with youth with moderate mental health problems. Many respondents identified that youth with mental health problems may not be receiving treatment. Increased public awareness about the prevalence and detrimental impact of

* Correspondence: Suzanne Tough, Professor and Scientific Director, Child Development Centre, 2888 Shaganappi Trail NW, Calgary, Alberta T3B 6A8, Canada. E-mail: suzanne.tough@albertahealthservices.ca.

youth mental health issues may help policy makers allocate resources to effective screening and treatment for youth with mental health concerns.

Introduction

Adequate levels of mental health literacy ('the knowledge and beliefs about mental disorders which aid their recognition, management or prevention' (1)) in the population is important for several reasons. First, it is estimated that in the course of a lifetime, almost everyone will either come into contact with a person with a mental health problem or will develop a mental health problem (1). Second, poor mental health literacy may delay treatment as people are unable to identify the signs and symptoms of mental health problems or be unable to clearly communicate these symptoms to care providers (2). As the majority of mental health problems begin before the age of 24 (3), understanding the public's knowledge of mental health problems in adolescents is crucial as this sets the context in which policy is developed, clinicians are trained and individuals seek care (4). Furthermore, an Australian study found that when dealing with mental health issues, youth (aged 15-25) were most likely to turn to family and friends for assistance before seeking out professional help (3). Therefore, it is important that members of the general public are able to recognize the signs and symptoms of mental health problems and are able to direct individuals to appropriate sources of care.

Poor mental health literacy is believed to contribute to public stigma towards individuals with mental health problems. This in turn can lead to social distancing ('the desire to avoid contact with a particular group of people' (5)) from individuals with mental health problems which can further impact an individual's ability to seek and receive treatment and successfully integrate into society (6). While the desire for social distance from adults with mental health issues has been widely reported on in the literature, the desire for social distance from children and youth afflicted with mental health problems is less clearly understood (5). A 2009 review of social distance from individuals with mental health problems concluded that social distance should routinely be measured as part of national health surveys as an indicator of public stigma and the impact of public health campaigns to reduce stigma towards individuals with mental health problems (5).

This study aimed to assess the mental health literacy of the general population, and to assess their desire for social distance from youth afflicted with moderate mental health problems.

Our sample

English-speaking men and women who were at least 18 years of age and were residing in Alberta Canada at the time of contact were involved in this population-based study. Participants were recruited through a random-digit dialing technique targeting landlines and cellular phones. If an individual was contacted on their cellular phone, they were given the opportunity to provide an alternative number for a scheduled call back. Potential participants were contacted up to 10 times at various times of day. Interviews took approximately 30 minutes to complete. Prior to beginning the questionnaire, participants were informed that their participation in this research was completely voluntary, that their individual responses would be kept confidential, and that they could end the interview at any time. An overall response rate of 21.2% (1203/5667) was obtained for this survey and on average it took 3.9 call attempts to complete an interview. This study was approved by the Arts, Science and Law Research Ethics Board at the University of Alberta.

The Alberta Survey is conducted annually by the Population Research Laboratory at the University of Alberta to understand public opinion on issues with relevance to public policy. Community groups, researchers and governmental organizations have the opportunity to add a group of questions to this survey each year.

To understand mental health literacy and a desire for social distance, respondents were asked the following 5 questions regarding their perceptions about youth mental health issues along with questions related to respondent demographics:

1. Generally, what percentage of youth between the ages of 15 to 19 do you think have some kind of mental health problem? (Open Ended)
2. Generally, what percentage of children between the ages of 12 to 14 do you think have some kind of mental health problem? (Open Ended)
3. What percentage of those between the ages of 12 to 19 with a mental health problem receive treatment? (Open Ended)
4. At what age do you think a mental health problem can develop? (Response options: before or after birth (up to 12 months), early childhood (13-59 months), childhood (5-9 years), puberty (10-13 years), teens (14-19 years), early adulthood (20-24 years), adulthood (≥25 years), any age)
5. How comfortable do you think you would feel in the company of a child or youth between the ages of 12-19 who has a moderate mental health problem in the following settings? (Response options: very uncomfortable, uncomfortable, neutral, comfortable, very comfortable)
   a. Work
   b. School
   c. Social setting (i.e., family gathering or party with friends or work colleagues)
   d. Community setting (i.e., sports, recreational activities, or church)

The following definition of a moderate mental health problem was provided to survey respondents upon request: An individual with a moderate mental health problem exhibits chronic and pervasive behaviours that interfere with the functioning and safety of the individual and other individuals around him/her. Typically a moderate mental health problem is characterized by a number of maladaptive behaviours, such as: an inability to establish or maintain satisfactory relationships with peers or adults; a general mood of unhappiness or depression; inappropriate behaviour of feelings under ordinary conditions; continued difficulty in coping with the everyday situations in spite of remedial intervention; physical symptoms or fears associated with personal, work or school problems; difficulties in accepting the realities of personal responsibility and accountability; and/or physical violence toward other persons and/or physical destructiveness toward the environment.

Data were collected between May and July 2010 using a computer-assisted telephone interview (Ci3 WINCATI, Sawtooth Software).This analysis was completed using Stata SE version 11 and significance was set at $p<0.05$. Descriptive statistics were used to describe the characteristics of study respondents. Categorical variables were expressed as frequencies and percentages with 95% confidence intervals (CI). Four multivariable logistic regression models were used to determine what demographic variables (marital status, employment, education, age, ethnicity, annual household income) were significantly associated with comfort in interacting with youth with moderate mental health problems in various settings (coded as very comfortable/comfortable vs. neutral/uncomfortable/very uncomfortable). All variables were initially entered into the model, the variable with the highest p-value was purposively removed from the model until all remaining variables had a p-value of <0.05.

Findings

Table 1. Respondent characteristics

Variable	Survey Respondents N (%, 95% CI)	2006 Canadian Census: Alberta Population (7) %
Location		
City	774 (64.4, 61.7 to 67.1)	---
Town/Village	238 (19.8, 17.6 to 22.1)	
Rural Area	189 (15.7, 13.7 to 17.8)	
Gender		
Male	598 (49.7, 46.9 to 52.5)	50.0
Female	605 (50.3, 47.5 to 53.1)	50.0
Marital Status*		
Married/Common Law	855 (71.4, 68.8 to 73.9)	64.8
Single/Divorced/Separated/Widowed	343 (28.6, 26.1 to 31.2)	35.2
Employment Status**		
Employed Full-Time	666 (60.1, 57.2 to 62.9)	Employment rate: 70.9%
Employed Part-Time	164 (14.8, 12.7 to 16.9)	---
Retired	227 (20.5, 18.1 to 22.8)	---
Unemployed	52 (4.7, 3.4 to 5.9)	Unemployment Rate: 4.3%
Highest Level of Education Completed		
Did not complete high school	96 (8.0, 6.5 to 9.6)	23.4
Completed high school	240 (20.1, 17.8 to 22.4)	26.2
Some post-secondary	137 (11.5, 9.7 to 13.3)	---
Completed post-secondary	584 (48.9, 46.0 to 51.7)	45.1
Post-graduate degree	138 (11.5, 9.7 to 13.4)	5.3
Median Age Group***	51.0	36.0
Ethnicity		
Caucasian	1021 (84.9, 82.8 to 86.9)	86.1
Other	182 (15.1, 13.1 to 17.2)	13.9
Median Personal Income	$50,000 to 54,999	$43,964
Children Reside in the Home		
No	805 (67.1, 64.5 to 69.8)	---
Yes	394 (32.9, 30.2 to 35.5)	

* Census results for marital status are for individuals age 20 and older

** Census results for employment are for individuals age 15 and older

*** Census results are for all Albertans, while survey participants had to be at least 18 years of age

This questionnaire was completed by a total of 1203 individuals. Approximately equal numbers of men and women participated in the survey (Table 1). The majority of respondents: lived in a city, were married or in a common law relationship, were employed full-time, had completed post-secondary education, had an annual household income ≥ ≥$80,000, were Caucasian, and did not currently have children residing with them in their homes (Table 1).

Respondents are reflective of the Alberta population as captured by the 2006 Canadian census (7) in terms of gender and ethnicity (Table 1). Respondents tended to have completed a higher level of education, have a higher income and be older than the average Albertan (Table 1).

Perceptions regarding the prevalence of youth mental health issues

Table 2. Respondent beliefs about youth mental health issues (n=1139)

Variable	N	% (95% CI)
What percentage of children between the ages of 12-14 do you think have some kind of mental health problem?		
0-10%	476	46.5% (43.5 to 49.6)
11-20%*	204	19.9% (17.5 to 22.4)
21-30%	151	14.8% (12.6 to 16.9)
31-40%	60	5.9% (4.4 to 7.3)
41-50%	71	6.9% (5.4 to 8.5)
>50%	61	6.0% (4.5 to 7.4)
What percentage of youth between the ages of 15-19 do you think have some kind of mental health problem?		
0-10%	358	34.7% (31.7 to 37.6)
11-20%*	229	22.2% (19.6 to 24.7)
21-30%	149	14.4% (12.2 to 16.6)
31-40%	102	9.9% (8.1 to 11.7)
41-50%	73	7.1% (5.5 to 8.6)
>50%	122	11.8% (9.8 to 13.8)
What percentage of youth between the ages of 12-19 with a mental health problem receive treatment?		
0-10%	495	50.2% (47.0 to 53.3)
11-20%	115	11.7% (9.6 to 13.7)
21-30%*	110	11.1% (9.2 to 13.1)
31-40%	54	5.5% (4.0 to 6.9)
41-50%	114	11.6% (9.6 to 13.5)
>50%	99	10.0% (8.2 to 11.9)
At what age do you think a mental health problem can develop?		
Before or after birth (up to 12 months)		
Early childhood (13-59 months)	159	14.0 (11.9 to 16.0)
Childhood (5-9 years)	199	17.5 (15.3 to 19.7)
Puberty (10-13 years)	207	18.2 (15.9 to 20.4)
Teens (14-19 years)	101	8.9 (7.2 to 10.5)
Early adulthood (20-24 years)	65	5.7 (4.4 to 7.1)
Adulthood (25+ years)	12	1.1 (0.5 to 1.6)
Any age*	10	0.9 (0.3 to 1.4)
	386	33.9 (31.1 to 36.6)

* correct response

Approximately 20% of respondents correctly identified that 11-20% of youth between the ages of 12 and 19 years suffer from mental health problems; and many respondents believed that mental health problems influenced fewer than 10% of youth (Table 2). On average, 11% of respondents correctly identified that 21-30% of youth aged 12-19 with mental health problems receive treatment for these issues (Table 2). Slightly over half of respondents believed that no more than 10% of youth with mental health problems received treatment for these problems. Approximately a third of respondents correctly identified that mental health problems can develop at any age, and only 2.0% of respondents believed that mental health problems could not develop until adulthood (Table 2).

Comfort interacting with youth with moderate mental health problems

Approximately two-thirds of respondents reported that they would be comfortable or very comfortable interacting with youth with moderate mental health problems in work, school, social and community settings (Table 3). Only 10% of respondents reported that they would be uncomfortable or very uncomfortable interacting with youth with moderate mental health problems in work, school, social and community settings (Table 3). The proportion of respondents who reported being comfortable/very comfortable interacting with youth with moderate mental health problems was slightly less for social and community settings than it was for work and school settings.

Table 3. Comfort interacting with youth aged 12-19 with moderate mental health problems in various settings (n=1174)

Variable	Work Setting N (% 95% CI)	School Setting N (% 95% CI)	Social Setting N (% 95% CI)	Community Setting N (% 95% CI)
Very Uncomfortable	55 (5.0, 3.7 to 6.3)	40 (4.1, 2.8 to 5.3)	30 (2.6, 1.7 to 3.5)	30 (2.6, 1.7 to 3.5)
Uncomfortable	66 (6.0, 4.6 to 7.5)	62 (6.3, 4.8 to 7.8)	63 (5.4, 4.1 to 6.7)	55 (4.7, 3.5 to 5.9)
Neutral	214 (19.6, 17.2 to 21.9)	197 (20.0, 17.5 to 22.5)	225 (19.2, 16.9 to 21.4)	222 (18.9, 16.7 to 21.2)
Comfortable	305 (27.9, 25.2 to 30.6)	267 (27.2, 24.4 to 29.9)	352 (30.0, 27.4 to 32.6)	350 (29.9, 27.2 to 32.5)
Very Comfortable	453 (41.4, 38.5 to 44.4)	417 (42.4, 39.3 to 45.5)	504 (42.9, 40.1 to 45.8)	515 (43.9, 41.1 to 46.8)

Age and ethnicity were significant predictors in all models examining comfort interacting with youth with moderate mental health problems (Table 4). Consistently, individuals who were 18-24 years old and of Caucasian ethnicity were more likely to report being comfortable or very comfortable interacting with youth with moderate mental health problems. Annual household income was a significant predictor in the models examining comfort in work, social and community settings (Table 4). In all models, a positive association was observed whereby the higher the annual household income the more likely individuals were to report that they were comfortable/very comfortable interacting with youth with moderate mental health problems. Education was a significant predictor in the models examining comfort in school and social settings (Table 4). In both scenarios, individuals who had not completed high school were the most likely to report being uncomfortable interacting with youth with moderate mental health problems. Marital status was only a significant predictor in the model examining comfort in a community setting (Table 4), where it was noted that individuals who were single, separated, divorced or widowed were significantly less likely to report being comfortable interacting with youth with moderate mental health issues (OR=0.64, 95% CI: 0.44-0.93).

Table 4. Significant predictors of comfort interacting with youth with moderate mental health problems in various settings

Variable	OR (95% CI)			
	Work Setting (n=828) OR (95% CI)	School Setting (n=730) OR (95% CI)	Social Setting (n=875) OR (95% CI)	Community Setting (n=876) OR (95% CI)
Age Categories				
18-24	Reference	Reference	Reference	Reference
25-34	0.26 (0.08 to 0.80)	0.67 (0.31 to 1.44)	0.31 (0.10 to 0.96)	0.19 (0.05 to 0.68)
35-44	0.31 (0.10 to 0.93)	0.58 (0.28 to 1.21)	0.52 (0.16 to 1.62)	0.26 (0.07 to 0.91)
45-54	0.28 (0.09 to 0.84)	0.48 (0.24 to 0.98)	0.30 (0.10 to 0.90)	0.20 (0.06 to 0.71)
55-64	0.25 (0.08 to 0.76)	0.41 (0.20 to 0.83)	0.28 (0.09 to 0.84)	0.17 (0.05 to 0.61)
65+	0.21 (0.07 to 0.64)	0.29 (0.14 to 0.61)	0.22 (0.07 to 0.69)	0.13 (0.03 to 0.45)
Annual Household Income				
<$39,999	Reference	Not included in final model	Reference	Reference
$40,000-$79,999	2.00 (1.17 to 3.40)		2.27 (1.35 to 3.83)	1.77 (1.03 to 3.03)
≥ $80,000	2.25 (1.36 to 3.71)		2.37 (1.44 to 3.89)	1.85 (1.08 to 3.18)
Ethnicity				
Caucasian	Reference	Reference	Reference	Reference
Other	0.49 (0.32 to 0.76)	0.56 (0.38 to 0.83)	0.48 (0.31 to 0.73)	0.43 (0.27 to 0.66)
Highest Level of Education Completed				
High School Incomplete	Not included in final model	Reference	Reference	Not included in final model
High School Complete		2.25 (1.25 to 4.03)	1.63 (0.85 to 3.13)	
Post-Secondary Incomplete		2.29 (1.22 to 4.29)	1.86 (0.92 to 3.77)	
Post-Secondary Complete		2.27 (1.34 to 3.85)	1.99 (1.09 to 3.63)	
Post-Graduate Degree		2.49 (1.31 to 4.75)	2.02 (1.00 to 4.11)	
Marital Status				
Married/Common Law	Not included in final model	Not included in final model	Not included in final model	Reference
Single/Divorced/Separated/ Widowed				0.64 (0.44 to 0.93)

Discussion

Mental health literacy in this sample appears to be low, as only 20% of respondents were able to correctly identify that 11-20% of youth (aged 12 to 19) suffer from mental health problems and only 11% of respondents were able to correctly identify that 21-30% of youth aged 12-19 with mental health problems receive treatment for these issues. Additionally, only one third of respondents were able to correctly identify that mental health problems can develop at any age. Generally, respondents did not believe that youth with mental health problems were receiving the treatment that they need. This has important implications for government policy as it may indicate public confidence in Alberta's publicly funded health care system in regards to youth with moderate mental health problems could be improved. Most respondents reported that they would be comfortable or very comfortable interacting with youth with moderate mental health problems in work, school, social and community settings indicating a low desire for social distance from youth with moderate mental health problems. Consistent predictors of comfort included: age 18-24, completion of high school, Caucasian ethnicity, and annual household income ≥$40,000/year.

While direct comparison with other studies is difficult due to the differing nature of how questions were asked, respondents in this survey appear to be more willing to interact with individuals with mental health issues. A 2006 US study found that the majority of survey respondents did not want to work or socialize with individuals with mental health problems (4), while only 10% of respondents in this study reported feeling uncomfortable or very uncomfortable interacting with youth in various settings. It is unknown if these large differences are due to methodological differences in how cases were presented and social distance was assessed, or the different population groups (adults vs. youth) that were the focus of the study, or if recent efforts to bring attention to the issue of mental health have influenced public opinion (8-10). Few studies have compared public opinion of child and adult mental health issues. A US study using data from the 1996 and 2002 General Social Surveys found survey respondents were significantly more likely to perceive childhood depression as a serious problem than adult depression and that the problem was unlikely to improve without treatment (11). It is unknown what impact these findings may have on social distance.

The socio-demographic predictors of comfort interacting with youth with moderate mental health problems identified in this study are comparable to that seen in the literature. Other studies that have examined socio-demographic predictors of social distance have consistently found that older individuals are less comfortable interacting with individuals with mental health problems (5, 6, 12, 13) and that gender is not associated with a desire for social distance (5).

This work is not without limitations. Respondents were asked broad questions about mental illness and not presented with specific case examples. While some survey researchers argue that generic questions are less likely to extract discriminating public responses (14), due to the nature of the survey we were not able to ask a series of questions based on case studies. Additionally, while case vignettes are a typical way public opinion has been gathered in similar studies, the public's ability to categorize each case as a mental illness is context dependent (15). A national US study found that while 88% of survey respondents were able to classify a case vignette describing a person with DSM-IV diagnosis of schizophrenia as having a mental illness, less than half of respondents classified individuals with alcohol dependence (49%) or drug addiction (44%) as having a mental illness (15). Furthermore, while we presume that individual responses to questions reflect actual behaviours, we did not assess behaviours directly. A social desirability bias may partially explain the low desire for social distance that is reported in this study in contrast to other studies of this nature;

however, this could also be because these questions specifically pertained to youth where there may be less need for concern about social distance. Additionally, a low response rate was obtained for this study; however, those that chose to participate are reflective of Alberta population (7), thus increasing the generalizability of these findings.

In conclusion, these results indicate strong public support for social inclusion and connectedness to youth with mental health conditions, while also highlighting gaps in knowledge about the prevalence of youth mental health conditions. Finally, the public correctly identified that it is only the minority of youth who receive treatment for these conditions. Additional treatment or intervention options for youth with mental health conditions would address a gap already identified by the public, and may improve outcomes for youth and their families.

Acknowledgments

Funding for this study was received from the Alberta Centre for Child, Family and Community Research. The authors would like to thank the Population Research Laboratory at the University of Alberta for their assistance with survey design and data collection. This manuscript was previously presented at the World Congress of Epidemiology meeting which was held in Edinburgh Scotland from August 7-11, 2011. None of the authors have any conflicts of interest to disclose.

References

[1] Jorm AF, Korten AE, Jacomb PA, Christensen H, Rodgers B, Pollitt P. Mental health literacy: A survey of the public's ability to recognise mental disorders and their beliefs about the effectiveness of treatment. Med J Aust 1997;166:182-6.

[2] Cotton SM, Wright A, Harris MG, Jorm AF, McGorry PD. Influence of gender on mental health literacy in young Australians. Aust NZ J Psychiatry 2006;40(9):790-6.

[3] Reavley NJ, Jorm AF. Young people's recognition of mental disorders and beliefs about treatment and outcome: findings from an Australian national survey. Aust NZ J Psychiatr 2011;45(10):890-8.

[4] Pescosolido B, Martin J, Long J, Medina T, Phelan J, Link B. A disease like any other? A decade of change in public reactions to schizophrenia, depression, and alcohol dependence. Am J Psychiatr 2010;167(11):1321-30.

[5] Jorm AF, Oh E. Desire for social distance from people with mental disorders. Aust NZ J Psychiatr 2009;43(3):183-200.

[6] Gaebel W, Baumann A, Witte A, Zaeske H. Public attitudes towards people with mental illness in six German cities: results of a public survey under special consideration of schizophrenia. Eur Arch Psychiatry Clin Neurosci 2002;252:278-87.

[7] Statistics Canada. 2006 Census of Population. Ottawa, ON: Statistics Canada catalogue no. 97-560-XCB2006008.

[8] World Health Organization. Atlas: Child and adolescent mental health resources: Global concerns, implications for the future. Geneva: WHO, 2005.

[9] Mental Health Commission of Canada. Toward recovery and well-being: A framework for a mental health strategy for Canada. Calgary, AB: Mental Health Commission Canada, 2009.

[10] Kirby M, Keon W. Out of the shadows at last: Transforming mental health, mental illness and addiction services in Canada. Ottawa: Standing Senate Committee Social Affairs Science Technology, 2006.
[11] Perry B, Pescosolido B, Martin J, McLeod J, Jensen P. Comparison of public attributions, attitudes, and stigma in regard to depression among children and adults. Psychiatr Serv 2007;58(5):632-5.
[12] Stuart H, Arboleda-Florez J. Community attitudes toward people with schizophrenia. Can J Psychiatr 2001;46:245-52.
[13] van't Veer J, Kraan H, Drosseart S, Modde J. Determinants that shape public attitudes towards the mentally ill: a Dutch public study. Soc Psychiatry Psychiatr Epidemiol 2006;41:310-7.
[14] Pescosolido B, Monahan J, Link B, Stueve A, Kikuzawa S. The public's view of the competence, dangerousness, and need for legal coercion of persons with mental health problems. Am J Public Health 1999;89(9):1339-45.
[15] Link B, Phelan J, Bresnahan M, Stueve A, Pescosolido B. Public conceptions of mental illness: labels, causes, dangerousness, and social distance. Am J Public Health 1999;89(9):1328-33.

In: Mental Health from an International Perspective
Editors: J. Merrick, S. Aspler and M. Morad
ISBN: 978-1-62948-519-5

Chapter 9

Cancer, pain and depression

Marisa Nosralla, Adriana M Issy, PhD, Luis R Gerola, MD, PhD and Rioko K Sakata, MD, PhD*

Department of Anesthesia, Universidade Federal de São Paulo, São Paulo, Brazil

Cancer-related pain results in mood changes and impairs the quality of life of patients. Some emotional manifestations of the disease and treatment side-effects may be similar therefore it is important to make adequate assessments. In this chapter we review depression in cancer and pain patients.

Introduction

Diagnosing a serious disease leads to different emotional reactions such as fear, uncertainty and guilt; and impairs the quality of life of patients. Among such diseases and especially with cancer there is a certain underlying life-threat existence, even in the event of a positive prognosis (1). Cancer patients present mood changes during the evolution of the disease, either in the initial stage or in the worsening of the medical condition. Diagnosis criteria for mood changes such as anxiety, sadness and depression are different from those which apply for psychiatric diseases (2-5). As there may be similarities among some emotional manifestations of the disease and treatment side-effects, there is a need for multidisciplinary focus in the assessment and treatment of patients aiming at reducing emotional suffering an aiding in the search of strategies for coping with the disease.

In suffering, pain is manifested on the physical level, but it may also be experienced in a subjective and individual manner. The emotional meaning which pain represents may interfere on symptom intensity, depending on the individual's personality, family and social support, spiritual and religious beliefs, cultural factors, and functional limitations of everyday life (6).

* Correspondence: Rioko Kimiko Sakata, R Três de Maio 61-51, V Clementino- SP- SP, CEP 04044-020 São Paulo, Brazil. E-mail: riokoks.dcir@epm.br.

Most cancer patients experience pain at some stage of the disease or treatment (3, 4). The presence of depression in patients with oncological pain has been reported in literature showing a higher incidence than in the general population (7). In the same way in which chronic pain causes depression, the presence of depression results in the increase of the intensity of pain. Therefore, both assessment and treatment are fundamental in order to improve quality of life.

Pain in cancer

Pain is very frequent symptom, present in approximately 70% of cancer patients during some stage of the disease (2). Pain in oncological patients may derive from: tumor (bone invasion; plexus and peripheral nerve compression and infiltration, organ distension or torsion, blood vessel obstruction, and mucosal necrosis or infiltration), therapeutical procedures (incision or scar, phantom limb pain, trauma neuritis, mucositis and actinia neuropathy), diagnosis procedures (biopsies, blood collection), paraneoplasic syndromes (deep vein thrombosis), and pain not related to the oncological disease.

Emotional meaning of pain

The emotional meaning of pain and of the disease depends on the individual's personality, that is, not only how he experiences the situation but also how he deals with pleasurable and frustrating experiences during their lifetime (2, 3). Pain may have an connotation of threat, punishment or judgment (8). The changes which take place in the life of an individual with cancer may be interpreted as an experience of either threat or death. A patient may believe he/she is being punished and sometimes feels responsible and this may impair his/her disposition to follow a treatment. He believes not to be worthy of help but, on the other hand, longs for care, attention and that people around motivate him to take care of themselves.

Pain produces profound and meaningful changes in an individual's life especially in cancer patients bringing loss of mobility, ties (social, professional and familiar) and of pleasurable moments. The concept of total pain comprises several other components besides those physical aspects associated with anatomical lesions.

Psychic pain is associated with fear of the unknown, uncertainty, insecurity, loss and death. An individual feels sadness, anger, outrage, despair, and depression. Pain is experienced by the person as something which threatens his integrity. Physical pain is socially and culturally more accepted whereas psychic pain is considered a sign of weakness of character. Patients seek relief for their psychological and emotional suffering by means of seeking medical assistance for their physical pain.

Social pain happens when a patient feels isolated, rejected and abandoned. Pain may bring some benefits to an individual such as receiving care and attention or the elimination of a difficult current situation one has to deal with. On the other hand, the patient becomes dependent and feels useless. Pathological behavior which impairs an efficacious treatment, may lead to the secondary gain of pain. A patient may feel his pain as his only and that no one can help ease the burden. Pain becomes the focus of his/her attention and complaining. The individual feels victim of such intense suffering and presents little disposition to deal with the situation. A more passive attitude is noted in addition to multiple complaints related or not to the pain status and to the expectation of an improvement which he does not believe in.

When there is loss of autonomy and abandonment similar pain may occur. With spiritual pain there is a lack of meaning in both life and death. As the disease progresses, a patient will display fear of life after death, of having to submit himself and of asking for forgiveness to God. Financial pain happens frequently (losses and difficulties). As the patient has to reduce his/her professional activities due to fatigue, drug side-effects, and the need to perform required exams, visits and treatments, the family's financial resources are affected (9-11).

Pain and psychological changes

When a cancer, relapse or non-successful treatment is diagnosed a period of initial shock and disbelief may happen followed by a period of crisis accompanied by mixed symptoms of anxiety and depression, irritability, and reduced appetite and changes in the sleep cycle (5).

Fear of changes in the appearance resulting from surgery sequelae and other treatments is experienced in an anguishing manner. Physical appearance changes (hair loss, weight gain or loss, and skin color and texture changes) and the need to use prostheses interfere with self-esteem. These changes are an everyday constant, even when patients want to forget about the disease. The sense of lack of control over the disease, one's body, and life permeates and one becomes dependent on physicians and family members (12, 13).

The future is unknown and long-term projects need to be restructured or postponed. Priority planning needs to be redone and there is a need for elaborating objectives which can be achieved in a short period of time. Anxiety sets in due to the doubts associated with the disease. Treatment efficacy, side-effects, fear of feeling uncontrollable pain, and the possibility of dying are present during the treatment (9-11). Intense pain is related to depression, impairing quality of life. It interferes in physical functioning, and in social interaction, increasing psychological suffering (4, 14-18).

Several factors may contribute to the high scores attributed to pain in surveys, especially in our society: lack of financial means for purchasing medication, inadequate use of pain killers, drug-related taboos, no knowledge of conduct on behalf of the professionals, and worsening of the clinical status at the time of referral to a specialized sector. Pain provokes transient or lasting emotional changes which may interfere on its treatment (19).

Chronic pain patients present mood disorders, including depression (20). The psychological morbidity risk is higher in the advanced disease, at relapse, when there is worsening of physical capacity, and when there is a family history of depression (4, 15, 21-24). Psychological factors such as anxiety, depression, and the meaning of pain to a patient, may intensify the perception of pain (2, 3).

Cancer patients who attribute pain to a non-oncological cause have reported less intensity in pain in relation to those who believe that pain represents progression of the disease (25). Suffering caused by the treatment or progression of the disease and the inadequate coping strategies, play a significant role in the intensity of the pain (3) and in mood disorders (26). Pain and psychological changes are associated with suicidal thoughts in cancer patients (2, 4,

5, 17, 23, 26, 27). Many oncology patients who experience suicidal thoughts have been associated with pain (2, 3).

Depression

Depression following cancer diagnosis is usually expected. Depression manifests itself as: dysphoria, feeling of hopelessness and abandonment, loss of self-esteem, feeling of uselessness or guilt, anhedonia and thoughts of desire to die or suicidal ideation (5, 28).

Depression is described according to the following basic characteristics: depressed mood during most part of the day, decreased interest and pleasure in almost every activity which would usually be enjoyable, lack of reaction to events or activities which usually provoke an emotional response, insomnia or hypersomnia, worse in the morning, evidence of mental slowing or noticeable psychomotor agitation, decreased or increased appetite, decreased or increased weight, reduced libido, fatigue or decreased energy levels, feelings of low self-esteem or inappropriate guilt, decreased capability in thinking, concentration or decision making and recurrent death or suicidal thoughts, suicide plan or attempt.

Decreased interest and pleasure in activities are important in assessing depression. Diagnosis must be performed based on a set of manifestations, associated with the individual's functional loss (21, 29). A depressed mood can vary from sadness which is a normal reaction towards loss and frustration to pathological depression in which signs and symptoms exceed the normal reaction to loss or grief (23). A patient with a depressed mood continues to mobilize his/her resources to deal with the disease despite the hopelessness, whereas in depression the patient has given up on fighting for life (21, 29).

Some factors may determine the prevalence of depression. Young patients display higher depression incidence, especially in a serious disease such as cancer where they feel that life has been interrupted, ambitions have not been achieved and there are unsettling feelings regarding the welfare of dependents. An existing prior relationship disorder and alcoholism, and the presence of pain increase the incidence of depression (21, 28, 30).

A cancer patient may experience depression due to the loss of his/her health and due to anticipatory loss, including death (27). The ability to concentrate and continue to perform daily activities is impaired and thoughts regarding the diagnosis and fear of the future may interfere in the emotional well-being of the patient. These manifestations may improve with family support, social support and explanations from the physicians regarding the treatment plan.

Depression changes physical capacity and quality of life of the patients (2, 22). Depression associated with pain, increases morbidity and mortality and increase in the intensity of pain besides the difficulty in coping with a stressful situation. It may be generating pain.

In a patient palliative care study, authors found the highest incidence of female depression (31). Some authors describe that women seek more treatment and express their symptoms more and there are some factors which may contribute to this behavior: physical (hormones and genetics), social and cultural and psychological influences, and a greater awareness and care with their body (14, 32). Some authors have reported that depression prevalence in cancer is higher in the elderly (18, 22, 31, 33, 34). It should be taken into consideration that cancer is more prevalent in the elderly. Other authors have observed more depression in youngsters (13, 31, 35).

The authors of a study reported that the symptoms of cancer patients are correlated with depression (24). In other studies, a significant relation between proximity of death and depression was not observed (13, 15). In another study, no correlation was found between educational level and depression. Despite, however, that individual with a higher level of schooling have more of an opportunity for learning about what cancer means and also have a better chance of obtaining treatment (35).

In some studies it has been observed that the prevalence of depression varied significantly in relation to the different concepts on depression, on the measuring tools used, on the studied populations and other variables (medication, disease stage and time of diagnosis) (22, 34, 36). All these factors interfere in the diagnosis of depression and may justify the differences in the study results.

Coping strategies

The efficacy of coping strategies during an individual's lifetime seems to perform a more important role in the experiencing of chronic pain than the variables of age or gender. The manner in which a person copes with the cancer and death itself varies greatly. Coping with the disease is associated with personal aspects (phase in life cycle, schooling, marital status, personality, capacity in coping with stressful situations and religious and spiritual beliefs), social (family and social support, community and financial resources), and physical (tumor type, site and extension and sequelae). Coping capabilities comprise psychological mechanisms and the development of alternatives to live despite the disease, reducing its negative impacts. Family and social support seem to be important in the reducing of depression incidence (13, 31).

In one study, a correlation between family and social support and quality of life was noticed in which it aided in decreasing the effects of physical symptoms (1). Family plays an important role in the care giving and emotional support of the oncological patient, especially when there is worsening of the disease, when intensified care and decision making for the patient who is very debilitated, is required (37, 38). Establishment of a good relationship with the caregiver allows for the expression of feelings and makes it easier to cope with the suffering caused by the disease (37, 38). Social support can be given via emotional assistance (care and interest) or instrumental (provision of material goods) (1, 21).

Some patients seek support in religion (39). The authors observed that individuals presenting spiritual well-being showed less anguish at the end of their lives as terminal patients, providing a positive contribution in the predisposition to hopelessness, desire to die and suicidal ideation, even after the effects of depression and of other variables have been controlled. Religious practices (praying, meditating, reading the Bible) are inversely related to physical health, indicating that those who experience a worse health condition are more inclined to seek faith as a resource for coping with the disease (40).

The spiritual aspect may not be important for the general population but for the population with a more fragile health-state it has become a contributor, with psychological and environmental aspects, during the disease (41). In conclusion, depression is an important factor in the increase of pain and assessment with intervention are fundamental.

References

[1] Manning–Walsh J. Social support as mediator between symptom distress and quality of life in women with breast cancer. J Obstet Gynecol Neonatal Nurs 2005;34(4):482-93.

[2] Breitbart W, Payne DK. Pain. In: Holland JC, ed. Psychooncology. New York: Oxford Univ Press, 1998:450–67.

[3] Breitbart W, Payne DK. Psychiatric aspects of pain management in patients with advanced cancer and aids. In: Chochinov HM, Breitbart W, eds. Handbook of psychiatry in palliative medicine. New York: Oxford Univ Press, 2000:131-59.

[4] Akechi T, Nakano T, Akizuki N, Okamura M, Sakuma K, Nakanishi T, Yoshikawa E, Uchitomi Y. Somatic symptoms for diagnosing major depression in cancer patients. Psychosomatics 2003;44(3): 244-48.

[5] Miller K, Massie MJ. Depression and anxiety. Jones Bartiett Publishers; 2006;12(5):388-97.

[6] Risdon A, Eccleston C, Crombez, McCracken L. How can we learn with pain? A methodological analysis of the diverse understandings of acceptance of chronic pain. Soc Sci Med 2003;56:375-86.

[7] Reyes–Gibby CC, Aday LA, Anderson KO, Mendonza TR, Cleeland CS. Pain, depression, and fatigue in community – dwelling adults with and without a history of cancer. J Pain Symptom Manage 2006; 32(2):118-28.

[8] Strang P. Cancer pain-a provoker of emotional, social and existencial distress. Acta Oncol 1998;37:641-4.

[9] Rowland JH. Developmental stage and adaptation: adult model. In: Holland JC, Rowland JH, eds. Handbook of psychooncology. New York: Oxford Univ Press, 1990:25-43.

[10] Fox BH. Psychosocial factors in cancer incidence and prognoses. In: Holland JM, ed. Psychooncology. New York: Oxford Univ Press, 1998:110–24.

[11] Barraclough J. Cancer and emotion: a practical guide to psychooncology, 3th ed. New York: John Willey, 1998:221.

[12] Portenoy RK, Foley KM. Management of cancer pain. In: Holland JC, ed. Handbook of psycooncology. New York: Oxford Univ Press, 1990:369-82.

[13] Eli K, Sanchez K, Vourlekis B, et al. Depression, correlates of depression, and receipt of depression care among low–income women with breast cancer or gynecological cancer. J Clin Oncol 2005; 23(13):3052-60.

[14] Turk DC, Okifuji A. Does sex make a difference in the prescription of treatments and the adaptation to chronic pain by cancer and non–cancer patients? Pain 1999;82:139-48.

[15] Buttler LD, Koopman C, Cordova MJ, Garlan RW, Dimiceli S, Spiegel D. Psychological distress and pain significantly increase before death in metastatic breast cancer patients. Psychosomat Med 2003;65:416-26.

[16] Chen ML. Pain and hope in patients with cancer: a role for cognition. Cancer Nurs 2003;26(1):61-7.

[17] O'Mahony S, Goulet J, Kornblith A, Abbatiello G, Clarke B, Kless-Siegel S, et al. Desire for hastened death, cancer pain and depression: report of a longitudinal observational study. J Pain Symptom Manage 2005;29(5):446-57.

[18] Mistakidou K, Tsilika E, Parpa E, Katsouda E, Galanos A, Vlahos L. Psychological distress of patients with advanced cancer: influence and contribution of pain severity and pain interference. Cancer Nurs 2006;29(5):400-5.

[19] Large RG. Psychological aspects of pain. Ann Rheum Dis 1996; 55:340-5.

[20] Derogatis LR, Morrow GR, Fetting J, Penman D, Piasetsky S, Schmale AM. The prevalence of psychiatric disorders among cancer patients. JAMA 1983;249:751-7.

[21] Wilson KG, Chochinov HM, Faye BJ, Breitbart W. Diagnosis and management of depression in palliative medicine. In: Chochinov HM, Breitbart W, eds. Handbook of psychiatry in palliative medicine. New York: Oxford Univ Press, 2000:25-49.

[22] Massie MJ. Prevalence of depression in patients with cancer. J Nat Cancer Inst Mon 2004;32:57-71.

[23] Wasan AD, Artamonov M, Nedeljkovic SS. Delirium, depression and anxiety in the treatment of cancer pain. Reg Anesth Pain Med 2005; 9(3):139-44.

[24] Doorenbos AZ, Given CW, Given B, Verbisky N. Symptom experience in the last year of life among individuals with cancer. J Pain Symptom Manage 2006;32(5):403-12.

[25] Daut RL, Cleeland CS. The prevalence and severity of pain in cancer. Cancer 1982;50:1913-8.

[26] Breitbart W, Passik SD. Psychiatric approaches to cancer patient. In: Breitbart W, Holland JC, eds. Psychiatric aspects in cancer patients. Washington, DC: Am Psychiatr Press, 1993:49-86.

[27] Massie MJ, Shakin EJ. Management of depression and anxiety in cancer patients. In: Breitbart W, Holland JC, eds. Psychiatric aspects in cancer patients. Washington, DC: Am Psychiatr Press, 1993:1-21.

[28] Massie MJ, Popkin MP. Depressive disorders. In: Holland JC. Psychooncology. New York: Oxford Univ Press, 1998:519-40.

[29] Cavanaugh SVA. Depression in the medically ill. Psychossomatics. 1995; 36:48-59.

[30] Chochinov MC, Keith GW, Enns M, Lander S. Prevalence of depression in the terminally ill: effects of diagnostic criteria and symptom threshold judgments. Am J Psychiatr 1994;151(4):537-40.

[31] Wilson KG, Chochinov HM, Skirko MG, Allard P, Chary S, Gagnon PR, et al. Depression and anxiety disorders in palliative cancer care. J Pain Symptom Manage 2007;33(2):118-29.

[32] Holdcroft A, Berkley K. Sex and gender diferences in pain and its relief. In: McMahon SB, Koltzenburg M. Wall and Melzack's textbook of pain, 5th ed. Philadelphia, PA: Elsevier Churchill Livingstone, 2006:1181-97.

[33] Rao A, Cohen HJ. Symptom management in the elderly cancer patients: fatigue, pain and depression. J National Cancer Institute Monograph, Oxford University Press. 2004;32:150-7.

[34] Miaskowski C. Gender diferences in pain, fatigue and depression in patients with cancer. JNCI Monogr 2004;32:139-43.

[35] Akhtar–Danesh N, Landen J. Relation between depression and sociodemographics factors. Int J Mental Health Systems 2007;1(4):1-4.

[36] Gagliese L, Melzack R. Pain in elderly. In: McMahon SB, Koltzenburg M. Wall and Melzack's textbook of pain, 5th ed. Philadelphia, PA: Elsevier Churchill Livingstone, 2006:1169-79.

[37] Porter LS, Keefe FJ, Lipkua I, Hurwitz H . Ambivalence over emotional expression in patients with gastrointestinal cancer and their caregivers: associations with patient pain and quality of life. Pain 2005;117:340-8.

[38] Fleming DA, Sheppard VB, Mangan PA, Taylor KL, Tallarico M, Adams I, Ingham J. Caregiving at the end of life: perceptions of health care quality and quality of life among patients and caregivers. J Pain Symptom Manage 2006;31(5):407-20.

[39] MC Clain CS, Rosenfeld B, Breitbart W. Effect of spiritual well – being on end of life despair in terminally – ill cancer patients. Lancet 2003;361:1603-7

[40] Rippentrop AE, Altaimer EM, Chen JJ, Found EM, Keffala VJ. The relationship between religion/ spirituality and physical health, mental health, and pain in a chronic pain population. Pain 2005;116: 311-21.

[41] WHOQOL SRPB Group. A cross–cultural study of spirituality, religion, and personal beliefs as components of quality of life. Soc Sci Med 2006;62:1486-97.

In: Mental Health from an International Perspective
Editors: J. Merrick, S. Aspler and M. Morad

ISBN: 978-1-62948-519-5

Chapter 10

Sleep and mood, pain, functional status and health-related quality of life in children with juvenile idiopathic arthritis

Dawn Hrelic, BS[1], Kelly Rouster-Stevens, MD[1], Harry Gewanter, MD[2] and Kathi J Kemper, MD, MPH*[1,3,4]

[1]Department of Pediatrics, Wake Forest University School of Medicine, Winston-Salem, North Carolina

[2]Pediatric and Adolescent Health Partners, Midlothian, Virginia

[3]Department of Social Science Health Policy, Public Health Sciences, Wake Forest University School of Medicine, Winston Salem, North Carolina and OSU Center for Integrative Health and Wellness, Columbus, Ohio, United States of America

Over 50% of pediatric pain patients suffer from sleep disorders. Many children with juvenile idiopathic arthritis (JIA) experience mild to moderate joint pain. We hypothesized that among pediatric patients with JIA a) sleep problems would be common; b) sleep disturbance would be correlated with mood (depression and anxiety); c) sleep disturbance and mood would be associated with pain, number of co-morbid conditions, functional status, and health related quality of life (HRQOL). Methods: We conducted a cross sectional survey of JIA patients six years and older from two clinical sites between June 1 and July 31, 2007. Demographic, health status, co-morbidity questions and the sleep survey were completed by parents; standardized measures of anxiety, depression, pain, HRQOL, and functional status were completed by the patients themselves. Results: Of 89 eligible patients, 49 (55%) completed all instruments. Sleep problems were present in 80% of patients. Sleep problems were significantly correlated with patient anxiety ($r=0.57$, $p<0.0001$) and depression ($r=0.47$, $p<0.0001$). Sleep

* Correspondence: Professor Kathi J Kemper, MD, MPH, Director, OSU Center for Integrative Health and Wellness, 503 McCampbell Hall, 1581 Dodd Dr, Columbus, OH 43210, United States. E-mail: kathi.kemper@osumc.edu.

problems, anxiety, and depression were all significantly associated with increased pain, number of co-morbid conditions, worse health status and HRQOL, and decreased functional status ($p<0.05$ for all). Conclusion: Sleep abnormalities in children with JIA are common, and are significantly related to mood, pain, overall health, functional status, and HRQOL. Pediatric rheumatologists should routinely ask about patients' sleep. More studies are needed to elucidate the causal relationships between sleep, pain, mood and health in these patients.

Introduction

Sleep abnormalities in children with chronic pain are common and adversely affect outcomes. Over 50% of pediatric pain patients suffer from sleep disorders (1-3). Obtaining sufficient sleep is extremely important to children. Sleep is critical to intellectual growth and development; it impacts school attendance, performance and participation in daily activities (1, 4). Physical and mental well-being are also negatively impacted by sleep disturbances (5, 6).

The relationship between sleep disturbances and pain is well documented: pain interferes with sleep and sleep problems exacerbate pain (7). In chronic pain patients, longer sleep time is associated with improvements in pain status (8). More than half of pediatric inflammatory disease patients experience sleep problems during exacerbations (9, 10). Sleep laboratory studies also link chronic pain to disrupted sleep patterns, including problems initiating or maintaining sleep, frequent stage shifts, and subjective perception of non-restorative sleep upon awakening (11, 12). Decreased sleep time, delayed sleep onset, and nighttime awakenings are also associated with increased pain intensity (1). Not surprisingly, pain duration correlates with degree of sleep difficulty and dissatisfaction (1).

It has been proposed that mood disorders also play a role in the relationship between pain and sleep, although less is known about the mechanism for these effects (13). Sleep disturbance is prominent in individuals undergoing stress, anxiety or depression (1, 14). On the other hand, in a survey of 105 pain clinic patients, sleep disturbances were prevalent in chronic pain patients, but were not always associated with an underlying mood disturbance(4).

Pain is an important issue for patients suffering from chronic inflammatory conditions such as juvenile idiopathic arthritis (JIA). A 2003 Sleep in America Poll revealed sleep difficulties in 72% of adults aged 55 years and older with arthritis (15). Similar findings have been documented among adult patients with rheumatoid arthritis (RA) and osteoarthritis (11, 16).

Surprisingly few studies have evaluated the prevalence of and relationship among sleep, mood, and HRQOL in juvenile idiopathic arthritis (JIA), the most frequent rheumatic disease of childhood (17). In a 2002 study of 25 JIA patients, self-reported sleep problems correlated with pain intensity (16). A 1998 study characterized sleep disturbance in 16 JIA patients through objective polysomnographic study of abnormal sleep, as well as through associations with daytime sleepiness, as evidenced by abnormal multiple sleep latency tests and longer afternoon naptimes (18). In a 2004 study of 59 children suffering from JIA, parents and children were asked to report on quality of life, physical, emotional, and social functioning (14). Negative relationships were established between pain and quality of life; however the pattern of these relationships was not consistent for reports from parents and children, emphasizing the importance of data from patient self-report (14).

Elucidating the frequency and relationships between these problems has important implications for caregivers of JIA patients. Therefore, we conducted this study to better understand the extent of sleep problems and their relationship with other factors. Based on previous research, we hypothesized that among pediatric patients with JIA: a) sleep problems would be common; b) sleep disturbance would be correlated with mood (depression and anxiety); c) sleep disturbance and mood would show strong associations with pain, functional status and quality of life.

Our sample

As part of a larger study (19), we conducted a cross sectional survey of pediatric patients with JIA between June 1 and July 31, 2007. Patients were eligible if they were diagnosed with JIA using the International League of Associations for Rheumatology classification(11); they were at least six years old; and they had received care at least once in the previous six months by a pediatric rheumatologist at Brenner Children's Hospital (KRS) or the at the private rheumatology practice of Harry Gewanter (HG) in Richmond, Virginia. Subjects were excluded if either the patient or parent/guardian did not speak English, or if both patient and parent/guardian declined to participate. Younger children were not included because the survey instruments had not been standardized for younger children.

Participants were recruited through letters from the attending rheumatologist at each site. For the overall study, approximately 165 letters were sent to parents, (distributed equally to each site) each of which contained $2 in cash, and an offer of $10 for return of completed questionnaires. The surveys included baseline demographic questions, overall health status, the patient's co-morbid conditions and a standardized measure of sleep disturbance, which were to be completed by parents with the patient's input; it also included standardized questions about pain, anxiety, depression, functional status and health related quality of life (described below), which were completed by the patients themselves.

Demographic information consisted of patient's age, gender, race/ethnicity, maternal education, and parental marital status. Parents were asked to rate the patient's overall health status (excellent/good/fair/poor); the duration of the child's disease; and the presence of comorbid conditions (e.g., abdominal pain, acne, ADHD, allergies, asthma, constipation or diarrhea, frequent infections, headaches, scoliosis, eczema, GERD, and other).

Patient questionnaires

Sleep

The 45-item Child Sleep Health Questionnaire (CSHQ) was used to assess sleep dysfunction. The CHSQ has been used internationally in pediatric research, including studies of children with recurrent and chronic pain (15, 16). It can be completed by children as young as 8 years old (12). The CSHQ covers 8 domains pertinent to childhood sleep: 1) Bedtime resistance, 2) sleep onset delay, 3) sleep duration, 4) sleep anxiety, 5) night wakings, 6) parasomnias (e.g., sleepwalking and night terrors), 7) sleep disordered breathing and 8) daytime sleepiness. The total sleep disturbance score includes all items of the 8 subscales and is a useful screening instrument in identifying sleep disturbances in school-aged children (12).

Caregivers completed the CSHQ by rating the frequency of sleep behaviors during a typical week. Items are scored on a 3-point scale ranging from "usually" (if the sleep behavior occurs 5-7 times per week), "sometimes" (2-4 times per week), to "rarely" (0-1 times per week). Some items are reverse scored; higher scores suggest more disturbed sleep. An overall score of 41 has been established as the cut-off indicating potential sleep disorder with a sensitivity of 0.80 and specificity of 0.72(12). Mean normal scores for Bedtime Resistance, Sleep Onset Delay, Sleep Duration, Sleep Anxiety, Night Wakings, Parasomnias, Sleep Disordered Breathing, and Daytime Sleepiness have been established at 7.06 (SD=1.89), 1.25 (SD=0.53), 3.41 (SD=0.93), 4.89 (SD=1.45), 3.51 (SD=0.89), 8.11 (SD=1.25), 3.24 (SD=0.63), and 9.64 (SD=2.80) respectively. The CSHQ has good internal consistency, test-retest reliability, and validity(12). Scores were used only for patients 8 years and older.

Anxiety

The Revised Children's Manifest Anxiety Scale (RCMAS), a 37-item self-report measure, was used to assess anxiety. The RCMAS is a revision of the Children's Manifest Anxiety Scale (20). It asks 37 "yes" or "no" questions to assess the presence or absence of various anxiety related symptoms. The RCMAS includes 28 anxiety items which yield three factors: 1) physiological anxiety, 2) worry/oversensitivity and 3) fear/concentration (9).

The RCMAS has been used internationally to assess anxiety in a range of populations for children as young as six years old (2, 3). Items answered "yes" are awarded 1 point, while items answered "no" are awarded 0 points. High scores indicate higher levels of anxiety. Normative data yields mean total anxiety scores of 13.84 (SD=5.79) (9). Normative means scores for physiological anxiety are 4.57 (SD=2.14), worry/oversensitivity are score of 5.39 (SD=2.34) and fear/concentration are 3.88 (SD=2.14) (9). The RCMAS has satisfactory internal consistency, test-retest reliability, and convergent and construct validities (9).

Depression

The Center for Epidemiological Studies Depression Scale for Children (CES-DC), a 20-item self report depression inventory, was used to assess depression (17). The CES-DC includes a list of 20 items, each making a specific statement, and asks the patient to identify the number of times he or she has felt or acted that way within the past week by answering "a lot," "some," "a little," or "not at all." Items are scored on a scale of 0-3. Questions which are phrased positively are scored in opposite order so that higher scores indicate increasing levels of depression. A cutoff score of 15 is suggestive of significant levels of depressive symptoms (21). The CES-DC has been used internationally for children 7 years and older (5, 17). It has good internal consistency, test-retest reliability, and concurrent validities (17). Scores were used only for patients seven years and older.

Pain

The Varni-Thompson Pediatric Pain Questionnaire (PPQ), a self reported visual analogue scale (VAS), was used for patients to give independent assessments of their current pain status and their worst pain during the previous week (6). It is reliable in documenting self reported pain in patients as young as five years old (1). The PPQ-VAS consists of a 100-mm horizontal line anchored on each side by a smiley or sad face, along with developmentally appropriate pain descriptors ("not hurting," "no discomfort," and "no pain," or "hurting a whole lot," "very uncomfortable," and "severe pain") (1). The patient is instructed to indicate pain levels by marking anywhere along the horizontal line. Scores are calculated by taking the average distance from the smiley face anchor, between the two items. Higher scores are associated with greater pain intensity. The PPQ-VAS has been shown to be a reliable and valid measure of perceived pain in juvenile arthritis and chronic pain populations (1, 4, 14).

Functional status

The Pediatric Quality of Life Inventory Present Functioning Visual Analogue Scales (PedsQLTM VAS) was used to measure patients' self reported functional status. It is a six item measure of anxiety, sadness, anger, worry, fatigue and pain at the present moment. The scoring system is based on the Varni/Thomson Pediatric Pain Questionnaire (PPQ) Pain Intensity VAS format, with 100mm lines anchored with a smiley or sad face at either end. The happy and sad faces are accompanied by developmentally appropriate descriptors such as "not/very afraid," "not/very angry," and "not/very tired (22). The PedsQLTM VAS Total Symptom Score is calculated by averaging the distance from the smiley face anchor of all six items. Higher scores indicate lower functional status.

Quality of life

The 22-item Pediatric Quality of Life Inventory (PedsQL) 3.0 Rheumatology Module was used to assess health related quality of life (HRQOL). The PedsQL 3.0 Rheumatology Module is multidimensional, encompassing five separate scales: 1) pain and hurt (4 items), 2) daily activities (5 items), 3) treatment (7 items), 4) worry (3 items), and 5) communication (3 items) (7). Patients are asked to describe the how often they find themselves in agreement with various statements, by responding "never" (0 points), "almost never" (1 point), "sometimes" (2 points), "often" (3 points), or "almost always" (4 points).27 Higher scores indicate worse HRQOL and therefore increased frequency of problems or symptoms. The PedsQL 3.0 Rheumatology Module has good reliability, validity, and responsiveness (7, 8).

Data analysis

Data for all questionnaires were entered by a research assistant blind to the patients' name. Data were entered into a secure Microsoft Excel database which was backed up nightly. Data values were checked by a separate research assistant and further checked for reasonable ranges; a 25% sample was triple checked against original paper copies to ensure accuracy. Standard descriptive statistics and pearson product-moment correlation coefficients were calculated using Microsoft Excel 2003®. This study was approved by the Wake Forest University School of Medicine Institutional Review Board.

Findings

Of the 165 surveys sent, 103 (62%) were returned. Of these, 89 (86%) met the criteria of the patient being 6 years or older. Of the 89 who met eligibility criteria, about half came from each practice site; demographic characteristics of respondents and patients were similar for the two sites. Of 89 eligible patients, 49 (55%) completed all questions on sleep, anxiety, and depression. The 89 eligible and the 49 who completed all questionnaires were similar in terms of demographic and disease characteristics (see table 1). Demographic and sleep disturbance surveys were generally completed by patients' mothers (98%) with input from the patients. Parents were mostly married (81%); 28% had completed high school and 71% had completed some college or higher education. The average patient age was 13 years, 28% were male, and 84% were Caucasian.

Table 1. Demographic information

	Anxiety, Depression, and Sleep **N (%)**	**Any Demographic Information** **N (%)**
	Both Locations 49 (100)	**Both Locations** 89 (100)
Age – median (mean ± sd)	13.0 (13.8 ± 3.8)	12.5 (13.0 ± 4.3)
Gender – N (%)	14 (28.6)	25 (28.1)
Race – N (%)		
Caucasian	40 (81.6)	75 (84.3)
African American	7 (14.3)	8 (9.0)
Hispanic	2 (4.1)	2 (2.2)
Other	0 (0.0)	4 (4.5)
JIA Duration in years – median (mean ± sd)	7.3 (7.4 ± 5.3)	5.3 (6.7 ± 5.1)
Maternal Education Level – N (%)		
12th Grade or Less	16 (32.7)	25 (28.1)
Post High School Education	33 (67.3)	63 (70.8)
Maternal Marital Status – N (%)		
Married	41 (83.7)	67 (81.7)
Divorced	8 (16.3)	15 (18.3)
Overall health, parental rating – N (%)		
Excellent	8 (16.3)	18 (20.2)
Good	29 (59.2)	46 (51.7)
Fair	11 (22.4)	18 (20.2)
Poor	1 (2.0)	1 (1.1)
Total with a Comorbidity – median (mean ± sd)	31 (63.3)	60 (67.4)
Abdominal Pain – N (%)	9 (18.4)	12 (13.5)
Acne – N (%)	8 (16.3)	15 (16.9)
ADHD– N (%)	3 (6.1)	9 (10.1)
Allergies – N(%)	10 (20.4)	27 (30.3)
Asthma– N (%)	1 (2.0)	4 (4.5)
Constipation or Diarrhea – N (%)	10 (20.4)	13 (14.6)
Frequent Infections – N (%)	5 10.2)	8 (9.0)
Headaches – N (%)	13 (26.5)	20 (22.5)
None – N (%)	18 (36.7)	29 (32.6)
Other, includes scoliosis, eczema, GERD – N (%)	10 (20.4)	17 (19.1)

Sleep

Parental reports on the CSHQ indicate a high prevalence of sleep-related problems in the patients (see table 2). Sleep disturbance, indicated by a total sleep disturbance score of greater than 41, was present in 80% of participants. The observed range of total sleep disturbance scores (33–66) matched the minimum and maximum allowed by the CSHQ indicating a wide distribution of sleep disturbance. Daytime sleepiness was the most frequently reported sleep problem, present in 72% of participants.

Table 2. Prevalence of specific problems

	Instrument Range	Observed Range	Median (Mean ± SD)	Abnormal Values N (%)
Parent Reported Sleep Disturbance (CSHQ)⁺	33 – 66	33 – 66	45.5 (46.3 ± 7.1)	59 (79.7)
Bedtime Resistance	6 – 18	6 – 16	7 (7.5 ± 2.0)	14 (18.9)
Sleep Onset Delay	1 – 3	1 – 3	2 (1.8 ± 0.8)	41 (55.4)
Sleep Duration	3 – 9	3 – 9	4 (4.4 ± 1.6)	30 (40.5)
Sleep Anxiety	4 – 12	4 – 12	4 (4.9 ± 1.6)	9 (12.2)
Night Wakings	3 – 9	3 – 7	3 (3.8 ± 1.1)	15 (20.3)
Parasomnias	7 – 21	7 – 17	8 (8.6 ± 1.7)	15 (20.3)
Sleep Disordered Breathing	3 – 9	3 – 7	3 (3.3 ± 0.8)	14 (18.9)
Daytime Sleepiness	8 – 24	8 – 24	14 (14.4 ± 3.5)	53(71.6)
Child Reported Anxiety (RCMAS)⁺	0 – 28	0 – 26	8 (8.7 ± 6.1)	12 (17.6)
Physiological Anxiety	0 – 9	0 – 9	3 (3.2 ± 2.2)	7 (10.3)
Worry/Oversensitivity	0 – 10	0 – 10	3 (3.5 ± 2.9)	10 (14.7)
Fear/Concentration	0 – 9	0 – 8	2 (2.0 ± 1.8)	4 (5.9)
Child Reported Depression (CES-DC)⁺	0 – 60	0 – 56	9 (11.5 ± 10.1)	23 (33.3)
Child Reported Pain Status (PPQ-VAS)⁺	0 – 10	0 – 10	2.5 (3.0 ± 2.8)	N/A
Child Reported Quality of Life (PedsQL RM)⁺	0 – 88	0 – 62	19 (21.1 ± 15.5)	N/A
Child Reported Functional Status (PedsQL™ VAS)⁺⁺	0 – 10	0 – 9.97	1.4 (2.0 ± 2.1)	N/A

+Higher scores indicate presence of the condition or an unfavorable status.

++Higher scores indicate a favorable status.

Anxiety and depression (mood)

Total anxiety (RCMAS) scores fell over a range of 0 to 26, with 18% of scores indicating significant levels of anxiety. Depression (CES-DC) scores ranged from 0 to 56, of a possible 60; 33% of patients' scores were suggestive of significant levels of depressive symptoms.

Correlations between sleep disturbance, mood, pain, HRQOL and functional status

The relationships between sleep disturbance, mood, pain, HRQOL, and functional status are shown in table 3. Sleep disturbance was strongly correlated with anxiety (r=0.57, p<0.0001) and depression (r=0.47, p<0.0001) (see table 3). Sleep problems and mood were associated with increased pain, number of co-morbid conditions, worse health status and HRQOL, and decreased functional status (p<0.05 for all). Examining the relationship between specific sleep disturbances and other problems revealed the most significant associations for night waking and parasomnias (see table 4).

Table 3. Relationships between Sleep Disturbance, Anxiety, Depression, Number of Comorbid Conditions, Pain, Health-Related Quality of Life, Functional Status, and Health Status by Pearson product-moment correlation coefficient, r

	Parent Reported Sleep Disturbance (CSHQ)$^+$	Patient Reported Anxiety (RCMAS)$^+$	Patient Reported Depression (CES-DC)$^+$	No. Comorbid Conditions	Patient Reported Pain Status(PPQ-VAS)$^+$	Patient Reported Quality of Life (PedsQL RM)$^+$	Patient Reported Functional Status (PedsQL^{TM} VAS)$^+$
Patient Reported Anxiety (RCMAS)$^+$	0.57*	---					
Patient Reported Depression (CES-DC)$^+$	0.47*	0.76*	---				
No. Comorbid Conditions	0.33***	0.29***	0.34***	---			
Patient Reported Pain Status(PPQ-VAS)$^+$	0.24****	0.44*	0.63*	0.34***	---		
Patient Reported Quality of Life (PedsQL RM)$^+$	0.29*	0.63*	0.60*	0.28***	0.69*	---	
Patient Reported Functional Status (PedsQL^{TM} VAS)$^+$	0.37**	0.67*	0.79*	0.29***	0.70*	0.70*	---
Parent Reported Health Status^{++}	-0.37**	-0.36**	-0.38**	-0.40*	-0.50*	-0.52*	-0.46*

+Higher scores indicate an unfavorable status or presence of condition.

++Higher scores indicate a favorable status.

*p<0.0001 **p<0.001 ***p≤0.01 ****p<0.05

Table 4. Relationship between various Sleep Disturbances and Anxiety, Depression, Number of Comorbid Conditions, Pain, Health-Related Quality of Life, Functional Status, and Health Status by Pearson product-moment correlation coefficient, r

	Reported Sleep Disturbance	**Bedtime Resistance (CSHQ)$^{+}$**	**Sleep Onset Delay (CSHQ)$^{+}$**	**Sleep Duration (CSHQ)$^{+}$**	**Sleep Anxiety CSHQ)$^{+}$**	**Night Wakings (CSHQ)$^{+}$**	**Parasomnias (CSHQ)$^{+}$**	**Sleep Disordered Breathing (CSHQ)$^{+}$**	**Daytime Sleepiness (CSHQ)$^{+}$**
Patient Reported Anxiety (RCMAS)$^{+}$	0.57*	0.20	0.22****	0.33***	0.19	0.47*	0.65*	0.25****	0.24****
Patient Reported Depression (CES-DC)$^{+}$	0.47*	0.28***	0.21****	0.22****	0.16	0.44*	0.49*	0.20	0.16
No. Comorbid Conditions	0.33***	0.03	0.03	0.12	0.07	0.36**	0.42*	0.22****	0.17
Patient Reported Pain Status(PPQ-VAS)$^{+}$	0.24***	0.14****	0.12	0.28***	-0.03	0.45*	0.14	0.01	0.03
Patient Reported Quality of Life (PedsQL RM)$^{+}$	0.29*	0.26****	0.34***	0.27***	0.15	0.35**	0.29***	0.12	0.33***
Patient Reported Functional Status (PedsQL™ VAS)$^{+}$	0.37**	0.24****	0.17	0.35**	0.08	0.43*	0.38**	0.11	0.05
Parent Reported Health Status^{++}	-0.37**	-0.08	-0.23****	-0.28***	-0.11	-0.32***	-0.34**	-0.05	-0.22****

+Higher scores indicate an unfavorable status or presence of condition.

++Higher scores indicate a favorable status.

*$p<0.0001$ **$p<0.001$ ***$p\leq0.01$ ****$p<0.05$

Discussion

As expected based on previous studies, sleep problems were common (80%) among pediatric patients with JIA. The most frequent specific sleep disturbance was daytime sleepiness (72% of participants). Greater sleep disturbance was correlated with increased scores for anxiety and depression. All three were associated with pain, overall health status, number of co-morbid conditions, functional status, and HRQOL. Specifically, night waking and parasomnias stood out among individual sleep problems as demonstrating strong associations with anxiety and depression.

These results are consistent with previous studies showing that sleep disturbance is common among pediatric chronic pain populations including those with recurrent headache, abdominal pain, and sickle cell disease (23-25). Despite their frequency, negative implications, and seemingly reciprocal relationship to pain status and psychological health, sleep quality and quantity are often ignored by medical professionals (26). The high prevalence of sleep problems within this population underlines the importance for clinicians to include sleep assessment as a regular aspect of JIA patient evaluation.

The data are also consistent with earlier studies showing that youth with arthritis are at increased risk for overall adjustment problems and internalizing symptoms (27,28). In addition to pain and physical limitations, JIA patients may harbor increased fears about the course of their disease and the certainty of their future (28). Clinicians caring for children with JIA should consider screening for depression and anxiety.

Although chronic pain patients may suffer from poor sleep quality as a function of depressed mood or anxiety rather than pain, the causal relationships among these problems have not been definitively established (29). Our data confirms that sleep disorders frequently accompany mood disturbances and pain. However, longitudinal studies are needed to determine causality. While the results of such studies are pending, it appears prudent to ensure that clinicians assess JIA patients for concomitant depressive and anxiety disorders as part of the overall plan to optimize the management of somatic symptoms.

Of the individual sleep disturbances, night waking and parasomnias were most highly correlated with anxiety and depression. Sleep disturbance, anxiety and depression may be expressed differently in children than in adults. For example, children may exhibit increased (or decreased) nap times, behavioral problems, learning disabilities, mental uneasiness, and physical restlessness (30). Sleep patterns may be useful in predicting and monitoring symptom severity, psychological disease status, and how well children are coping with their illness.

Daytime sleepiness was the most frequent disturbance in this study, present in 72% of patients. Previous studies have reported similar trends of daytime sleepiness in 6-18 year olds with migraine and adults with chronic pain (15, 31). Modest sleep loss and daytime sleepiness are associated with increased secretion of pro-inflammatory cytokines (32, 33). This study did not explore patient's sleep and wake time or delve into physiologic characteristics such as cytokine levels. Future research investigating the relationship of sleep, symptom severity and cytokine levels would be useful.

This study has several strengths as well as limitations. The strengths include the inclusion of patients from both private and academic practices, in two separate states which enhances generalizability; the use of standardized instruments which enhances validity; and the use of patient-completed instruments which enhances sensitivity. Limitations include its modest sample size; its cross-sectional nature which limits the ability to draw inferences about causal relationships; and its focus on self-report rather than objective measures such as cytokine levels

Despite its limitations, this data has important implications for future clinical care and research. Because sleep problems are so common in this population and may contribute to decreased function and poor quality of life, clinicians who care for children with JIA should consider routinely screening for sleep problems. Because sleep problems were significantly correlated with anxiety and depression, clinicians should consider additional screening for these problems among JIA patients who report significant sleep disturbances. Future studies should explore the causal relationships between these factors, and how improvements in one or more symptoms might improve overall quality of life.

Acknowledgments

We thank Debbie Dirkse and Kaylene Hood for distributing and collecting questionnaires. We thank the families who participated. We thank Paula Stant for assistance in questionnaire preparation, data entry and manuscript preparation. Supported from NIH K24 AT2207. Author contributions: DH developed the research questions, analyzed the data and drafted the manuscript, KRS participated in developing the research questions, recruiting patients and editing the manuscript, HG participated in developing the research questions, recruiting patients and editing the manuscript and KK participated in developing the research questions, supervised data collection and data analysis and edited and reviewed the manuscript.

References

[1] Varni JW, Thompson KL, Hanson V. The Varni/Thompson Pediatric Pain Questionnaire. I. Chronic musculoskeletal pain in juvenile rheumatoid arthritis. Pain 1987;28(1):27-38.

[2] von Essen L, Enskar K, Kreuger A, Larsson B, Sjoden PO. Self-esteem, depression and anxiety among Swedish children and adolescents on and off cancer treatment. Acta Paediatr 2000;89(2):229-36.

[3] Murphy DA, Marelich WD, Hoffman D. Assessment of anxiety and depression in young children: support for two separate constructs. J Clin Child Psychol 2000;29(3):383-91.

[4] Gragg RA, Rapoff MA, Danovsky MB, Lindsley CB, Varni JW, Waldron SA, et al. Assessing chronic musculoskeletal pain associated with rheumatic disease: further validation of the pediatric pain questionnaire. J Pediatr Psychol 1996;21(2):237-50.

[5] Fendrich M, Weissman MM, Warner V. Screening for depressive disorder in children and adolescents: validating the Center for Epidemiologic Studies Depression Scale for Children. Am J Epidemiol 1990;131(3):538-51.

[6] Melzack R. The McGill Pain Questionnaire: major properties and scoring methods. Pain 1975;1(3):277-99.

[7] Varni JW, Seid M, Knight TS, Uzark K, Szer IS. The PedsQL 4.0 Generic Core Scales: sensitivity, responsiveness, and impact on clinical decision-making. J Behav Med 2002;25(2):175-93.

[8] Varni JW, Burwinkle TM, Limbers CA, Szer IS. The PedsQL as a patient-reported outcome in children and adolescents with fibromyalgia: an analysis of OMERACT domains. Health Qual Life Outcomes 2007;5:9.

[9] Reynolds CR, Richmond BO. What I Think and Feel: a revised measure of Children's Manifest Anxiety. J Abnorm Child Psychol 1997;25(1):15-20.

[10] Norvell N, Brophy C, Finch AJ, Jr. The relationship of anxiety to childhood depression. J Pers Assess 1985;49(2):150-3.

[11] Petty RE, Southwood TR, Manners P, Baum J, Glass DN, Goldenberg J, et al. International League of Associations for Rheumatology classification of juvenile idiopathic arthritis: second revision, Edmonton, 2001. J Rheumatol 2004;31(2):390-2.

[12] Owens JA, Spirito A, McGuinn M. The Children's Sleep Habits Questionnaire (CSHQ): psychometric properties of a survey instrument for school-aged children. Sleep 2000;23(8):1043-51.

[13] Brunner HI, Johnson AL, Barron AC, Passo MH, Griffin TA, Graham TB, et al. Gastrointestinal symptoms and their association with health-related quality of life of children with juvenile rheumatoid arthritis: validation of a gastrointestinal symptom questionnaire. J Clin Rheumatol 2005;11(4):194-204.

[14] Sawyer MG, Whitham JN, Roberton DM, Taplin JE, Varni JW, Baghurst PA. The relationship between health-related quality of life, pain and coping strategies in juvenile idiopathic arthritis. Rheumatology (Oxford) 2004;43(3):325-30.

[15] Heng K, Wirrell E. Sleep disturbance in children with migraine. J Child Neurol 2006;21(9):761-6.

[16] Bloom BJ, Owens JA, McGuinn M, Nobile C, Schaeffer L, Alario AJ. Sleep and its relationship to pain, dysfunction, and disease activity in juvenile rheumatoid arthritis. J Rheumatol 2002;29(1):169-73.

[17] Faulstich ME, Carey MP, Ruggiero L, Enyart P, Gresham F. Assessment of depression in childhood and adolescence: an evaluation of the Center for Epidemiological Studies Depression Scale for Children (CES-DC). Am J Psychiatry 1986;143(8):1024-7.

[18] Zamir G, Press J, Tal A, Tarasiuk A. Sleep fragmentation in children with juvenile rheumatoid arthritis. J Rheumatol 1998;25(6):1191-7.

[19] Rouster-Stevens K, Nageswaran S, Arcury TA, Kemper KJ. How do parents of children with juvenile idiopathic arthritis (JIA) perceive their therapies? BMC Complement Altern Med 2008;8(1):25.

[20] Casteneda AM, BC; Palermo, DS. The children's form of the Manifest Anxiety Scale. Child Dev 1956;27:317-26.

[21] Weissman MM, Orvaschel H, Padian N. Children's symptom and social functioning self-report scales. Comparison of mothers' and children's reports. J Nerv Ment Dis 1980;168(12):736-40.

[22] Sherman SA, Eisen S, Burwinkle TM, Varni JW. The PedsQL Present Functioning Visual Analogue Scales: preliminary reliability and validity. Health Qual Life Outcomes 2006;4:75.

[23] Miller VA, Palermo TM, Powers SW, Scher MS, Hershey AD. Migraine headaches and sleep disturbances in children. Headache 2003;43(4):362-8.

[24] Hargrave DR, Wade A, Evans JP, Hewes DK, Kirkham FJ. Nocturnal oxygen saturation and painful sickle cell crises in children. Blood 2003;101(3):846-8.

[25] Huntley ED, Campo JV, Dahl RE, Lewin DS. Sleep characteristics of youth with functional abdominal pain and a healthy comparison group. J Pediatr Psychol 2007;32(8):938-49.

[26] Ranjbaran Z, Keefer L, Stepanski E, Farhadi A, Keshavarzian A. The relevance of sleep abnormalities to chronic inflammatory conditions. Inflamm Res 2007;56(2):51-7.

[27] LeBovidge JS, Lavigne JV, Donenberg GR, Miller ML. Psychological adjustment of children and adolescents with chronic arthritis: a meta-analytic review. J Pediatr Psychol 2003;28(1):29-39.

[28] Barlow JH, Shaw KL, Harrison K. Consulting the 'experts': children's and parents' perceptions of psycho-educational interventions in the context of juvenile chronic arthritis. Health Educ Res 1999;14(5):597-610.

[29] Sayar K, Arikan M, Yontem T. Sleep quality in chronic pain patients. Can J Psychiatry 2002;47(9):844-8.

[30] Atkinson JA-I, S; Slater, MA. Subjective sleep disturbance in chronic back pain. Clin J Pain 1988;14(4):311-4.

[31] Merkelbach S, Schulz H. What have fatigue and sleepiness in common? J Sleep Res 2006;15(1):105-6.

[32] Vgontzas AN, Zoumakis M, Papanicolaou DA, Bixler EO, Prolo P, Lin HM, et al. Chronic insomnia is associated with a shift of interleukin-6 and tumor necrosis factor secretion from nighttime to daytime. Metabolism 2002;51(7):887-92.

[33] Vgontzas AN, Zoumakis E, Bixler EO, Lin HM, Follett H, Kales A, et al. Adverse effects of modest sleep restriction on sleepiness, performance, and inflammatory cytokines. J Clin Endocrinol Metab 2004;89(5):2119-26.

In: Mental Health from an International Perspective
Editors: J. Merrick, S. Aspler and M. Morad
ISBN: 978-1-62948-519-5

Chapter 11

Hatha yoga and depression

Jana Whiddon, PhD, LMHC, ERYT-500* ***and Adam Bazini, PhD, LMHC***

Counselor Education Department, Capella University, Minneapolis, Minnesota and Counseling Department, Webster University, Webster Groves, Missouri, United States of America

Due to the rise of individuals affected by depression and the challenges with traditional treatments it is imperative that alternative treatments, yoga in particular, be integrated into mainstream treatments. Yoga is based on the practice of mind and body unity. Without this congruity, the mind will become restless and agitated resulting in depressive symptoms, poor overall health, and decreased mental clarity. The practice of yoga is believed to reduce these effects and restore good mental and physical health. Methods: A true experimental method, specifically a randomized control-group pretest-posttest design was used to investigate the effects of Hatha yoga on depression in adults. The study was conducted in a mid-sized, urban city in Central Florida and studied twenty-six adults who suffered from mild, moderate, to severe depression and who were in outpatient treatment at the time of the study. Participants in the experimental group practiced Hatha yoga for one and a half hours, three times per week, for eight weeks with a certified yoga instructor. Those in the control group were on a wait list. The Beck Depression Inventory-II was utilized as a pretest and posttest measure and an independent sample t-test was used to analyze the data. Results: The results showed that the BDI-II depression scores for the individuals in the experimental group were significantly lower than the control group. Limitations: The main limitation is the small sample size. Conclusions: The study supports previous research that Hatha yoga is a viable and effective alternative adjunct treatment for reducing depressive symptoms.

* Correspondence: Jana Whiddon, 215 East Bay St #3, Lakeland, FL 33801, United States. E-mail: jwhi99@aol.com.

Introduction

For thousands of years, Yogi's and practitioners of the art of yoga have emphasized the physical and psychological aspects of yoga practice and the resulting benefits to physical and mental health. Bridging the gap between the mind and body with the breath can allow the individual to increase self-confidence, increase the level of tolerance, expand the capacity to deal with and accept change, and appreciate the gift of life. Yoga is based on the practice of mind and body unity. Without this congruity, the mind will become chronically restless and agitated resulting in poor health and decreased mental clarity. The practice of yoga is believed to combat these effects and restore good mental and physical health (1). Yoga not only improves physical and mental health, it also bestows a sense of self-reliance, a sense of harmony with the laws of the universe, and enhances our innate potential (2).

Psychotherapy and yoga alter an individual's feelings about him or her self, alleviating anxiety, and nurturing a measure of self-control. The difference lies in the ultimate goals. The goal of psychotherapy is narrow, focusing only on the individual's adjustment to society, whereas the goal of yoga is to maximize joy and unfold human potential (2). Unlike Western psychological theory which states that our mental difficulties stem from a combination of life experiences, stressors, genetic factors, and/or cognitive and behavioral challenges, yoga philosophy proposes that our difficulties originate from separation from our true nature. This separation causes suffering manifesting in many affective, cognitive, and behavioral symptoms. Inherent in the beliefs of yoga philosophy is the notion that we are just right as we are, however, over time we have forgotten this. Loosing sight of this truth leads to the separation. Yoga challenges individuals to identify false and illusionary perceptions, beliefs, and patterns and to be present and non-judgmental of emotional challenges such as depression, anxiety, anger, fear and other conflicts (3).

In yoga philosophy, the practice of the eight limbs guides an individual on a more clear path to unity. Pantanjali Maharishi, creator of The Yoga Sutras, outlined the eight limbs, or basic beliefs, of yoga. Hatha yoga is commonly comprised of the first four beliefs: Yama, Niyama, Asana, and Pranayama. Yamas are the moral commandments such as attitudes towards others, nonviolence, truthfulness, non-stealing, conservation of energy, and lack of greed. The Niyamas are ethics dealing with self-purification such as purity of the body and mind, contentment, self-study, and self-surrender. Asana is the practice of physical postures incorporating awareness, balance, and comfort in order to revitalize the body. The physical is more accessible and often people can integrate physical experiences with increased efficiency. Finally, the fourth of the eight limbs is Pranayama which is the practice of rhythmic breath control leading to the enhancement of subtle energy flow energizing the body and mind (3).

The state of depression

Modern age is the age of stresses and strains. There has been a significant change in lifestyles in the twenty-first century making individuals scurry beyond capacity, resulting in a myriad of physical and emotional dysfunctions, especially depression. Depression is a serious medical condition that has a tremendous impact on society. It affects multiple aspects of an individual's life such as physical health, work performance, financial welfare, relationships, and overall quality of life. Approximately 20.9 million Americans suffer from a mood disorder, which includes Major Depressive Disorder, Dysthymic Disorder, and Bipolar Disorder. Of these statistics, 6.7% of U.S. adults suffer from Major Depressive Disorder and 1.5% from Dysthymia (4, 5). In addition, general medical centers and mental health treatment centers report that major depression is one of the most prevalent and disabling conditions for which individuals seek treatment (6). The World Health Organization reports Major Depressive Disorder is the leading cause of disability in the United States for ages 15-44 (7).

The cost of depression is astonishing. Estimates of the direct and indirect costs of depression to the nation in 2000 totaled 83.1 billion dollars (8). This includes inpatient and outpatient treatment, medication treatment, lost work time, and a decrease in work productivity. The economic burden of depression is likely to be higher due to other potentially important indirect costs of depression. These include physical ailments, substance abuse disorders, cigarette smoking, other mental illnesses that occur in conjunction with depression, work related problems such as absenteeism and decreased productivity, and the general decline in quality of life (8).

Although there are many effective treatments available for depression, less than 20% of individuals who have depressive symptoms seek treatment during the initial year of onset. Many factors influence the decision to avoid seeking treatment such as societal stigma, fear of discrimination and judgment by friends, co-workers, and even family members, and a feeling of personal failure due to a perceived inability to cope effectively with stressors and problems (9). The traditional treatments for depression such as psychotherapy or pharmacological treatment can be timely, costly, and frequently ineffective (10). Unfortunately, symptom recovery rates for the traditional treatments are no more than 50% to 60% and rates of full sustained remission are even lower (11). Although many of the antidepressants prescribed to treat depression may alleviate some symptoms, they can have unpleasant side effects that interfere with an individual's ability to function at a desired level. The iatrogenic effect of medicating depression is sometimes trading one negative symptom for another. Therefore, alternative interventions which are low-cost and do not have negative side effects need to be incorporated into the mainstream (12).

Nontraditional approaches such as aerobic exercise, running and swimming, and anaerobic exercise, weight lifting and stretching, have been documented to have antidepressant affects and have been proposed as an adjunct and even a replacement for traditional treatment approaches (13-17). Considered even more nontraditional, many Eastern approaches, such as yoga and meditation, are making an appearance into mainstream allopathic medicine in the United States. Although there has been a surge of studies over the past decade, it is still limited as to the full empirical support they have in treating depression.

Yoga as treatment for depression

A dearth of empirical evidence exists in support of yoga in the treatment of depression; however, there has been a surge of interest in this area within the medical, mental health, and research communities. Shapiro et al. (18) conducted an experimental study using Iyengar yoga as a complimentary treatment for depression. There were seventeen participants in three treatment groups practicing various Iyengar techniques for a total of twenty sessions. Utilizing various assessments, for psychological and physiological constructs, results showed a decrease in depression, anger, and anxiety. Eleven of the seventeen participants went into remission of the depressive symptoms after participating in the yoga groups. Change occurred after each session as well as a cumulative effective of the practice. Unfortunately, limitations existed due to the small sample size, high drop out rate, and lack of a control group (18).

Woolery et al. (19) conducted an experimental study examining the effects of Iyengar style yoga on young adults with mild depressive symptoms. Twenty three participants completed the study with ten in the experimental group who practiced Iyengar yoga one hour, twice per week, for five weeks. A battery of tests were given before and after the first, fifth, and last classes. The results indicated a significant decrease in depression related symptoms.

Lavey's (20) study on the effects of yoga on mood for psychiatric inpatients suggests that yoga was associated with improved mood as well as other psychological factors on the Profile of Mood States. The participants were 113 inpatients at a New Hampshire psychiatric hospital with various diagnoses such as psychotic disorders, mood, anxiety disorders, adjustment and personality disorders. Yoga class was held once weekly and assessment was administered before and after the class. Although this was not a controlled study, it is further preliminary support that practicing yoga would improve negative emotions (20).

In another study using an alternative treatment for depression there were forty-six dysthymic patients who received Sudarshan Kriya Yoga (SKY), a yogic breath practice, for three months. At the completion of this study 68% of the patients attained remission (21). A year later in another study SKY was compared to electroconvulsive therapy (ECT) and imiprimine, an antidepressant medication. Each SKY session was followed by 10 to15 minutes of Yoga Nidra, which is a state of deep relaxation. Forty-five hospitalized individuals with melancholic depressive symptoms were randomly assigned to one of the three treatment groups. They were assessed prior to the start of the study, every week for four weeks, and at the completion of the study. The SKY group received the treatment once daily six days a week, the ECT group received three treatments per week and the imipramine group received a single daily oral dose of 150 mg. The results showed that all three groups had significant reductions in BDI scores although there was no between-group difference. SKY produced a 67% remission rate after just four weeks of treatment (22).

Savasana is an asana, or posture, that Yogies believe is extremely important and highly therapeutic for curing depression and anxiety. While in this position the individual engages in slow, rhythmic, diaphramatic breathing. A study examined the effectiveness of savasana as a therapeutic intervention to alleviate depression. It included 50 subjects, 25 in the experimental and 25 in the control group, who suffered from severe depression. The subjects in the experimental group practiced this yoga asana thirty minutes daily for thirty consecutive days. The differences in mean scores between pretests and post tests revealed a statistically significant decrease in depression scores for the experimental group and no significant differences in the control group supporting the hypothesis that savasana is an effective intervention for alleviating or decreasing depression (23).

These studies and others suggest that yoga alone or in combination with other psychotherapeutic approaches may play a useful role in mental health particularly in psychological constructs as they are related to depression (24-26). Although the initial indication is such, there is a need for more empirically-based and controlled studies to support the benefits of yoga in depression. This study was a controlled trial examining the effects of Hatha yoga on depression.

Our study

The purpose of this study was to determine the effects of practicing Hatha yoga on levels of depression for the adult participants The research question asked if the practice of Hatha yoga would produce a difference between experimental and control group's depression scores on the Beck Depression Inventory – II (BDI-II). The corresponding hypothesis was that there would be a significant difference in levels of depression between the experimental and control groups. In order to test this hypothesis this study utilized an experimental method, specifically a randomized control-group pretest-posttest design.

Participants were randomly recruited by placing notices in various public areas and via an advertisement in the local newspaper. Each respondent participated in a phone interview with the researcher assessing for appropriateness based on identified inclusion and exclusion criteria. All respondents were included in the study. The number of participants in the experimental group and the control group was 12 and 14, respectively. The experimental group was comprised of 17% males and 83% females with a mean age of 45 years. The control group was comprised of 7% males and 93% females with a mean age of 43 years.

A group meeting with all of the screened participants took place where the purpose, procedures of the study, confidentiality, and informed consent were explained. Each subject completed a demographic data sheet and the BDI-II then was randomly assigned to the Hatha yoga group or the wait-list control group. The Hatha yoga classes were held for 90 minutes, three times a week, for eight weeks. The yoga sessions followed the series as described in The Schedule of Hatha Yoga Practice (Appendix A). The Hatha yoga sessions incorporated pranayama, asana, savasana, and dharana. The BDI-II was given as a posttest measure after the completion of the final class to all participants in the experimental and control groups.

The test instrument selected for use in this study is the BDI-II. The BDI-II was selected due to its wide use in assessing the severity of depression, its administration time, and ease in scoring. The psychometric properties of the BDI-II are sound. In testing for reliability, coefficient alpha estimates with outpatients was .92 and for a non-clinical sample it was .93. The test-retest reliability coefficient was high, .93 over a week's span. Evidence for concurrent validity was demonstrated through a moderately high correlation with the Hamilton Psychiatric Rating Scale for Depression-Revised ($r = .71$) in outpatients (27).

Findings

The research question guiding this study inquired if the practice of Hatha yoga would produce a difference between experimental and control groups' depression scores on the BDI-II. The analysis assessing the differences in posttest scores between the experimental and control groups did reveal a statistically significant decrease in the BDI-II posttest scores for depression for the experimental group. The BDI-II pretest scores were obtained at the beginning of the study to show participant's level of depression, in addition the scores were used in a statistical analysis to ascertain the degree of group equivalency for the experimental and control groups.

There was a wide range of pretest scores for both groups. The range of scores for the experimental group was 19-45 and for the control group the range of scores was 19-41. The BDI-II categorizes depression in the following manner; minimal 0-13, mild 14-19, moderate 20-28, and severe 29-63 (27). For the experimental group one participant's score was in the mild range for depression, five participants scored in the moderate range, and six participants scored within the severely depressed range. For the control group one participant fell within the mildly depressed range, four participants scored in the moderate range, and nine participants scored in the severely depressed range. The mean pretest score on the depression inventory for the experimental group was 29.58 with a standard deviation of 8.096, while the mean pretest score for the control group was 30.64 with a standard deviation of 7.110.

At the completion of the eight-week study, both the experimental and control groups were re-tested using the BDI-II to assess if the groups differed significantly. The mean posttest score for the experimental group was 5.08 and the standard deviation was 2.503. The mean posttest score for the control group was 27.00 with a standard deviation of 4.169. The experimental group showed a range of 0 to 10 while the control group had a range of scores of 19 to 33. All participants in the experimental group had posttest scores that fell within the minimal range of depression on the BDI-II. The control group participants' posttest scores continued to show a range with one that fell within the mild range, nine were in the moderate range, and four were in the severe range of depression.

An independent sample t-test was used to determine if the experimental and control groups differed on the BDI-II posttest. The analysis did show a significant difference in the posttest scores for the experimental and control groups, $t(24) = -15.893$, $p < .05$ (two-tailed). Table 1 shows the t-test summary for the experimental and control groups' posttest scores. The BDI-II posttest scores show a mean difference of 21.92 points between the experimental and control groups, with the experimental group showing the larger decrease in depression scores. In other words, the experimental group, who practiced Hatha yoga three times per week for eight weeks, showed a larger decrease in depressive symptoms than the control group, which did not participate in the Hatha yoga program. Therefore the research hypothesis is supported by the data that the practice of Hatha yoga does produce a difference in experimental and control group's depression scores on the BDI-II.

Table 1. Independent Samples t-test Assessing Control and Experimental Group Posttest Scores

N	Experimental Group	Control Group	t	df	Sig.	Mean Difference	95% Upper	Conf. Int. Lower
26	5.08	27.00	-15.893	24	.000	-21.92	-24.763 -	19.007

Discussion

The results of this study coincide with previous research showing the antidepressant effects of Hatha yoga with adults (18, 19, 27). The individuals in this study who participated in the

Hatha yoga treatment group not only showed a more significant decrease in depressive symptoms as compared to those who did not participate in the Hatha yoga treatment, but also showed a substantial decrease in depressive symptoms with all of the individuals scoring in the minimal range for depression on the BDI-II posttest. It is important to highlight that all of the participants in this study were in some type of outpatient traditional treatment for the depression at the time of the study. These results are vital to individuals who are suffering from depression and are either reluctant to seek treatment or who have been unsuccessful in conventional treatments. Furthermore, with the estimation that over 8% of the population is diagnosed with some type of depression, it is imperative that effective, inexpensive, easily accessible, and non-stigmatizing treatments for depression be discovered and mainstreamed (4, 5, 28).

Yoga as a treatment for depressive disorders has tremendous potential for four specific reasons. First, there are minimal side effects when compared to medication treatment. Second, it is more cost-effective than psychotherapy and medication therapy. Third, yoga is less time-consuming than traditional medication treatment programs. Fourth, it has implications as a preventative measure for recurring depressive episodes (23). Given these important characteristics, exercise could, if research studies continue to reflect its effectiveness in treating depression, become the preferred intervention. Employing yoga as a treatment could decrease and even eliminate obstacles that conventional treatments generate; thus, individuals may be more likely to view yoga as a socially acceptable intervention for depression.

This study utilized a sound methodology safeguarding internal validity through specific methods; however additional research utilizing larger sample sizes would increase external validity. Although it was a controlled experiment, the number of participants who completed the study totaled fewer than thirty. Utilizing a larger sample size would increase the generalizability of the results. In addition, having a representative sample across gender and ethnicity would strengthen the external validity of the results. It can also be recommended that this study be replicated with clinical and non-clinical populations.

The results from this study are compelling enough to warrant further investigation of the effects of Hatha yoga treatment on depression. As previously mentioned, if this research study were replicated a larger sample should be used in order to improve the generalizability of the results. It is also recommended that additional testing times occur during the treatment which would help determine when the participant's depressive symptoms began to decrease and the point at which the participant reached a substantial benefit. In addition, a study could be conducted that investigated the long-term effects of Hatha yoga practice. This could include testing at intervals such as three months, six months, and nine months after the completion of treatment. It would also be valuable to determine whether individuals who practice Hatha yoga as a treatment for depression have a higher rate of compliance than those who participate in the conventional treatments. Another recommendation for further research would be to compare the timeline of improvement between a Hatha yoga treatment group and a traditional treatment group for depression. Finally, from a theoretical perspective, further research is needed to identify the mechanism of change inherent in alternative treatments such as Hatha yoga.

Conclusion

With the continuous rise of depression and the challenges faced by the public to obtain quality healthcare, providing alternatives to the costly traditional treatment methods is warranted. The overall estimated cost of depression soared from $44 billion in 1990 (29) to $83.1 billion in 2000 (8). These costs include inpatient and outpatient treatments, pharmacological treatment as well as decreased productivity at work and lost work time. There are also costs associated with depression that cannot be measured such as emotional turmoil and interpersonal problems (29). Although there are benefits of traditional treatments such as pharmacology and psychotherapy, they boast only moderate results in the treatment of depressive symptoms (11). This warrants the necessity of having empirically supported holistic alternative treatments for depression such as yoga.

The philosophy of yoga also provides a holistic way to view the person with depression. The literal meaning of yoga is union and although the essential union is between the mind and body, many levels of unions exist, such as the union of movement and breath, the union of muscle and muscle, the union of thought and action, and the union of desire and intent (30). It is within these unions that an individual may transcend the superficial and reach contentment and harmony. In practical terms yoga involves the release of human potential. It is not about becoming more flexible, stronger, or fit. These are incidental side effects. Yoga is about unlocking the full power of the body and the full power of the mind. As yoga practice increases, potential fulfills itself. In regular practice an individual will experience deeper relaxation, enhanced calmness, heighten concentration, and improved alertness. Most importantly an individual will experience increased levels of self-confidence, determination, and contentment (30). Yoga can also affect mood in a positive way by creating internal awareness, providing time for oneself, and by focusing on the present by disregarding cognitive chatter (13). With further theoretical and empirical support the holistic approach of yoga can be a viable compliment to the traditional treatments for depression.

Acknowledgments

Many valuable individuals were involved in supporting this research. First and foremost is the current and past Faculty at Barry University – Orlando campus was integral in this process. Also, thank you to the courageous people who committed themselves to facing depression with strength and perseverance.

References

[1] Kraftsow, G. Yoga for wellness. New York: Penguin, 1999.
[2] Ramaswami, S. Yoga and healing. In: Sheikh AA, Sheikh KS, eds. Healing east and west: Ancient wisdom and modern psychology. New York: John Wiley, 1996.
[3] Satchidananda SS. The yoga Sutras of Patanjali. Virginia: Integral Yoga Publ, 1990.

[4] Kessler RC, Chiu WT, Demler O, Walters EE. Prevalence, severity, and comorbidity of twelve-month DSM-IV disorders in the National Comorbidity Survey Replication (NCS-R). Arch Gen Psychiatry 2005;62(6):617-27.

[5] US Census Bureau. US Census Bureau Population Estimates by Demographic Characteristics. Table 2: Annual Estimates of the Population by Selected Age Groups and

[6] Sex for the United States: April 1, 2000 to July 1, 2004. URL: http://www.census.gov/popest/national/asrh/ (accessed February 8 2010).

[7] Motabai R. Residual symptoms and impairment in major depression in the community. Am J Psychol 2001;158(10):1645-51.

[8] The World Health Organization. The global burden of disease: 2004 update, Table A2:

[9] Burden of disease in DALYs by cause, sex and income group in WHO regions, estimates for 2004. URL: http://www.who.int/healthinfo/global_burden_disease/GBD_report_2004update_part4.pdf

[10] O'Connor EA, Whitlock EP, Gaynes BN, Beil TL. Screening for depression in adults and older adults in primary care: An updated systematic review. Ann Intern Med 2009;151(11):793-803.

[11] O'Neal, H, Dunn, A, Martinsen, E. Depression and exercise. Int J Sport Psychol 2000;31: 110-35.

[12] Martinsen EW. Interaction of exercise and medication in the psychiatric patient. In: Morgan WP, Goldston SE, eds. Exercise and mental health. Washington, DC: Hemisphere Publ, 1987.

[13] Friedman, MA, Detweiler-Bedell, JB, Leventhal, HE, Home, R, Keitner, GI, Miller, IW. Combined psychotherapy and pharmacotherapy for the treatment of major depressive disorder. Clin Psychol Sci Pract 2004;2:47-68.

[14] Craft LL, Landers DM. The effects of exercise on clinical depression and depression resulting from mental illness: A meta-analysis. J Sport Exerc Psychol 1998;20:339-57.

[15] Berger, B, Owen, D. Mood alteration with yoga and swimming: Aerobic exercise may not be necessary. Percept Mot Skills 1992;75:1331-43.

[16] Babyak, M, Blumenthal, J, Herman, S. Exercise treatment for major depression: Maintenance of therapeutic benefit at 10 months. Psychosom Med 2000;62:633–8.

[17] Craft, L, Perna, F. The benefits of exercise for the clinically depressed. Prim Care Companion. J Clin Psychiatry 2004;6:104–11.

[18] Doyne EJ, Ossip-Klein DJ, Bowman ED, Osborn KM, McDougall-Wilson IB, Neimeyer RA. Running versus weight lifting in the treatment of depression. J Consult Clin Psychol 1987;55(5):748-54.

[19] Martinsen E, Hoffart A, Solberg O. Comparing aerobic with nonaerobic forms of exercise in the treatment of clinical depression: A randomized trial. Compr Psychiatr 1989;30(4):324-31.

[20] Shapiro D, Cook I, Davydov D, Ottaviani C, Leuchter A, Abrams M. Yoga as a complementary treatment of depression: Effects of traits and moods on treatment outcome. eCAM [Online]. URL: http://ecam.oxfordjournals.org/cgi/content/full/nel114v1

[21] Woolery A, Myers H, Sternlieb B, Zeltzer L. A yoga intervention for young adults with elevated symptoms of depression. Alternative Ther Health Med 2004;10(2):60-3.

[22] Lavey R, Sherman T, Mueser K, Osborne D, Currier M, Wolfe R. The effects of yoga on mood in psychiatric inpatients. Psychiatr Rehabil J 2005;28(4):399-402.

[23] Janakiramaiah N, Gangadhar BN, Naga Venkateska Murthy PJ, Shetty TK, Subbakrishna DK, Mete BL, et al. Therapeutic efficacy of sudarshan kriya yoga (SKY) in dysthymic disorder. Nimhans J 1998;17:21-8.

[24] Janakiramaiah N, Gangadhar B, Naga Venkatesha Murthy P, Harish M, Subbakrishna D, Vedamurthachar A. Antidepressant efficacy of sudarshan kriya yoga (SKY) in melancholia: A randomized comparison with electroconvulsive therapy (ECT) and imipramine. J Affect Disord 1999;57(1-3):255-9.

[25] Khumar S, Kaur P, Kaur S. Effectiveness of savasana on depression among university students. Indian J Clin Psychol 1993;20:82-7.

[26] Anantharaman, R, Kabir R. A study of yoga. J Psychol Res 1984;28(2):97-101.

[27] Berger, BG, Owen, DR. Stress reduction and mood enhancement in four exercise modes: swimming, body conditioning, Hatha yoga, and fencing. Res Q Exerc Sport 1988;59(2):148-59.

[28] Kamei T, Toriumi Y, Kimura H, Ohno S, Kumano H, Kimura K. Decrease in serum cortisol during yoga exercise is correlated with alpha wave activation. Percept Mot Skills 2000;90:1027-32.

[29] Beck AT, Steer RA, Brown GK. Beck Depression Inventory-II Manual, 2nd ed. Texas: Psychol Corp, 1996.
[30] Nemeroff C. Progress in the battle with the black dog: Advances in the treatment of depression. Am J Psychol 2001;158(10):1555-7.
[31] Greenberg PE, Stiglin LE, Finkelstein SN, Berndt ER. The economic burden of depression in 1990. J Clin Psychol 1993;54(11):405-18.
[32] Devereux, G. Hatha yoga. London: Harper Collins, 2001.

Appendix A

Schedule of Hatha Yoga Practice

WEEK 1 – 4

Dirga Pranayama – Three Part Breath
Tadasana – Mountain Pose
Surya Namaskar A – Sun Salutation A series (modified)x 4
Padangusthasana – Foot Big Toe Pose
Utthita Trikonasana – Extended Triangle Pose
Utthita Parsvakonasana – Extended Side Angle Pose
Prasarita Padottanasana – Separate Leg Toe Pulling Pose
Virabhadrasana I – Warrior I Pose
Virabhadrasana II - Warrior II Pose
Utthita Hasta Padagusthasana – Standing Toe Pointing Pose
Vrksasana – Tree Pose
Virabhadrasana III – Warrior III Pose
Kapotasana - Pigeon Pose
Dandasana – Seated Pose
Paschimottanasana – Seated Forward Bend
Purvottasana – Eastern Intense Stretch Pose
Janu Sirsasana A - Head-to-Knee Forward Bend
Baddha Konasana – Bound Angle Pose
Savasana – Corpse Pose
Pavanamuktasana - Wind Removing Pose
Setu Bandha Sarvangasana – Bridge Pose
½ Salamba Sarvangasana – ½ Supported Shoulder stand
Paschimottanasana – Seated Forward Bend
Ardha Matsyendrasana – Half Lord of the Fishes Pose
Marichyasana C – Spinal Twist
Kapalbhati in Vajrasana - Blowing in Firm pose
Shavasana – Corpse Pose
Yoga meditation in Padmasana – Lotus or Easy Pose

WEEK 5-8:

Dirga Pranayama – Three Part Breath
Tadasana – Mountain Pose
Surya Namaskar A – Sun Salutation A series (modified)x 4
Padangusthasana – Foot Big Toe Pose
Ardha-Chandrasana - Half Moon Pose
Utthita Trikonasana – Extended Triangle Pose
Utthita Parsvakonasana – Extended Side Angle Pose
Prasarita Padottanasana – Separate Leg Toe Pulling Pose
Virabhadrasana I – Warrior I Pose
Virabhadrasana II - Warrior II Pose
Vrksasana – Tree Pose
Tuladandasana – Balancing Stick Pose
Dandayamana-Dhanurasana - Standing Bow Pulling Pose
Kapotasana - Pigeon Pose
Ardha-Kurmasana - Half Tortise Pose
Dandasana – Seated Pose
Paschimottanasana – Seated Forward Bend
Purvottasana – Eastern Intense Stretch Pose
Ustrasana - Camel Pose
Balasana – Child Pose
Sasangasana - Rabbit Pose
Shavasana – Corpse Pose
Supta Padangesthasana A – Sleeping Big Toe Pose
Supta Padangesthasana B – Sleeping Big Toe Pose
Supta Padangesthasana C – Sleeping Big Toe Pose
Setu Bandha Sarvangasana – Bridge Pose
Sarvangasana – Shoulderstand
Paschimottanasana – Seated Forward Bend
Ardha Matsyendrasana – Half Lord of the Fishes Pose
Marichyasana C – Spinal Twist
Savasana – Corpse Pose
Yoga meditation in Padmasana – Lotus or Easy Pose

SECTION TWO: CHILDREN, YOUTH AND FAMILIES

In: Mental Health from an International Perspective
Editors: J. Merrick, S. Aspler and M. Morad

ISBN: 978-1-62948-519-5

Chapter 12

Immigrant families: Cultural and psychological issues

Olivier Taïeb, MD, PhD[1], Thierry Baubet, MD, PhD[2], Dalila Rezzoug, MD[3], Jordan Sibeoni, MD[4] and Marie Rose Moro, MD, PhD[4*]

Department of Child and Adolescent Psychiatry and General Psychiatry, Avicenne Hospital, Bobigny and Department of Adolescent Psychiatry, Cochin Hospital, Paris, France

Abstract

Whether they are African or Asian, children of immigrant families live in risk-fraught situations in which they may be exposed to serious trauma. Immigrant families often live in extreme conditions. Although research has described these conditions, intervention is still inadequate. How many times have we heard that working among these families does not involve treatment, but requires only the basic needs families have to fulfill – survival, where to find food, where to sleep, where to bury their dead. Yet psychological care of immigrant children and families has a lot to teach us. We set out here to share what we have learnt about immigrant families with infants.

Introduction

Culture and parenthood, in the meaning shared by psychoanalysts, psychologists, psychiatrists and paediatricians, and also philosophers, teachers, social workers and policy-makers, is the challenge of the twenty-first century (1). It is tempting to suggest that the most important issue is for each individual to find their own style of parenthood, to transfer or pass

* *Correspondence:* Professor Marie Rose Moro, MD, PhD, Department of Adolescent Psychiatry, Cochin Hospital, AP-HP, Paris 5 University, Inserm U 699, Paris, France. E-mail: marie-rose.moro@cch.aphp.fr.

on the bond, the tenderness, the protection of self and others. Oddly enough, the English *parenthood* has only recently appeared in other languages (French, Spanish, or Italian) as a neologism (such as *parentalité* in French). It is as if we have just realised how precious what we have in our hands was, and that parents all over the world possess it. We have seen parents, those who are vulnerable or find themselves in difficult or inhuman situations, worry so much about finding strategies to survive, mentally or materially speaking – that it becomes difficult or impossible for them to pass on anything but the precariousness of their surrounding world. This is why it is important to study migratory situations, since these situations lead the parents to changes and in some cases to breakdowns that make the establishment of parent-infant relationships more complex. Indeed, migrations are nowadays part of modern societies, which are multiform and multicultural, and migration should be a focus of our clinical concerns. This is all the more true because once this variable is taken into account, the risk is converted into creative potential, for both the children and their families and also for caregivers, as will be seen hereafter from a French experience in infant care set up in Avicenne Hospital and Jean Verdier Hospital in the Paris suburbs (2-6). Better understanding, better care, better provision for migrants and their children are the challenges for early prevention and clinical care in today's society.

Parenthood

You are not born a parent, you become one. Parenthood is made of complex ingredients. Some of them are community ingredients, and belong to the society as a whole; they change over time, they can be historical, legal, social and cultural. Others are more personal and private, they may be conscious or unconscious, they belong to each parent as separate persons and future parents, to the couple, and to the family history of each parent. What are played out here are the parts that are passed on and the parts that remain hidden, childhood traumas, and the way each individual has patched them up. There is also another set of factors belonging to the child, who changes the people who gave birth to him or her. Certain infants are more gifted than others, some are born within an environment that makes things easier; others, due to the circumstances of their birth (prematurity, neonatal distress, physical or mental handicap), have several obstacles to overcome, and must develop numerous, often costly, strategies to enter into a relationship with the distressed parent. Many authors along with Cramer, Lebovici and Stern have shown that the infant is an active partner in the parent-infant interaction, and thereby in the construction of parenthood (7, 8). Indeed, the infant contributes to the emergence of the maternal and paternal identities when the parents are taking care of him or her by handling, feeding and giving pleasure within a process of exchange of actions and feelings that are a central part of the first moments of life (9).

There are many ways of being a father and being a mother, as it has been broadly shown by sociologists and anthropologists (10-14). Professionals have to leave room for these potentials to emerge. Yet it is a difficult task which implies to refrain from any form of judgement on the "best way" to be a father or a mother. Indeed, it is tempting for any professional to think he or she knows better than the parents what the “good” parental behaviour is and what the child’s needs and expectations are. Social and cultural elements contribute to the construction of parental functioning (15-17). Cultural elements have a preventive function and give the opportunity to anticipate the issue of how to become a parent as it gives a meaning to the daily ups and downs of parent-child relations, and preventing distress from setting in.

Early on, cultural elements mingle and become profoundly entangled with individual, family and social elements (18-21). Pregnancy, on account of its initiatory nature, recalls our mythical, cultural and fantasised belonging. How can we protect ourselves in exile? How can we have fine and healthy children? In some places the pregnancy must be concealed, in others certain fish should not be eaten, or certain tubers that soften when cooked. In others places, the husband should not eat certain sorts of meat while his wife is pregnant, or dreams must be kept and interpreted and the demands made complied with, because in dreams it is the child who is speaking (14). In exile these elements belong to the private sphere and can find themselves in contradiction with new, outside, medical, cultural and social manners of thinking; then comes the moment of childbirth. Here again there are many ways of giving birth, receiving the child, presenting him to the world and thinking about his otherness and sometimes his distress. There are also all sorts of "trivial" things that are reactivated in situations of crisis, reawakening representations that may have remained dormant, or that were thought to be outlived.

In the name of a sort of empty universality and simplistic ethics, we professionals do not integrate these complex manners of thinking in the design of prevention and care provision, nor in our theorising. The issues we approach rarely integrate the cultural dimension of parenthood, and above all we do not view these ways of thinking and doing things as being useful in establishing an alliance, understanding, anticipating and providing care. We feel that technique is unclothed, that it has no cultural impact, and that it is enough to observe a protocol for the action to be correctly implemented.

Yet several clinical experiences (6) show that once these different representations are shared, efficiency is patent. From a theoretical point of view they renew our manners of thinking, lead us to "de-centre" and complicate our models and to set aside our over-hasty judgement. Apprehending this otherness allows migrants women to experience the different stages of their pregnancies and parenthood in a non-traumatic manner, and to become familiar with other ways of thinking and other techniques. Migration does entail the need to change. But ignoring otherness is not only to miss the creative side of the encounter, but also to take the risk that these women will never find their place in our prevention and health systems, and it also restricts them to solitude of thought and living. Exchanges with others enable us to change; we need to build together, exchange ideas, and confront perceptions with those of other people. If not, people's thoughts tend to close in on them and its own mechanisms and this can lead to rigidity and withdrawal.

Psychic and cultural transparency

Besides these social and cultural dimensions, paternal and maternal function can be upset by manifestations of individual mental functioning, or by earlier suffering that has not found relief. It usually appears in a sudden and violent manner when the line of descent is being enacted: for instance, the various forms of post-partum depression, and even psychoses, leading on to loss of meaning. The mother vulnerability in this period is well known and has been theorised, in particular via the concept of "psychic transparency"(*transparence psychique*). What transparency means is that, in the perinatal period, the mental functioning of the mother is easier to read and to perceive than it usually is (22, 23). Indeed, the alterations occurring during pregnancy are accompanied by a more ready, more explicit expression of desires, conflicts, and impulses. In addition, childhood conflict is relived, reactivated in particular by oedipal revival. Later, functioning becomes opaque again. This psychic transparency is less recognised in fathers, who also experience upheavals relating to the reliving of their own conflicts, to the re-enacting of their own status as a son, and to the shift from being a son to being a father. The perinatal period thus enables regression and expression that are quite specific to it.

Exile merely potentiates this psychic transparency and this will be expressed by both parents in both mental and cultural spheres. On the one hand, it is expressed in the mental sphere by the reliving of conflicts and the expression of emotions. On the other hand, it is expressed in the cultural sphere in the same way but relying on cultural representations, and ways of doing and saying things specific to each culture. All these cultural elements, which we thought belonged to the preceding generation, are reactivated, and suddenly become valuable and alive. Thus it is appropriate to suggest the concept of cultural transparency to address and represent what the parents are experiencing. Their relationship with their culture and their parents is altered.

Early prevention

In this reality in which different levels interact one with another, the psychological dimension has a specific position in terms of prevention and care. Prevention, indeed, starts with the pregnancy. Some mothers-to-be experience difficulties to think about their expected child. It is then important to help them to invest in and eventually welcome their future baby despite their solitude – which is social and, even more, existential.

Sharing a culture makes it possible to anticipate what will happen, to think about it, and to establish protection. The culture is a base on which we can build a place for the child to be born. The setbacks in this construction of the parent-infant bond find cores of meaning within the experience of the social group; but these meanings are far more difficult to apprehend in a migrant situation. What remains as fixed elements in this case are the body and the individual mental makeup, since everything else has become shifting and precarious. Women living in their communities but excluded from their own societies, equally isolated, also find themselves alone in the task of humanising the child, a common task to all births. The child is a stranger that the mother must learn to know and recognise.

In the perinatal period, adjustments are needed between mother and infant, and also between husband and wife. Dysfunction in the relationship could occur and is sometimes unavoidable, but it is often short-lived if early intervention is possible. To intervene early, demands need to be recognised in their somatic or functional "translations" – these demands are often difficult to express because individuals do not know to whom address them and how. It is therefore important to learn how to recognise the distress and doubts of migrant women through small clues (somatic complaints, complaints concerning the child, requests for social assistance). Most of all, they should be allowed to say things, in their own language if necessary, through other women in their community.

Early prevention is available from the start of life in prevention centres, maternity wards, paediatric departments, infant welfare centres and GP consultations. This perinatal prevention work is essential because the period is crucial for the child's development and for the construction of the child's place in the family.

Care represents an issue as important as prevention. Day-to-day difficulties of migrant or socially underprivileged families and their children are leading us to alter our psychological care provision techniques and our theories so as to adapt them to increasingly complex clinical situations (24).

This also leads us to alter our own frameworks in order to adequately cater for these children and their parents, and to refer them on to specialised consultations if necessary, within a network enabling links and to-and-fro movements between prevention and care facilities: this complementary functioning is essential. The aim is to enable the parent to move from the inside to the outside that he or she is afraid of, and to be what Michel Serres (25) called the "weaver" working to seam together two worlds set apart by a sudden catastrophe.

The tree of life

Each of us, according to Serge Lebovici, carries a trans-generational mandate: it can be said that our "tree of life" sends its roots down into the earth that has soaked up the blood from the wounds caused by the childhood conflicts of our parents (7, 8, 26). Yet our roots, he says, can enable the tree of life to develop and blossom, if they are not too buried in the soil that they become inaccessible. Generally – and happily so – filiation, with its neurotic conflicts, does not prevent the processes of cultural affiliation. The child's tree of life, that is to say the mandate he or she is given via trans-generational transmission, thus brings the grandparents' generation into his or her psychic life through the childhood conflicts of his or her parents, whether it is pre-conscious or repressed (7, 8).

More contemporary conflicts, and in particular migratory trauma, can also take their place in this tree of life, and such events give new meaning, in the aftermath, to childhood conflict and traumas. This is the case for migratory traumas. When the weight of transmission is too heavy, and translation too direct, filiation for the child becomes a "pathology of destiny" (26). This is when there are "ghosts in the nursery" (27). These are visitors that re-emerge from the parents' forgotten past, visitors that were "not invited to the christening". In favourable circumstances the ghosts are driven away from the nursery and return underground.

But in some unfavourable circumstances these representations of the past in the present take over the field, settle there, and seriously affect the mother-infant relationship. Here is the therapeutic challenge: to create and co-create, with the mother and those around her - starting from the child as an interactive partner-, the conditions to identify the ghosts, and rather than chasing them away to negotiate with them and, in a way, to humanise them. Once again, the task is to make something human even out of trauma, whatever its nature is, here breakdown arising from exile.

Pregnancy and childbirth in exile

Traditionally, childbirth is an initiatory moment in which the mother-to-be is necessarily supported by other women from the group: accompaniment, preparation for the different events, interpretation of dreams and so forth (2). Migration leads to several breaks in this supportive process that constructs meaning. First, there is a loss of the accompaniment by the group, by the family, by cultural and social support, and an inability to give a culturally acceptable meaning to dysfunction, such as the mother's sadness, feelings of inability, or inharmonious mother-infant relations. In addition, migrating women are confronted with medical methods that do not allow traditional protective strategies. For these women, western medical practice can be violent, indecent, traumatic and even "pornographic" (a word used by several patients). We became acutely aware of the scale of the violation experienced by the pregnant migrant women since the beginning of our work with them. The women referred in our practice are migrants from the rural areas of North Africa, sub-Saharan Africa, or Sri Lanka. For city-dwellers, these effects are also present, but probably in less explicit manner.

A case story

Medina, a Soniké woman from Mali had been referred for post-partum depression, apparently accompanied by elements of delirium, but this later was shown to be the cultural expression of a traumatic experience, following trans-cultural evaluation. There was no delirium, only trauma, even if its expression was unusual. Medina is a tall woman with a deeply sad look in her eyes. At our first encounter she was wearing a bright yellow *boubou* and a cloth of the same colour covering her hair. On her serious face there were ritual scarifications: a vertical line on the chin, two horizontal lines on the cheek-bones, and a small vertical mark on the forehead. She spoke Soniké in a monotonous voice. From time to time a few tears ran down her cheeks. She took no notice and went on talking about her complete incomprehension of what had happened to her while her son, Mamadou, was still in her womb. On that day she had Mamadou on her back, he was two months old and her first child: Mamadou was very small as he was not feeding well; he was crying a lot and moaning painfully. Medina was not able to breast feed him, he sucked the breast very feebly, and in addition she was convinced she had no milk, or that her milk was not nourishing enough for the child. Medina had been in France for one year, where she had come to join her husband in the country for the previous eight years.

There are several moments that can take the form of genuine mental and cultural violations for these women from rural areas. But before any analysis is made, it is important to emphasise that what is violent is the fact that actions are performed without preparation. These technical acts are closely linked to the western cultural context. For those who do not share it, these acts, by their implicit content, become truly inductors of mental violation. Women can neither imagine nor anticipate them. The conclusion to be drawn is not that such acts should not be performed, which would be quite unacceptable both in terms of ethics and in terms of public health.

To refrain from practising these acts would lead to exclude the women further from our healthcare system, and would contribute to socially marginalise them. On the contrary, we have to ensure that these acts are efficacious and fulfil their purpose. To adapt our care and prevention strategies we need to apprehend this otherness. Thus, instead of being an obstacle to interaction, it can become the opportunity for a new encounter.

Reporting the pregnancy

Traditionally, pregnancy should be hidden as long as possible, or at least it should be spoken of as little as possible so as not to arouse envy among sterile women, women who have not had a boy, women who have had too few children, or women who are outsiders. This explains the fear that Medina experienced when she went to see the social worker for her to complete the required pregnancy certificate forms. She felt threatened and unprotected. Anything could happen to her, she could even be "bewitched" and lose the child she was carrying. This fear was with her throughout her pregnancy, and even when the child was born she was still terrified: the child was not protected, he could at any time return to the world of the ancestors; it means that he could die.

The ultrasound scan

In hospital things continued along the same lines for Medina. They took "photos" that showed what she had in her womb, that showed "what God was still keeping hidden" she said. For her, the scan was almost pornographic. Especially because the medical team had shown her the images almost without comment, since she understood very little French. These images without words and without accompaniment were very violent. The practitioner performing the scan did not understand her refusing to look; he talked to her, encouraged her to look and not to worry... She closed her eyes to avoid seeing. He interpreted this refusal to look at the images as a difficulty investing herself in the child. In contrast, for other migrant women in the habit of asking for divinatory acts during pregnancy, such as the Mina or Awa women from Togo or Benin, the scan is sometimes associated with these practices, in which case it is felt to be familiar. Every situation is unique.

Childbirth

Then Medina gave birth, on her own, without an interpreter, with the virtually compulsory presence of her husband, who was brought into the labour room because things were not going well. A caesarean was envisaged but the husband was terrified and he refused. Finally they waited a little, and Medina was calmed by bringing in thc labour room another Soniké woman who had just given birth in the same ward. Then, she said, the child consented to come out "on his own". We now know the importance to allow for physiological labour every time it is possible, that is to say as long as the lives of the mother and the child are not at risk.

For Medina there was the recurrent idea that the child she had born and that came into the world in these conditions was not protected, he was in danger, and so was she. In this case it was the category "lack of protection of mother and child", and also its cultural consequence, vulnerability towards an "attack by witchcraft", that was the right category for us to envisage, as was confirmed in subsequent work with Medina.

Medina did indeed begin to feel calmer following certain cultural acts that contributed to shoring up the breach, the inadequate protection: the couple asked their families in Mali to perform protection rites for their son Mamadou, so that the child was brought into the generational chain and the wider family. At the same time, we explored the mother's sadness with her, and her lost support, by bringing to life cultural representations that had lost their meaning because of exile and family conflict; in other words the cultural prop was partly reconstructed in the therapeutic group: she had left Mali without her father's consent, and therefore her first child was unprotected. This work of co-construction of cultural meaning was the first step for the construction of a framework.

In the second stage, the many losses that Medina had suffered were approached. Her mother died when she was born and she had been brought up by her father's other wife. In addition she was distressed and sad in her life of exile, separated from her sisters, one of them died before she could have seen her again. Supported by the group (4) and the framework offered, Medina went on to elaborate her sadness, she found meaning for everything that had happened during her all-too-lonely pregnancy, and she constructed a secure relationship with her son Mamadou. The protection of the maternal grandfather requested and obtained by Medina then took effect.

In the preventive sphere, it can be seen from this story, and many others like it, that there is a need to enable pregnant women to have a culturally acceptable representation of what is done to them. They can then build an individual strategy enabling them to shift from one world to another without having to relinquish their own representations – thus constructing a genuine *métissage* or cultural hybridisation.

In intra-cultural situations, through pregnancy and childbirth women put themselves in the line of mothers and grandmothers, thus find efficient support (whether family, medical of friendly). In a trans-cultural situation women will no longer find the support required to shore up their internal disarray, this leads to a "potentiation of the mechanisms of confusion through exile" (28).

Other attitudes can be seen among mothers and need to be understood to be linked to the trauma of certain exiles, and the way in which this reactivates previous conflict. There is first of all the apparent "opting out" of certain mothers: it is as if they were saying that the abilities are with someone else, with the foreigners. Then, they go on to over-hasty acculturation: everything that comes from me is bad, and everything good comes from outside. Or, conversely, there is the development of a cultural rigidity: women tend to return to practices that may be outlived in their original families, and there is, more importantly, a loss of their adaptive flexibility to any culture, and more rigidity in behaviour; there are above all thoughts that are secondary to a trauma that cannot be expanded upon.

Pregnancy and childbirth in a situation of migration reactivate the loss of a framework. When events are not carried by the group, their traumatic nature is enhanced. Thus it is for childbirth, the time of a breach in the maternal shell, both mental and physical, which is often a factor that reactivates the sufferings of exile.

Thus it can be seen that caring for migrant women and their infants is a quite specific task: if there is a pathology of exile, the pathology cannot be positioned on the level of content, since it is invariant and universal; however its nature can be sought in the functioning of the "containers", and the internal and external frameworks.

The infant

The infant develops within a cultural shell that pre-exists before his or her birth. What is the nature of the infant? Where is he from? These questions on the child's ontology have been with human beings through time and under all latitudes. The questions seek to apprehend the otherness of the infant by establishing him or her within ontological representations that are specific to each cultural group. The infant is a stranger who will have to be identified (28).

These questions, and their answers, pervade the whole of family discourse. Overall, they try to determine whether the infant is a "virgin" being, or whether he or she has arrived already possessing his/her own abilities. In North Africa it is sometimes said that the infant is an angel until his/her first chuckles – they say that the infant is pure as long as he or she has not opened his mouth, and if he or she dies he or she will go straight to heaven. In India in some families it is sometimes said that the infant is a trans-migrant, loaded with baggage containing tendencies and experiences from his previous life (11). In certain West African countries it is said that the infant is not human, he is a stranger from another world, a visiting stranger, who may leave again without notice if the world of humans does not please him. Thus it is the infant that decides his own death, and this strange ability is significant of the infant's otherness. In so-called traditional societies where infant mortality is still high, this ontological representation is an attempt to give an acceptable meaning to this unacceptable event. In other places, the infant will only really achieve human status when he or she has reached the age of talking and walking: the risk of mortality decreases markedly after two years old. In Mongolia in certain regions it is only with the first haircut – between the ages of two and five – that the child shifts from an intermediate being to a human being (29). In Western Europe between the two world wars popular representations saw an infant carrying no trace of any sort, a dough or clay that was to be shaped; educational prerogative belonged to the parents, who were supposed to shape the infant in their own image. Later academic theory, with child psychiatrists such as Lebovici, Cramer or Brazelton, set out very different representations: the infant came to be thought to arrive in the world with a baggage of abilities that the adults had the task of bringing out (7). If this theory had such success, it is because popular representation had already noted, beyond prevalent discourse, the specific abilities of the very young infant.

The "enculturation" of the infant as defined by Margaret Mead in 1928 and 1930 is enacted through the body, care, and mothering, and also through education, speech, and the implicit components of discourse (30,31). Enculturation is the incarnation of culture in each one of us. Culture embeds itself in perceptions and sensations as the child grows. In Niger, in order to be considered handsome, Peul infants should have a thin nose; among the Touaregs, the mother will pull and pinch the child's nose, a symbol of honour. In West Africa, Bambara women massage their infants energetically so that later they will have "sure feet in the bush" and become brave hunters (14). Thus each of these mothers implicitly passes on a fundament value belonging to the group to her child. This enculturation is part of what Devereux has referred to as the cultural "envelope" or shell, a shell that clothes each one of us and forms a sort of second skin (32). Enculturation of the human child becomes a more delicate matter when it occurs in a cultural environment that is not the one in which the mother and those around her have grown up. The mother, undergoing the multiplicity of the worlds around her, is more prone to states of confusion, and even perplexity, and this will make her function of "object-presenting" to the baby more difficult (33). The mother will in this case transfer her own perception of the world, a kaleidoscope perception, sometimes pervaded with anxiety. Her classic function of guarding the infant from over-excitation is compromised, she has difficulty presenting the world "in small doses" so that the child is constantly at risk from encountering the world in a traumatic manner. However certain interactive patterns, even if altered by migration, retain coherence and are performed and passed on with sufficient serenity to enable good-quality mothering. For instance, this is what happens with massages performed on the infants.

Enculturation transits via specific interaction modes – the voice, the ways of looking and touching, kinetic stimulations. These patterns are variously implemented according to the cultural group into which the infant is born. Thus mothers in sub-Saharan Africa and Asia do not talk much to their babies and avoid visual interaction: the voice and the eyes can be filled with evil intentions.

There are various practices aiming to counter the effects of the evil eye or the evil tongue. It is easy to understand that in this cultural context the voice and the eyes are not the main channels for interaction. Our "quite natural" way of smiling and talking to babies is thus often seen as threatening by mothers from other cultures.

Naming the infant is the first step to humanisation. In sub-Saharan Africa, to affiliate a child to the community and to the mother, the main task is to set the child apart from the "other world" he or she is supposed to come from: the superhuman and supernatural world of the ancestors and the genies. Generally, when the infant is seven days old, the ritual of naming the child is performed, and this will consist in identifying which ancestor (or which genie) is returning in the child. The infant is indeed a messenger moving from one universe to another, and correct identification of the ancestor will apprehend the message the child brings. It is when the ancestor has been correctly identified that the infant can embark on a process of humanisation. There is then a breaking-off between the superhuman world and the human world.

This breaking off is the *sine qua non* condition for the infant to be able to develop harmoniously and finally settle among humans. In this mode of humanising the infant, the primary separation is seen first of all as occurring between the ancestor and the infant. This separation enables the child to settle into the primary relationship with the maternal figure. In this logic, the infant is not at first in a symbiotic relationship with his mother. The child does not belong to the mother. If there is symbiosis, it is with the "other world", the world of the ancestors. So long as this symbiosis is sustained the child cannot become human, and may present serious somatic or mental dysfunction, described by different aetiological theories, such as the child-ancestor or the *djinna* baby (6, 24, 34).

Through the naming ritual and primary separation, a whole theory of the humanisation of the infant can be seen: as long as those receiving the child have not settled their accounts with their ancestors and forerunners, the child runs the risk of paying dearly. Psychoanalysis confirms this, studies on trans-generational issues in particular. The naming rituals as practised in sub-Saharan Africa are an attempt to guard against subsequent serious disorder by forcing each member of the community to see him or herself as part of a chain of generations, in a trans-generational interaction that is cleared of major conflicts that could hinder the child's development.

Conclusion

The consequences to be drawn for day-to-day work with parents and future parents are considerable (4,6,35,36). The task, for psychologists and psychiatrists, midwives and child nurses, obstetricians and nurses, social workers and child education specialists, is to attempt quite simply to do their jobs better by adapting to these families from elsewhere. This work is sometimes seen as fraught with difficulty, yet once one becomes involved, it proves to be rewarding and fascinating.

To be affected and "transported" by these parents and their infants is necessary to allow them to draw on their own resources.

References

[1] Gauchet M. L'enfant du désir. Le Débat 2004;(132):98-121.

[2] Moro MR. Parents en exil. Psychopathologie et migrations. Paris: Presses Universitaires de France, 1994.

[3] Moro MR. Psychopathologie transculturelle des enfants et des adolescents. Paris: Dunod, 2000.

[4] Moro MR. Parents and infants in changing cultural context: Immigration, trauma and risk. Infant Ment Health J 2003;24:240-64.

[5] Moro MR. Aimer ses enfants ici et ailleurs. Histoires transculturelles. Paris: Odile Jacob, 2007.

[6] Moro MR, Neuman D, Réal I. Maternités en exil. Mettre des bébés au monde et les faire grandir en situation transculturelle. Grenoble: La pensée sauvage, 2008.

[7] Lebovici S. Le nourrisson, la mère et le psychanalyste. Paris: Le Centurion, 1983.

[8] Lebovici S. On intergenerational transmission. From filiation to affiliation. Infant Ment Health J 1993;14:260-72.

[9] Delaisi De Parseval G, Lallemand S. L'art d'accommoder les bébés, 100 ans de recettes françaises de puériculture. Paris: Le Seuil, 1980.

[10] Devereux G. L'image de l'enfant dans deux tribus: Mohave et Sedang. Rev Neuropsychiatr Infantile Hygiène Ment Enfant 1968;4:25-35.

[11] Stork H. Enfances indiennes. Etude de psychologie transculturelle et comparée du jeune enfant. Paris: Le Centurion, 1988.

[12] Rabain-Jamin J. La famille africaine. In: Lebovici S, Weil-Halpern F, eds. Psychopathologie du bébé. Paris: Presses Universitaires de France, 1989:722-7.

[13] Rabain-Jamain J, Wornham WL. Transformation des conduites de maternage et des pratiques de soin chez les femmes migrantes d'Afrique de l'Ouest. Psychiatr Enfant 1990,33.287-319.

[14] Lallemand S, Journet O, Ewombe-Moundo E. Grossesse et petite enfance en Afrique noire et à Madagascar. Paris: L'Harmattan, 1991.

[15] Bornstein MH, ed. Handbook of parenting. Mahwah, NJ: Erlbaum, 2002.

[16] Bornstein MH, Cote LR. Mothers' parenting cognitions on cultures of origin, acculturating cultures, and cultures of destination. Child Dev 2004;75:221-35.

[17] Tamminen T. How does culture promote the early development of identity? Infant Ment Health J 2006;27:603-5.

[18] Moro MR, Ferradji T, eds. Nourritures d'enfance. L'autre, Cliniques, Cultures et Sociétés, Vol. 1 (1). Grenoble: La pensée sauvage, 2000.

[19] Kotchick BA. Putting parenting in perspective: A discussion of the contextual factors that shape parenting practices. J Child Fam Studies 2002;11:255-69.

[20] Moro MR, Serre G, eds. Désirs d'enfant. L'autre, Cliniques, Cultures et Sociétés, Vol. 3 (2). Grenoble: La pensée sauvage, 2002.

[21] Cauce AM. Parenting, culture, and context: Reflections on excavating culture. Appl Dev Sci 2008;12:227-9.
[22] Bydlowski M. La transparence psychique de la grossesse. Études freudiennes 1991;(32):2-9.
[23] Bydlowski M. La dette de vie, itinéraire psychanalytique de la maternité. Paris: Presses Universitaires de France, 1997.
[24] Réal I, Moro MR. De l'art d'humaniser les bébés. Clinique transculturelle des processus de socialisation précoce. Champ Psychosomatique 1998;15:91-108.
[25] Serres M. Discours et parcours. In Lévi-Strauss C, ed. L'identité. Paris: Presses Universitaires de France, 1977:25-39.
[26] Coblence F. Serge Lebovici. Paris: Presses Universitaires de France, 1996.
[27] Fraiberg S. Fantômes dans la chambre d'enfants, Paris: Presses Universitaires de France, 1999.
[28] Moro MR, Nathan T, Rabain-Jamin, J, Stork, H, Si Ahmed J. Le bébé dans son univers culturel. In: Lebovici S, Weil-Halpern F, eds. Psychopathologie du bébé. Paris: Presses Universitaires de France, 1989:683-750.
[29] Fontanel B, D'Harcourt C. Bébés du monde. Paris: La Martinière, 1998.
[30] Mead M. Moeurs et sexualité en Océanie. Paris: Plon, 1963.
[31] Mead M. Une éducation en Nouvelle-Guinée. Paris: Payot, 1973.
[32] Devereux G. Essais d'ethnopsychiatrie générale. Paris: Gallimard, 1970.
[33] Winnicott W. L'enfant et sa famille. Paris: Payot, 1979.
[34] Nathan T, Moro MR. Enfants de djinné. Evaluation ethnopsychanalytique des interactions précoces. In: Lebovici S, Mazet P, Visier JP, eds. Evaluation des interactions précoces. Paris: Eschel, 1989: 307-40.
[35] Koniak-Griffin D, Logsdon MC, Hines-Martin V, Turner CC. Contemporary mothering in a diverse society. JOGNN 2006;35:671-8.
[36] Seeman MV. Cross-cultural evaluation of maternal competence in a culturally diverse society. Am J Psychiatry 2008;165:565-8.

In: Mental Health from an International Perspective
Editors: J. Merrick, S. Aspler and M. Morad

ISBN: 978-1-62948-519-5

Chapter 13

Temperament, intellectual functioning and social behaviour in children

Efrat Zion, BSc(Hons), DPsych(Clin) and Vickii B Jenvey, BA, BEd, MEd, PhD*

School of Psychology and Psychiatry, Monash University, Clayton, Victoria, Australia

In this chapter we investigated how individual differences among children, together with their intellectual functioning, influence their socially competent and antisocial behaviour. The contribution of temperament characteristics (level of emotionality, activity, sociability, and shyness) and intellectual functioning to social competence and antisocial behaviour was examined in 100 primary-school-aged children ($M = 10.7$ years $SD = .88$) who attended both regular and special schools. The best and most consistent predictors of children's socially competent and antisocial behaviour were their level of emotionality and their intellectual functioning or the type of school they attended. Additionally, teachers rated all children significantly higher on their level of social competence and significantly lower on their level of antisocial behaviour than did parents. Results of this study support a multidimensional model of social competence and antisocial behaviour, with both temperament characteristics in interaction with intellectual functioning contributing to the development of socially competent and antisocial behaviour in children.

Introduction

A growing body of research has demonstrated that the development of social skills is important for successful functioning with peers, adults and family during childhood, and for adjustment at later stages of development. Nevertheless, there is conflicting research as to what best contributes to socially competent and antisocial behaviour among children.

* Correspondence: Vickii B Jenvey, BA, BEd, MEd, PhD, School of Psychology, Psychiatry and Psychological Medicine, Monash University, Building 17, Clayton Campus, Wellington Road, Clayton, Victoria 3800, Australia.E-mail: vickii.jenvey@monash.edu.

Various theories have been proposed in an attempt to explain the processes involved in socially competent behaviour (1), the cognitions required for socially competent behaviour (2, 3), or other aspects of children's functioning, such as emotionality and emotional regulation (4). Other researchers emphasise the combined contribution of intelligence, temperament, and family environment to antisocial behaviour, but such models are restricted to explaining the social development of boys only (5, 6).

It has been suggested that socially skilled individuals can adapt well to their environment and avoid verbal and physical conflicts by effective communication with others (7). Hence, socially skilled individuals behave in ways that fit with the social demands and conditions of the environmental context in which they find themselves (8). Further, social competence is required to build positive peer relationships, and to deal with unreasonable behaviour of others (9), and for achieving academic success (10, 11). In contrast, children with inadequate social skills tend to display conduct problems and hyperactivity (10), unpopularity with peers and adults, and difficulties in getting along with their teachers (7). However, exceptions to this finding have also been shown (12, 13). Consequently, it has been argued that antisocial behaviour and social competence are not direct opposites of each other (14).

Moreover, children's social skills (such as getting along with others, cooperating with others, turn taking etc.) are influenced by different social contexts, such as home and school settings (15), and whether children attend a regular school or a special school (16, 17). However, findings about the influence of contextual differences on children's social functioning vary across studies. Additionally, children's manifestation of social skills has been linked to their temperament style (18, 19).

For these reasons, this study will focus on three factors that have previously been identified as potential contributors to social competence and antisocial behaviour in middle childhood: temperament, intellectual functioning, and school type (regular or special school). School type has been included, because in Australia, special schools are schools whose function is to offer specialised academic and developmental programmes for children who have a range of developmental delays and disabilities, many of whom are intellectually disabled children.

Temperament and social behaviour

Certain temperament dimensions, including negative emotionality or reactivity, emotional regulation and attentional regulation, and approach/sociability, have been consistently associated with children's level of social skilfulness. Studies investigating the association between temperament dimensions and social skills have consistently found a stronger association between temperament characteristics and negative, as opposed to prosocial developmental outcomes (18).

Lemerise and Arsenio (4) integrated emotional regulation, together with the temperament dimension of emotionality and mood state, within a model of social functioning among children. Additionally, Guralnick (15) adapted Crick and Dodge's (1) social information processing model to explain the behaviour of children with developmental delays. In Guralnick's (15) model, one of the processes that governs social strategies among intellectually disabled children is emotional regulation.

Previous studies that have examined the relationship between emotionality and social behaviour usually have examined the contribution of emotionality to antisocial behaviour, while overlooking positive social behaviours. One of the few exceptions is the study by Martin (20) in which low negative emotionality was facilitated the development of social competence at school. A number of studies by Eisenberg and her colleagues also found an association between emotionality and social skilfulness, one of which examined the contribution of emotionality to both socially competent and antisocial behaviour (21). These authors showed that young adolescents, who were rated high in social functioning were also rated overall as relatively low on negative emotionality and high on regulatory abilities during early adolescence, as well as at earlier stages of development (21). Further, young adolescents who were consistently rated low in social functioning over time were rated higher on negative emotionality and lower on emotional regulation than those who were consistently rated high on social functioning over time (21).

Another temperament dimension that has been associated with social behaviour is shyness. However, there have been some conflicting findings with respect to the association between temperamental shyness (or temperamental inhibition) and social behaviour. In a school context, temperamental shyness in preschool children was associated with internalising problems and a lack of social competence in preschool (22). In another study, parent-rated shyness was inversely correlated with aggression, sociability, and prosocial behaviour in children aged 4-5 years months (23). Anxious and shy children have also been found to have a reduced risk of delinquency (24, 25). Consistent with this finding, adolescents who had been rated highly on temperamental inhibition at 21 months of age, were rated significantly lower on total number of externalising behaviour disorders, delinquent behaviour, and aggressive behaviour scales of the Child Behavior Checklist (CBCL), than those who were rated as uninhibited during infancy (26).

Apart from temperament characteristics, another factor which has been found to contribute to children's social skilfulness is their intellectual functioning.

Intellectual functioning and social behaviour

Bellanti and Bierman (27) found that children with low cognitive ability and inattentiveness showed prosocial skill deficits (teacher-rated) and aggression (teacher-rated), and these placed those children at risk for social maladjustment and poor peer relationships. In other studies, lower IQ scores in preschool-aged children were associated with increased risk of disruptive and antisocial behaviour at later stages of development (see 28).

It has been suggested that low IQ, derived from a standardised measures of intelligence, and which involves significant deficits in a child's knowledge and reasoning skills, impedes social development by delaying the development of positive social skills, and leads to social withdrawal and poor peer relationships (29). According to Guralnick's (15) model of social competence in children with disabilities, children with mild intellectual disability have difficulties interacting with peers as they have deficits in cognitive skills that are associated with deficits in other areas important for social development. These include deficits in communication skills and social information processing, and lead to difficulties in using appropriate interaction strategies. Another association between intellectual functioning and social behaviour is proposed by Moffitt and colleagues (5, 6, 30), who showed that low intelligence (assessed with the Peabody Picture Vocabulary test at age 3, the Stanford Binet Intelligence Scales at age 5, and the WISC-R at ages 7, 9, and 11), among other factors, led to the development of severe antisocial behaviour in boys and girls. Thus, it is important to investigate children across the range of intellectual abilities, including children with intellectual disability.

Influence of context on social behaviour

In addition to a need to elucidate the relative contribution of temperament and intellectual functioning to socially competent and antisocial behaviours in children, it is important to investigate how these different attributes influence children's social functioning across different social contexts, such as home and school. Differences have been found between parent and teacher ratings of behavioural problems in both typically developing children (31), and children with intellectual disability (32). Additionally, parents have been found to rate some of their children's problem behaviours as more problematic than do teachers (33). Similarly, parents have been found to rate conduct problems more severely than teachers (32, 34), and report more behavioural and emotional problems in children than teachers when rating children's behaviour on the Child Behavior Checklist (35). While these findings suggest that there are differences in parents' and teacher's perceptions of children's behaviour, it may also indicate that children's behaviours are modified to some degree by the different social environments.

In assessing children's social skills, it is therefore important to assess both positive and negative aspects of social behaviour. Fewer studies have examined what contributes to positive social behaviour or social competence, in comparison with studies that have examined contributors to antisocial behaviour. In order to assess contextual influences on children's social behaviour, informants from children's home and school settings should both provide information about children's social behaviour and temperament across different social contexts.

Our study

The main objective of the present research was to examine potential factors that contribute to social competence and antisocial behaviour among elementary-school-aged children, who are typically developing or intellectually disabled across different social contexts (home and school, including both regular school and special school). Previous research indicated that children's social skills are likely to differ in the school and home environments, because different demands are placed on children in each setting. Additionally, awareness of the type of school children attend might further aid in understanding the potential for different contextual influences to impact upon social skill development. The findings of this study have the potential to enhance our understanding of the complex interaction of factors that predispose some children to socially effective functioning and others to more socially disruptive behaviour. Two research questions were posed:

- To what degree do temperament characteristics (emotionality, activity, sociability, and shyness), intellectual functioning, and school type (whether children attend a regular or a special school) contribute individually or in combination to both social competence and antisocial behaviour among typically developing and intellectually disabled children?
- Does the influence of temperament and intellectual functioning on social behaviour, differ across home and school contexts?

Participants and their parents and teachers were recruited from several regular and special schools across a wide range of Melbourne (Australia) suburbs. This range of schools form which participants were recruited ensured that both typically developing children and children with delayed development were from families of diverse socioeconomic backgrounds.

Participants were 100 children aged 9-12 years (59 boys and 41 girls, M = 10.7 years SD = .88), their parents who completed questionnaires about their children's behaviours (79% were mothers, 17% were fathers, and 4% were other carer-givers), and the class teachers who completed questionnaires about students' behaviours. Sixty participants were recruited from regular schools and 40 participants were recruited from three different types of special schools (see table 1 for descriptive data of each special school type).

Table 1. Descriptive data of special schools

School Type	Range of disability	Number of schools	Number of students
Special school	Mild intellectual disability (IQ range 50-69)	5	27
Special developmental school	Moderate to severe intellectual disability (IQ below 50)	5	12
Physical disability school	Physical disability	1	1

Table 2. Principal diagnoses of participating children

Diagnosis	Frequency
Intellectual disability/ Global developmental delay (unknown aetiology)*	12
Attention Deficit Hyperactivity Disorder with Intellectual Disability	8
Down Syndrome	7
Chromosomal abnormality/ rare genetic disorder	7
Cerebral Palsy with Intellectual Disability	5
Epilepsy with Intellectual Disability	2
Attention Deficit Disorder with Intellectual Disability	1

* This group included two children who attend regular schools, and were reported by their teachers to have an intellectual disability

Most of the students recruited from these special schools (and some students from the regular schools) had diagnoses of other disabilities in addition to intellectual disability (see table 2) as reported by their parents, and reflect the profile of intellectually-disabled children, many of whom have multiple disabilities. Children were excluded from the study if they had a dual diagnosis of autism with intellectual disability, if they had language delays that affected their ability to follow instructions in the administration of the K-BIT, and children whose parents' English was not proficient enough to complete questionnaires. Thus, the remaining participants were representative of the broader Australian intellectually-disabled population, in terms of their aetiologies and associated disabilities and their potential for assessment with the K-BIT to yield a valid measure of their global cognitive functioning.

Measures

Kaufman Brief Intelligence Test (K-BIT, 36, 37) was administered to children to assess intellectual functioning. This instrument was chosen in order to provide an estimate of the child's level of intellectual functioning. The K-BIT yields standardised scores, with an overall IQ (M = 100; SD = 15), as measured by the K-BIT IQ Composite (37).

School Social Behavior Scales, Second Edition (SSBS-2, 14). This instrument is a rating scale designed to be used by teachers and other school personnel to evaluate both positive (i.e., Social Competence) and negative (i.e., Antisocial Behavior) behaviours of children and youth aged 5 to 18 years in school settings. The author reports that the instrument is mainly for screening students who are at risk of developing severe behaviour problems (14), as well as a research instrument for studying the social-behavioural characteristics and patterns of children and youth. The SSBS-2 was used for this latter purpose in the current study.

The SSBS-2 yields standardised scores (T-scores: M = 50; SD = 10). Higher Social Competence scores indicate greater levels of social adjustment, and higher Antisocial Behavior scores indicate greater levels of social-behavioural problems (14). Scores on the Social Competence scale are ranked as follows: High Functioning (above 80th percentile), Average (20th to 80th percentile), At-Risk (5th to 20th percentile), High Risk (below 5th percentile). Scores on the Antisocial Behavior scale are ranked as follows: Average (below 80th percentile), At-Risk (80th to 95th percentile), and High Risk (96th percentile and higher) (14).

Home and Community Social Behavior Scales (HCSBS, 38). This instrument is a parent-rated version of the SSBS-2 (14) for evaluating Social Competence and Antisocial Behavior of children and youth, aged 5 to 18 years, in home and community settings. The HCSBS and SSBS-2 are similar conceptually and similar in item content, number of items, and rating format (38).

EAS Temperament Survey for Children: Parental Ratings (39). This is a questionnaire designed to be completed by parents to assess their child's temperament. This questionnaire assesses temperament in children aged 1-9 years, but has also been used with adolescents (11-16 year-olds) with acceptable reliability (40). Four dimensions of temperament are measured: Emotionality, Activity, Sociability, and Shyness.

EAS Temperament Survey for Children: Teacher Ratings (39). This questionnaire contains similar items to the one completed by parents except for some items that relate to children's behaviour in the school and classroom context. The survey also yields a score for each of the four temperament dimensions of Emotionality, Activity, Sociability, and Shyness.

Procedure

Parents and teachers completed the questionnaires in their own time and returned them by mail. Children were administered the K-BIT during school hours in a room set aside to enable privacy during the testing phase.

Findings

Data were analysed in terms of the standardised scores on the Social Competence and Antisocial Behavior scales of the HCSBS and the SSBS-2, the K-BIT IQ Composite scores, and the scores on each of the four temperament dimensions in the Parent and Teacher versions of the EAS Temperament Survey for Children. Frequency distributions were computed for all the dependent variables (teacher-rated Social Competence, teacher-rated Antisocial Behaviour, parent-rated Social Competence, and parent-rated Antisocial Behaviour) and independent variables (school type, K-BIT IQ Composite score and either teacher-rated or parent rated Emotionality, Activity, Sociability and Shyness). Correlations were computed among each of the dependent variables and the continuous independent variables (K-BIT IQ Composite score and either the teacher-rated or parent rated temperament dimensions). Four stepwise regression analyses were conducted to determine statistically the most effective overall prediction model (using the six independent variables) for each of the four dependent variables. Prior to analysis, examination of the assumptions of Multiple Regression analysis, for each of the regression models, revealed that the assumptions of linearity, homoscedasticity, and independence of the residuals were not violated. These were examined through inspection of residual plots. Further, the assumption of multicollinearity was examined with correlations among the independent variables, as well as VIF values, and this assumption was also not violated.

Table 3. Descriptive statistics of variables measured

	Mean Score (*SD*)		
	Total Sample (*N* = 100)	Regular school (*n* = 60)	Special school (*n* = 40)
Independent variables			
K-BIT IQ Composite	84.44 (25.55)	102.30 (11.88)	57.65 (14.74)
Emotionality (teacher-rated)	2.14 (.98)	1.93 (.97)	2.44 (.94)
Activity (teacher-rated)	3.51 (.90)	3.51 (.86)	3.52 (.98)
Sociability (teacher-rated)	3.89 (.81)	3.89 (.74)	3.90 (.92)
Shyness (teacher-rated)	2.53 (.83)	2.45 (.82)	2.66 (.83)
Emotionality (parent-rated)	2.85 (.98)	2.73 (.92)	3.03 (1.05)
Activity (parent-rated)	3.71 (.84)	3.63 (.84)	3.83 (.85)
Sociability (parent-rated)	3.40 (.84)	3.62 (.73)	3.08 (.89)
Shyness (parent-rated)	2.45 (.90)	2.56 (.94)	2.29 (.82)
Dependent variables*			
Social Competence (teacher-rated)	50.65 (8.95)	53.90 (8.74)	45.78 (6.87)
Antisocial Behaviour (teacher-rated)	49.35 (8.63)	47.03 (8.38)	52.83 (7.89)
Social Competence (parent-rated)	46.47 (11.20)	51.70 (9.06)	38.63 (9.45)
Antisocial Behaviour (parent-rated)	54.88 (13.69)	48.80 (8.56)	64.00 (14.93)

* These are the standardised scores.

A power analysis revealed that, for this study to detect medium effect sizes (*d* = .15), at a power of .80, for α = .05, with 6 independent variables, a minimum sample size of 97 participants was required. With a sample of 100 participants obtained in this study, there is adequate power (.81) to detect medium effect sizes.

In order to maintain adequate power in the data analyses, and investigate more global social behaviours, predictions were only made from the two major scales of the HCSBS and SSBS-2, rather than from each of the subscales. By making predictions from the subscales of these instruments, the power of the predictions would be reduced.

Descriptive statistics for the study variables are given in table 3. Independent sample t-tests were performed to find out whether there were any significant differences between regular school students and special school students, in terms of their K-BIT IQ Composite. It was found that students attending regular schools had a significantly higher K-BIT IQ Composite than those attending special schools, t(98) = -16.70, p = .00 (two-tailed), d = -3.33.

Home context

Correlations between the social behaviour scales and the K-BIT and temperament dimensions. Correlational analyses were carried out to assess the relationship between each of the dependent variables (parent-rated Social Competence, and parent-rated Antisocial Behaviour) and the independent variables (K-BIT IQ Composite score and parent rated Emotionality, Activity, Sociability and Shyness). Scores on the Social Competence scale was significantly and positively correlated with the K-BIT IQ Composite, r = .56, p< .01, while scores on the Antisocial Behaviour scale was significantly and negatively correlated with the K-BIT IQ Composite, r = -.44, p<.01. The Social Competence scale was significantly correlated with Emotionality, r = -.49, p<.01, and Sociability, r = .29, p<.01. The Antisocial Behaviour scale was also significantly correlated with Emotionality, r = .47, p<.01, and Sociability, r = -.25, p<.05, as well as Activity, r = .23, p<.05.

Table 4. Summary of stepwise regression analysis for variables predicting parent-rated social competence (N = 100)

Variable	*B*	*SE B*	β	R^2	R^2 change	*F* of R^2 change
Step 1				.33	.33	48.29**
School Type (special/regular)	13.08	1.88	.58			
Step 2				.50	.17	32.21**
School Type (special/regular)	11.62	1.66	.51			
Emotionality (parent-rated)	-4.72	0.83	-.41			
Step 3				.52	.02	4.66*
School Type (special/regular)	12.32	1.66	.54			
Emotionality (parent-rated)	-4.22	0.85	-.37			
Shyness (parent-rated)	-2.00	0.92	.16			

* *p*<.05.

** *p*<.01.

Contributors to Social Competence at home and in the community. Stepwise regression analysis was used to obtain the most effective overall prediction model for parent-rated Social

Competence. Results of the stepwise regression are presented in table 4. Results suggested that the best single predictor of parent-rated Social Competence was school type, accounting for 33% of the variance in parent-rated Social Competence, hence this was entered first in the equation. Prediction was then significantly improved by the addition of parent-rated Emotionality, which accounted for another 17% of variance, and lastly by the addition of parent-rated Shyness which accounted for an additional 2% of variance. The total model accounted for 52% of the variance in parent-rated Social Competence, and the model was statistically significant, F (3, 96) = 34.72, p = .00. Adding the variables of the K-BIT IQ Composite, parent-rated Activity and parent-rated Sociability scores did not significantly improve the predictive power of the model.

Contributors to Antisocial Behaviour at home and in the community. Stepwise regression analysis was used to obtain the most effective overall prediction model for parent-rated Antisocial Behaviour. Results of the stepwise regression are presented in table 5. Results suggested that the best single predictor was School Type, accounting for 30% of the variance in parent-rated Antisocial Behaviour, hence this was entered first into the equation. Prediction was then significantly improved by the addition of parent-rated Emotionality, which accounted for another 15% of variance. The total model accounted for 45% of the variance in parent-rated Antisocial Behaviour, and the model was found to be statistically significant, F(2, 97) = 40.42, p = .00 Adding the variables K-BIT IQ Composite, parent-rated Activity, parent-rated Sociability and parent-rated Shyness did not significantly improve the predictive power of the existing model.

Table 5. Summary of stepwise regression analysis for variables predicting parent-rated antisocial behaviour (N = 100)

Variable	*B*	*SE B*	β	R^2	R^2 change	*F* of R^2 change
Step 1				.30	.30	41.77**
School Type (special/regular)	-15.20	2.35	-.55			
Step 2				.45	.15	27.70**
School Type (special/regular)	-13.48	2.11	-.49			
Emotionality (parent-rated)	5.57	1.06	.40			

** *p*<.01

School context

Correlations between the social behaviour Scales and the K-BIT and temperament dimensions. Correlational analyses were carried out to assess the relationship between each of the dependent variables (teacher-rated Social Competence, and teacher-rated Antisocial Behaviour) and the continuous independent variables (K-BIT IQ Composite score and teacher-rated Emotionality, Activity, Sociability and Shyness). The Social Competence score was significantly and positively correlated with the K-BIT IQ Composite, r = .53, p<.01, while scores on the Antisocial Behaviour scale were significantly and negatively correlated with the K-BIT IQ Composite, r = -.30, p<.01. The Social Competence score was significantly correlated with Emotionality, r = -.46, p<.01, Sociability, r = .36, p<.01, and

Shyness, r = -.36, p<.01. The Antisocial Behaviour scale was also significantly correlated with Emotionality, r = .53, p<.01, and Sociability, r = -.22, p<.05.

Contributors to Social Competence at school. Stepwise regression analysis was used to obtain the most effective overall prediction model for teacher-rated Social Competence. Results of the stepwise regression are presented in table 6. Results suggested that the best single predictor was K-BIT IQ Composite accounting for 28% of the variance in teacher-rated Social Competence, hence this was entered first into the equation. Prediction was then significantly improved by the addition of teacher-rated Emotionality which accounted for another 14%, and then by the addition of teacher-rated Sociability which accounted for an additional 6%. The total model accounted for 48% of the variance in teacher-rated Social Competence, and the model was found to be statistically significant, F(3, 96) = 29.87, p = .00 Adding variables of school type, teacher-rated Activity and teacher-rated Shyness did not significantly improve the predictive value of the model.

Table 6. Summary of stepwise regression analysis for variables predicting teacher-rated social competence (N = 100)

Variable	*B*	*SE B*	β	R^2	R^2 change	*F* of R^2 change
Step 1				.28	.28	38.19**
K-BIT IQ Composite	0.19	0.03	.53			
Step 2				.42	.14	24.51**
K-BIT IQ Composite	0.16	0.03	.47			
Emotionality (teacher-rated)	-3.51	0.71	-.39			
Step 3				.48	.06	10.62**
K-BIT IQ Composite	0.17	0.03	.49			
Emotionality (teacher-rated)	-2.63	0.73	-.29			
Sociability (teacher-rated)	2.83	0.87	.26			

** *p*<.01.

Table 7. Summary of stepwise regression analysis for variables predicting teacher-rated antisocial behaviour (N = 100)

Variable	*B*	*SE B*	β	R^2	R^2 change	*F* of R^2 change
Step 1				.28	.28	39.01**
Emotionality (teacher-rated)	4.67	0.75	.53			
Step 2				.33	.05	6.83*
Emotionality (teacher-rated)	4.35	0.74	.50			
K-BIT IQ Composite	-0.07	0.03	-.22			

* *p*<.05.
** *p*<.01.

Contributors to Antisocial Behaviour at school. Stepwise regression analysis was used to obtain the most effective overall prediction model for teacher-rated Antisocial Behaviour. Results of the stepwise regression are presented in table 7. Results suggested that the best single predictor was teacher-rated Emotionality, accounting for 28% of the variance in teacher-rated Antisocial Behaviour, hence this was entered first into the equation. Prediction was then significantly improved by the addition of the K-BIT IQ Composite score, which accounted for another 5% of the variance. The total model accounted for 33% of the variance in teacher-rated Antisocial Behaviour, and the model was found to be statistically significant, $F(2, 97) = 24.08$, $p = .00$ Adding information on school type, teacher-rated Activity, teacher-rated Sociability, and teacher-rated Shyness did not significantly improve the predictive value of the model.

Home versus school contexts

Differences in social competence and antisocial behaviour between home and school contexts. Paired samples t-tests were performed to find out whether there were any significant differences between parent and teacher ratings, in terms of Social Competence and Antisocial Behaviour. It was found that parents rated their children significantly lower on their level of Social Competence compared with teachers, $t(99) = 4.84$, $p = .00$ (two-tailed), $d = .48$. It was also found that parents rated their children significantly higher on their level of Antisocial Behaviour than teachers, $t(99) = -4.82$, $p = .00$ (two-tailed), $d = .48$. However, both the teachers and parents rated participants as being in the average level of social competence and antisocial behaviour.

Differences in temperament between home and school contexts. Paired samples t-tests were performed to find out whether there were any significant differences between parent and teacher ratings, in terms of each of the temperament dimensions. It was found that parents rated their children significantly more highly on the Emotionality dimension of temperament, than teachers, $t(99) = 6.84$, $p = .00$ (two-tailed), $d = .68$. It was also found that parents rated their children as significantly less sociable than teachers, $t(99) = -4.89$, $p = .00$ (two-tailed), $d = .49$.

There were no significant differences between parent and teacher ratings of the child's level of Activity, $t(99) = 1.93$, $p = .06$ (two-tailed), and Shyness , $t(99) = -0.82$, $p = .41$ (two tailed).

Discussion

The fact that high emotionality was a significant predictor of poor social competence and high levels of antisocial behaviour, supports both Guralnick's (15, 41), and Lemerise and Arsenio's (4) proposal that emotionality contributes strongly to social functioning in children. Further, these results support the findings of Martin (20), who found that low negative emotionality promoted social competence at school, and Eisenberg and colleagues (most recently for example 21), who found an association between emotionality and socially competent (positive) and antisocial (negative) behaviour.

The results of this study are consistent with those of other studies where difficult temperament characteristics, including negative mood or emotionality, have been identified as predictive of oppositional or conduct disorder diagnoses (42, 43), and externalising behaviour problems (44-47). Even in the absence of a clinical diagnosis of an antisocial behaviour disorder, emotionality was still clearly the strongest predictor of antisocial behaviour in children.

The finding that the level of shyness, as rated by parents, was a significant predictor of parent-rated social competence of children in their home and community is consistent with previous research where associations have been found between shyness and social behaviour. However, there have been conflicting findings in the literature with regard to the direction of this association and it remains inconclusive. That is, whether shyness contributes positively or negatively to social behaviour. The present study found that shyness added to the predictive power of a model of social competence in the home setting (together with the independent variables of school type and emotionality, and only contributed 2%); yet shyness alone was not significantly associated with social competence. This does not yet clarify the possible contribution of temperamental shyness to social competence, and any association remains to be clearly delineated. Usually, studies have investigated the effects of shyness alone on antisocial behaviour, rather than its association with social competence. Hence, this study is one of the few that suggests that shyness has some relationship with more positive aspects of social behaviour. It appears that temperamental shyness does contribute to social behaviour, however its contribution appears to be quite variable among children and has different consequences for different children. Thus, shyness does not have a unique and specific effect on social behaviour, but when interacting with other factors, such as emotionality and school type, it is a significant predictor of social competence.

It may be that temperamental shyness does not have a direct linear relationship with social competence. Perhaps greater clarity in the operationalisation of shyness is required; a clearer definition may have assisted parents to reflect more accurately on this behaviour in their children. It seems plausible that a high level of shyness might lead to a reduced level of peer-related social competence, because shy children avoid social interaction (39) and withdraw from peers, yet the present results did not support this interpretation.

It was found that a high level of sociability, as rated by teachers, was associated with a high level of teacher-rated social competence. There have been very few studies that have examined the contribution of (any) temperament characteristics to social behaviour at school, particularly linking temperament to socially competent behaviour. In the Australian Temperament Project, teacher-rated sociability contributed to social skills (48). This finding can be explained in terms of the differing demands for sociability in a wide range of classroom and playground activities. For example, it is important for children to be able to take turns, participate in group activities and games and ask for help from teachers and peers to effectively negotiate social situations in that particular school environment (e.g., classroom or playground).

While similarities with previous studies have been found, findings about temperament in this study are unique. Firstly, the participants were of primary school age, as opposed to participants in other temperament studies where infants have mostly been investigated. Secondly, the participants in this study included both typically developing and intellectually disabled children. Intellectually disabled children are frequently overlooked in research investigating individual differences among children. Thirdly, temperament dimensions were related to both social competence and antisocial behaviour in both typically developing and intellectually disabled children. Hence, this suggests that intellectually disabled children display the same range of temperamental individuality as do typically developing children, and this differs from existing studies of intellectual disability and temperament, where a temperamental pattern of low persistence, high sensory threshold, and high activity was found to be associated with specific developmental delays (e.g., 43).

Contribution of intellectual functioning to social behavior

Intellectual functioning (as measured by the K-BIT IQ Composite) was a significant predictor of teachers' ratings of children's social competence and antisocial behaviour. Therefore the contribution of intellectual functioning, in the present study, is significant only in relation to children's social functioning in the school setting. Similar findings have been consistently shown in previous studies (27, 28), and findings are also consistent with Guralnick's (15) model of social competence in children with disabilities, and Moffitt and colleagues' (5, 6, 30) research in which low intelligence, among other factors, was shown to be predictive of the development of severe antisocial behaviour in boys and girls. This finding (of intellectual functioning being a predictor of social behaviour), was not replicated for parent-ratings of children's social functioning in the home context, where school type appeared to be a more powerful predictor, and thus it was included in the predictive model instead of intellectual functioning. It has been suggested that behaviour problems are more highly correlated with cognitive deficits when teacher ratings of behaviour are used than when parent ratings are used (49). This may be because teachers focus on optimising children's cognitive functioning in a structured context, and therefore cognitive functioning may be more important for that environment. Parents engage in less structured, and more informal learning situations. Hence, there are differential effects of temperament and intellectual functioning on children's social behaviour at home and at school. Such a finding also underlines the importance of having different informants rate the same children's behaviour across different social contexts.

Influence of context on social behavior

Considering the relative influence of home and school on social behaviour, it was found that parents rated their children significantly lower in social competence, and significantly higher in antisocial behaviour than did teachers. This is consistent with previous research where differences have been found between parent and teacher ratings of behavioural problems (31-35).

In attempting to explain these findings, different researchers have offered different explanations. One point of view maintains that children are likely to behave differently in different contexts (31), because of the different structures of those settings (50) and the different social demands of those settings. It may also be attributable to children having different relationships with their parents when compared with their teachers and this leads to the potential for biased perceptions that parents or teachers may develop about their children/students. Additionally, these findings may be due to the fact that the home environment is usually more diverse than school, and offers a broader range of experiences. For instance, at school, there are more demands to interact with a larger social group and the school environment is highly structured and supervised, and children use the materials and toys provided by the school for play. In contrast, at home, there are fewer people to interact with, children use their own toys for play, they have fewer constraints on their activities, and they are less closely supervised than at school.

The study only focused on a limited range of variables and there are obviously other factors that are likely to contribute to children's social behaviour. Nevertheless, increased understanding of the differential influences of home, community, and school contexts on children's expression of temperament and social skills, from the results of this study, would be valuable for designing interventions to improve children's social competence and reduce antisocial behavioural tendencies.

Conclusion

The findings of this study point to the complex multifaceted nature of children's socially competent and antisocial behaviour in different social environments. A combination of particular temperament characteristics and intellectual functioning, rather than each of these independently, best explains the level of positive and negative social behaviour in children. Social contexts (home and school) were identified as important influences on how children's social skills were manifested and temperament characteristics were expressed. This latter finding was attributed to the differential influence of parents or teachers in those settings, as well as differing demands on children's social behaviour in those settings.

References

[1] Crick NR, Dodge KA. A review and reformulation of social information-processing mechanisms in children's social adjustment. Psychol Bull 1994;115:74-101.
[2] Bandura A. Social foundations of thought and action: A social cognitive theory. Englewood Cliffs, NJ: Prentice-Hall, 1986.
[3] Bandura A. Social learning theory. Englewood Cliffs, NJ: Prentice-Hall, 1977.
[4] Lemerise EA, Arsenio WF. An integrated model of emotion processes and cognition in social information processing. Child Dev 2000;71:107-18.
[5] Moffitt TE. Adolescence-limited and life-course-persistent antisocial behavior: A developmental taxonomy. Psychol Rev 1993;100:674-701.
[6] Moffitt TE, Caspi A, Dickson N, Silva PA, Stanton W. Childhood-onset versus adolescent-onset antisocial conduct problems in males: Natural history from ages 3 to 18 years. Dev Psychopathol 1996;8:399-424.
[7] Matson JL. Enhancing children's social skills. New York: Pergamon, 1988.
[8] Sheridan SM, Maughan DP, Hungelmann A. A contextualized framework for social skills assessment, intervention, and generalization. Sch Psychol Rev 1999;28:84-103.
[9] Kelly JA. Social skills training: A practical guide to interventions. New York: Springer, 1982.
[10] Coolahan K, Fantuzzo J, Mendez JL, McDermott P. Preschool peer interactions and readiness to learn: Relationships between classroom peer play and learning behaviors and conduct. J Educ Psychol 2000;92:458-65.
[11] Walker HM, Hops H. Increasing academic achievement by reinforcing direct academic and/or facilitating nonacademic responses. J Educ Psychol 1976;68:218-25.
[12] Sutton J, Smith PK, Swettenham J. Bullying and "theory of mind': A critique of the "social skills deficit" view of anti-social behaviour. Soc Dev 1999;8:117-27.
[13] Vaughn BE, Vollenweider M, Bost KK, Azria-Evans MR, Snider JB. Negative interactions and social competence for preschool children in two samples: Reconsidering the interpretation of aggressive behavior for young children. Merrill-Palmer Quart 2003;49:245-78.
[14] Merrell KW. School social behavior scales, 2nd ed. Eugene, OR: Assessment-Intervention Resources, 2002.
[15] Guralnick MJ. Family and child influences on the peer-related social competence of young children with developmental delays. Ment Retard Dev Disabil Res Rev 1999;5:21-9.

[16] Freeman SFN, Alkin MC. Academic and social attainments of children with mental retardation in general education and special education settings. Remedial Spec Educ 2000;21:3-18.
[17] Diamond KE. The development of social competence in children with disabilities. In: Smith PK, Hart CH, eds. Blackwell handbook of childhood social development Blackwell handbooks of developmental psychology. Malden, MA: Blackwell, 2002:572-87.
[18] Sanson A, Hemphill SA, Smart D. Temperament and social development. In: Smith PK, Hart C, eds. Blackwell handbook of childhood social development. Malden, MA: Blackwell, 2002:97-115.
[19] Sanson A, Hemphill SA, Smart D. Connections between temperament and social development: A review. Soc Dev 2004;13:142-70.
[20] Martin RP. Child temperament and common problems in schooling: Hypotheses about causal connections. J Sch Psychol 1994;32:119-34.
[21] Murphy BC, Shepard SA, Eisenberg N, Fabes RA. Concurrent and across time prediction of young adolescents' social functioning: The role of emotionality and regulation. Soc Dev 2004;13:56-86.
[22] Coplan RJ, Bowker A, Cooper SM. Parenting daily hassles, child temperament, and social adjustment in preschool. Early Childhood Res Quart 2003;18:376-95.
[23] Russell A, Hart C, Robinson CC, Olsen SF. Children's sociable and aggressive behaviour with peers: a comparison of the US and Australia, and contributions of temperament and parenting styles. Int J Behav Dev 2003;27:74-86.
[24] Kerr M, Tremblay RE, Pagani L, Vitaro F. Boys' behavioral inhibition and the risk of later delinquency. Arch Gen Psychiatr 1997;54:809-16.
[25] Loeber R, Keenan K. Interaction between conduct disorder and its comorbid conditions: Effects of age and gender. Clin Psychol Rev 1994;14:497-523.
[26] Schwartz CE, Snidman N, Kagan J. Early childhood temperament as a determinant of externalizing behavior in adolescence. Dev Psychopathol 1996;8:527-37.
[27] Bellanti CJ, Bierman KL. Disentangling the impact of low cognitive ability and inattention on social behavior and peer relationships. J Clin Child Psychol 2000;29:66-75.
[28] Rutter M, Giller H, Hagell A. Antisocial behavior by young people. New York: Cambridge Univ Press, 1998.
[29] Guralnick MJ, Groom JM. Correlates of peer-related social competence of developmentally delayed preschool children. Am J Ment Defic 1985;90:140-50.
[30] Moffitt TE, Caspi A. Childhood predictors differentiate life-course persistent and adolescence-limited antisocial pathways among males and females. Dev Psychopathol 2001;13:355-75.
[31] Achenbach TM, McConaughy SH, Howell CT. Child/adolescent behavioral and emotional problems: Implications of cross-informant correlations for situational specificity. Psychol Bull 1987;101:213-32.
[32] Tasse MJ, Lecavalier L. Comparing parent and teacher ratings of social competence and problem behaviors. Am J Ment Retard 2000;105:252-9.
[33] Cheramie GM. The AAMD Adaptive Behavior Scale - School Edition, Part Two: Test-retest reliability and parent-teacher agreement in a behavior disordered sample. Percept Motor Skills 1994;79:275-83.
[34] Hart EL, Lahey BB, Loeber R, Hanson KS. Criterion validity of informants in the diagnosis of disruptive behavior disorders in children: A preliminary study. J Consult Clin Psychol 1994;62:410-4.
[35] Verhulst FC, Akkerhuis GW. Agreement between parents' and teachers' ratings of behavioral/emotional problems of children aged 4-12. J Child Psychol Psychiatr Allied Disciplines 1989;30:123-36.
[36] Kaufman AS, Kaufman NL. Australian adaptation of the Kaufman Brief Intelligence Test (K-BIT). Adaptation package. Circle Pines, MN: Am Guidance Service, 1996.
[37] Kaufman AS, Kaufman NL. Kaufman Brief Intelligence Test. Circle Pines, MN: Am Guidance Service, 1990.
[38] Merrell KW, Caldarella P. Home and Community Social Behavior Scales. Eugene, OR: Assessment-Intervention Resources, 2002.
[39] Buss AH, Plomin R. Temperament: Early developing personality traits. Hillsdale, NJ: Erlbaum, 1984.
[40] Goodyer IM, Ashby L, Altham PME, Vize C, Cooper PJ. Temperament and major depression in 11 to 16-year-olds. J Child Psychol Psychiatr Allied Disciplines 1993;34:1409-23.

[41] Guralnick MJ. A hierarchical model for understanding children's peer-related social competence. In: Odom SL, McConnell SR, McEvoy MA, eds. Social competence of young children with disabilities: Issues and strategies for intervention. Baltimore: Brookes, 1992:37-64.
[42] Maziade M. Should adverse temperament matter to the clinician? An empirically based answer. In: Kohnstamm GA, Bates JE, Rothbart MK, ed. Temperament in childhood. Chichester: Wiley, 1989.
[43] Maziade M, Caron C, Cote R, Boutin P, Thivierge J. Extreme temperament and diagnosis. Arch Gen Psychiatr 1990;47:477-84.
[44] Bates JE, Maslin CA, Frankel KA. Attachment security, mother-child interaction, and temperament as predictors of behavior-problem ratings at age three years. Monogr Soc Res Child Dev 1985;50:167-93.
[45] Bates JE, Bayles K. The role of attachment in the development of behavior problems. In: Belsky J, Nezworski T, ed. Clinical implications of attachment. New York: Erlbaum, 1988:253-99.
[46] Nelson B, Martin RP, Hodge S, Havill V, Kamphaus R. Modeling the prediction of elementary school adjustment from preschool temperament. Personal Individual Diff 1999;26:687-700.
[47] Rothbart MK, Ahadi SA, Hershey KL. Temperament and social behavior in childhood. Merrill-Palmer Quart 1994;40:21-39.
[48] Prior M, Sanson A, Smart D, Oberklaid F. Pathways from infancy to adolescence: Australian Temperament Project 1983-2000. Melbourne: Aust Inst Fam Stud, 2000.
[49] Szatmari P, Offord DR, Siegel LS, Finlayson MAJ, Tuff L. The clinical significance of neurocognitive impairments among children with psychiatric disorders: Diagnosis and situational specificity. J Child Psychol Psychiatr 1990;31:287-99.
[50] Vitaro F, Gagnon C, Tremblay RE. Teachers' and mothers' assessment of children's behaviors from kindergarten to grade two: Stability and change within and across informants. J Psychopathol Behav Assess 1991;13:325-43.

In: Mental Health from an International Perspective
Editors: J. Merrick, S. Aspler and M. Morad
ISBN: 978-1-62948-519-5

Chapter 14

Parental satisfaction, treatment outcome and children's mental health services

***Stephanie Rosso, PhD*[*1] and Diomaris E Jurecska, PsyD*[1, 2]**
[1]Children's Hospital and Research Center Oakland, Oakland, California
[2]Graduate Department of Clinical Psychology, George Fox University, Newberg, Oregon

Abstract

In this chapter we explore the relationship between customer satisfaction and symptom reduction at a hospital-based behavioral pediatrics clinic for children from low socioeconomic and diverse backgrounds. Parental/customer satisfaction and levels of functioning were assessed by a modified version of the Family Satisfaction Questionnaire (FSQ). Methods: Over a 3-year period, data were collected regarding overall parental satisfaction, access to service, symptom reduction, and increase in functioning. Results: Clinician/staff ability and access to service were the stronger predictors of parental satisfaction. Cultural sensitivity and service ability were strongly associated with overall satisfaction. Conclusion: These results suggest that accessibility to services and cultural sensitivity are vital to the therapeutic relationship and treatment success when working with diverse populations.

Introduction

In the United States alone, one in every four to five youth meets criteria for a psychiatric diagnosis (1). An extensive body of literature supports the indication that most psychiatric

* *Correspondence:* Stephanie Rosso, PhD, Clinical Director of the Behavioral Pediatrics Clinic, Children's Hospital and Research Center Oakland, 747 52nd Street, Oakland, California 94609, United States. E-mail: srosso@mail.cho.org.

disorders emerge during childhood or adolescence, making early intervention and prevention vital to future youth's life outcomes (1-4). Recent trends show that externalizing disorders such as attention deficit and hyperactivity disorder (ADHD) have the highest national prevalence rates when compared to internalized childhood disorders (1). Current studies indicate that the presence of untreated psychiatric disorders leads to comorbidity and predicts severe impairment at the individual level (5). Barriers to mental health access for children are based on epidemiological, cultural, as well as economic factors (6-8).

In terms of demographics, both Hispanic and African American children are significantly less likely to access mental health services when compared to their Caucasian counterparts (1). Current statistics also show an unequal distribution between the genders regarding behavioral diagnoses with male rates being significantly higher than female (5). Fortunately, statistics indicate that some externalizing behaviors, such as ADHD, have the highest service rates 59.8% (1). Although externalizing childhood behaviors are present in a broad range of families; they are more prominent in families where risks outnumber protective factors (6). Barriers to mental health services, specifically for children, are strongly associated with poverty, culture, and being from minority groups (6-8).

Studies in adult services show that patient feedback is a key predictor of treatment efficacy. However; perception of quality of care in child and family services are not part of the current methods of treatment outcome evaluations (9). A lack of effective interventions has been associated with children's mental health services. Therefore, providing evidence-based treatment (EBT) has been identified as one of the key components for moving forward in efficacy research with this population (10). Efforts to promulgate best practices or EBT without including patient's perspective can be counterproductive to treatment. Specifically, when working with families, parental satisfaction needs to be identified as one of the key predictors of treatment success (11-16).

Despite this knowledge, customer satisfaction has often been neglected when evaluating outcomes of mental health services for children. A comprehensive review of the literature revealed less than a dozen studies asking how parents perceive the quality of psychiatric care for their children. Therefore, the aim of the study was to explore the relationship between overall satisfaction and treatment outcomes in children's mental health services.

Our study

The Behavioral Pediatrics Clinic (BPC) at Children's Hospital & Research Center Oakland provides psychological evaluations and behavioral interventions to children ages 3 to 12 who are experiencing difficulties with affect and behavioral regulation, attention, learning, and developmental issues. We value a multidisciplinary viewpoint and collaborate as a team with developmental behavioral pediatricians, and nurse practitioners who have had specialized training. We work from an integrative model of therapy, borrowing from psychodynamic, family systems, attachment theory, and cognitive behavioral therapy. As a teaching hospital, our services are provided by licensed clinical psychologists, pre-doctoral interns, and occupational therapists.

The total sample consisted of 72 survey parental responses, of which 70% were male and 30% were female. In terms of ethnic makeup, 38 were African American (52.8%), 17 were

Hispanic American (23.6 %), 8 were European American (11.1%), 2 were Asian American (2.8%), and 1 was Native American (1.4%). The age reflects a range from 4 to 14 years with $M = 8.97$ ($SD = 2.5$). The entire sample had documented mental health diagnoses, while some of the most common diagnoses were: ADHD, autism spectrum disorder (ASD), mood disorder NOS, and adjustment disorder NOS. Inclusion criteria were having a child in treatment at BPC for at least three months.

An adaptation of the Family Satisfaction Questionnaire used with the Center for Mental Health Services (CMHS) Comprehensive Community Mental Services for Children and their Families Program Consumer Survey was used to assess parental satisfaction (16). Our modified version contained 15 Likert-type scale questions, and with five-ordered response levels ranging from *strongly disagree*, to *strongly agree*. Items in the questionnaire were aimed at providing insight into the following areas:

Overall satisfaction with services received;
Changes in the patients levels of functioning at school and home (symptoms reduction);
Cultural sensitivity from both the staff and providers;
Effectiveness of treatment; and
Access to services.

Questionnaires were given to parents while they were in the waiting room. They were invited to provide feedback to the clinic for the purpose of improving our services. Parents were asked to complete this questionnaire at their own convenience; the questionnaire included a verbal explanation that participation was voluntary, that participants could discontinue involvement at anytime without penalty, and that only aggregate data would be reported. All surveys were collected during the month of May for a period of up to four weeks. Completed surveys were received (48% response rate) from 72 parents of a potential 150 children. This study followed the American Psychological Association's ethical guidelines to protect the confidentiality of participants' records, including de-identification of data. The Institutional Review Board of Children Hospital & Research Center Oakland authorized this project. The data were analyzed using SPSS for Macintosh to produce descriptive statistics (means and standard deviations) and to calculate Pearson product-moment correlation and multiple linear regressions.

Findings

Our main goal was to assess the relationship between consumer satisfaction and the perception of improvement in the BPC (see descriptive of all the pertinent variables in table 1). To examine this association, we first conducted simple correlations among the primary variables (overall satisfaction, clinician and staff availability, access to services, communication with staff, spirituality and religion, effectiveness of interventions, respect from staff, cultural/ethnicity sensitivity, active participation in treatment, overall functioning, school functioning, and coping skills; see Table 2). Overall parental satisfaction with services was generally positive: the item mean ± *SD* was 4.67 ± .68 on a scale of 1to 5, with higher scores indicating greater satisfaction. Overall satisfaction was significantly associated with clinician and staff availability, access to services, effectiveness of interventions, and respect from staff. Additionally, respect from staff was strongly associated with sensitivity to cultural and religious (spiritual) beliefs. Effectiveness of interventions was strongly correlated with respect from staff, and moderately associated with overall satisfaction, overall functioning, school functioning, and increase of coping skills. Lastly, we performed a multiple regression analysis for the overall satisfaction score. In this analysis, we treated the overall score as the dependent variable and entered the clinical availability, access to services, effectiveness of interventions, and respect from staff scores as independent variables. This procedure allowed us to determine the strength of the association among the variables. Results indicated that clinician and staff availability significantly predicted overall satisfaction, $b = .546$, $t(65) = 6.078$, $p< .001$. The other variable that also explained a significant proportion of variance in overall satisfaction was access to services, $b = .328$, $t(65) = 3.785$, $p< .001$ in overall satisfaction $R^2 = .899$, $F(4,65) = 144.958$, $p< .001$.

Table 1. Descriptive Statistics

Variables	*N*	*M*	*SD*
Overall Satisfaction	72	4.67	.628
Clinician & staff availability	*71*	4.65	.657
Access to services	72	4.65	.632
Communication with staff	71	4.76	.430
Spirituality/ religion	69	4.67	.533
Effectiveness of interventions	70	4.53	.717
Respect from staff	72	4.75	.524
Cultural/ethnic sensitivity	69	4.68	.469
Overall functioning	71	4.03	.820
Active participation in treatment	70	4.59	.597
School functioning	70	3.87	.910
Coping skills	71	3.83	.910

Note: *M* = Mean, *SD* = Standard Deviation.

Discussion

Findings from the current study corroborate those of previous investigations noting a significant association between patient's relationships with providers and staff as an indicator of customer satisfaction (13, 17). An unexpected finding in our study was that changes in levels of functioning were not strongly associated with overall customer satisfaction. These results are inconsistent with other outcome evaluation studies (18, 19).

For example, Barber, Tischler, Healy (19) found that the highest predictor of consumer satisfaction of parents regarding their children's mental health services was the reduction of symptoms.

Table 2. Summary of Intercorrelations

	1	2	3	4	5	6	7	8	9	10	11	12
1. Overall Satisfaction	----	.915**	.876**	.749**	.654**	.807**	.813**	.692**	.579**	.533*	.447**	.446**
2. Availability/Response	.915**	----	.795**	.675**	.614**	.807**	.770**	.762**	.737**	.499**	.465**	.452**
3. Access to Services	.876**	.795**	----	.793**	.684**	.768**	.840**	.696**	.602**	.504**	.366**	.316**
4.Communication w/ Staff	.749**	.675**	.793**	----	.847**	.635**	.922**	.836**	.466**	.332**	.193	.151
5. Spirituality & Religion	.654**	.614**	.684**	.847**	----	.601**	.797**	.802**	.506**	.365**	.168	.086
6. Effectiveness	.807**	.807**	.768**	.635**	.601**	----	.745**	.582**	.640**	.554**	.476**	.454**
7. Respect from Staff	.813**	.770**	.840**	.922**	.797**	.745**	----	.770**	.522**	.450**	.394**	.326**
8. Cultural Sensitivity	.692**	.762**	.696**	.836**	.802**	.582**	.770**	----	.553**	.275*	.165	.132
9. Participation	.579**	.737**	.602**	.556**	.506**	.640**	.522**	.553**	----	.271*	.158	.158
10. Overall Functioning	.533**	.499**	.504**	.332**	.365**	.554**	.450**	.275*	.271*	----	.723**	.735**
11. School Functioning	.447**	.465**	.356**	.193	.168	.476**	.394**	.165	.158	.723**	----	.815**
12. Coping Skills	.446**	.452**	.316**	.151	.086	.454**	.326**	.132	.158	.735**	.815**	----

Note. Intercorrelations for pertinent variables **Correlation is significant at the 0.01 level (2-tailed). *Correlation is significant at the 0.05 level (2-tailed).

An explanation for this inconsistent finding may be the wide range of treatment length observed in the sample. Consistent with our philosophy, cultural sensitivity was strongly associated with parent's satisfaction. It appears that when delivering family services to diverse groups, cultural competence is vital for treatment success. Cultural context is an important consideration in studies of mental health services and customer satisfaction as some cultures might value their connection with the clinicians and the staff even higher than the goals of treatment (15, 20). On a comprehensive literature review, Hernandez, et al. (21) provided an institutional model for cultural competence. Their model states that "cultural competence occurs when there is compatibility among four important factors: community context, cultural characteristics of local populations, organizational infrastructure, and direct service support" (12).

In examining the effectiveness of children's mental health services provided by the BPC, several limitations to this study emerged. First, although all the treatments provided at BPC have elements of EBT modalities, they were significant differences among provider's approaches. It is also important to note that the diversity and needs of this population makes it difficult to have each child receive the same treatment. Our sample presents with significant differences in cognitive, and language abilities, which make treatment standarization a challenge. Although these results contribute to the literature on the effectiveness of mental health services provided to children, parents were the responders of the survey, and our findings do not provide information on the children's satisfaction (22). Finally, the design and analyses make it impossible to infer causality.

The results of the current study point to a number of future directions. First, consistent with the US Public Health Service report (23) more research exploring predictors of success in mental health services delivered to children, adolescent, and families is needed (22). Perhaps, a start is establishing criteria of specific treatments modalities, and settings as best practices for specific disorders. Second, researches would also benefit from an understanding of the role that culture has on the development of the therapeutic relationship and treatment success with diverse patients. Finally, further research is needed to address the various forms of research methodology to access specialized populations. A combination of qualitative, quantitative, and longitudinal methods may be best suited for studying these populations.

References

[1] Merikangas KR, He JP, Brody D, Fisher PW, Bourdon K, et al. Prevalence and treatment of mental disorders among US children in the 2001-2004 NHANES. *Pediatrics* 2010;125:75-81.

[2] Merikangas KR, He JP, Burstein M, Swendsen J, Avenevoli S, Case B, et al. Service utilization for lifetime mental health disorders in U.S. Adolescents: Results of the national comorbidity survey-adolescent supplement (NCS-A). *J Am Acad Child Adolesc Psychiatry*, 2011;50(1):980-9.

[3] Osofsky JD, Lieberman AF. A call for integrating a mental health perspective into systems of care for abused and neglected infants and young children. Am Psychol 2011; 66(2):120-8.

[4] *Simpson GA, Cohen RA, Pastor PN, Reuben CA. Use* of *mental health services* in the *past 12 months* by *children aged 4-17 years*: *United States, 2005-2006. NCHS Data Brief* 2008;8.

[5] Swendsen J, Conway KP, Degenhardt L, Glantz M, Jin R, Merikangas KR, et al. Mental disorders as risk factors for substance use, abuse, and dependence: results from the 10-year follow-up of the national comorbidity survey. J Addiction, 2010:105(6):1117-28.

[6] Copeland VC, Snyder K. Barriers to mental health treatment services for low-income African American women whose children receive behavioral health services: an ethnographic investigation. Soc *Work Public Health* 2011;26(1):78-95.

[7] Lopez C, Bergren MD. Latino disparities in child mental health services.J *Child*AdolescPsychiatrNurs 2008;21(3):137-45.

[8] Merikangas KR, Nakamura EF, Kessler RC. Epidemiology of mental disorders in children and adolescents. Dialogues Clin Neurosci 2009;11(1):7-20.

[9] Higa-McMillan CK, Powell C, Daleiden EL, Mueller CW. Pursuing an evidence-based culture through contextualized feedback: Aligning youth outcomes and practices. Prof Psychol Res Pract 2011;42(2):137-44.

[10] La Greca AM, Silverman WK, Lochman JE. Moving beyond efficacy and effectiveness in child and adolescent intervention research. J Consult Clin Psych 2010;77(3): 373-82. .

[11] Biering P, Jensen VH. The Concept of Patient Satisfaction in Adolescent Psychiatric Care: A Qualitative Study. J *Child* Adolesc Psychiatr Nurs 2011;24(1):3–10.

[12] Buston K. Adolescents with mental health problems: What do they say about health services? J Adolesc 2002;25(2):231-42.

[13] Garland AF, Saltzman MD, Aarons GA. Adolescent satisfaction with mental health services: Development of a multidimensional scale. J Eval Prog Plan 2000;23(2):165–75.

[14] Hart A, Saunders A, Thomas H. Attuned practice; a service user study of specialist child and adolescent mental health. Epidemiol Psichiatr Soc 2005;14(1):22–31.

[15] Kazak AE, Hoagwood K, Weisz JR, Hood K, Kratochwill TR, Vargas LA, Banez, GA. A meta-systems approach to evidence-based practice for children and adolescents. Am Psychologist 2010;65(2):85-97.

[16] Brunk M, Koch JR, McCall B. Report on parent satisfaction with services at Community Services Boards. Richmond, VA: Virginia Department Mental Health Mental Retardation Substance Abuse Services, 2000.

[17] Kaplan S, Busner J, Chibnall J, Kang G. Consumer satisfaction at a child and adolescent state psychiatric hospital. J Psychol Serv 2001;52(2):202-6.

[18] Godley SH, Fiedler EM, Funk RR. Consumer satisfaction of parents and their children with child/adolescent mental health services. J Eval Prog Plan 1999; 21(1):31-45.

[19] Barber AJ, Tischler V, Healy E. Consumer satisfaction and child behavior problems in child and adolescent mental health services, J Child Health Care 2006;10(1):9-21.

[20] Biever JL, Gómez JP, González CG, Patrizio N. Psychological services to Spanish-speaking populations: A model curriculum for training competent professionals. Training Educ Prof Psychol2011;5(2):81-7.

[21] Hernandez M, Nesman T, Mowery D, Acevedo-Polakovich ID, Callejas LM. Cultural competence: A literature review and conceptual model for mental health services. Psychol Serv 2009;60(8):1046-50.

[22] Steele RG, Roberts MC, eds. Handbook of mental health services for children, adolescents, and families. New York: Springer, 2005.

[23] Satcher D.Report of the Surgeon General's conference on children's mental health: A national action agenda; Washington, DC: Department Health Human Services, 2001.

In: Mental Health from an International Perspective
Editors: J. Merrick, S. Aspler and M. Morad
ISBN: 978-1-62948-519-5

Chapter 15

Risk behaviors among young adults

Liat Korn, PhD[*] and Hagit Bonny-Noach, PhD
Department of Health Management, School of Health Sciences, Ariel University, Ariel, Department of Sociology and Anthropology, Department of Criminology, School of Social Sciences, Ariel University, Ariel and Department for Youth Care Work, School of Education, Beit Berl Academic College, Kfar Saba, Israel

In this chapter we examine the prevalence of health risk behaviors (such as cigarette and hookah smoking, alcohol consumption and marijuana use), and deviant and delinquent behaviors (such as theft, property damage, drug abuse, cheating on exams and various driving violations) among undergraduate students at an academic institute in Israel. The novelty of this study is its investigation of a broad variety of health risk and deviant behaviors as a whole among undergraduate students, and the understanding of their contribution to predicting cannabis use. This study used a structured, self-reported anonymous questionnaire dealing with health, welfare and risk behaviors. The questionnaire was distributed among 1,574 undergraduate students at a large academic institute in Israel. The mean age of the sample subjects was 27 (SD=6.64). The findings demonstrate that approximately one fourth of the students reported cheating on exams. Additionally, around one fourth reported smoking marijuana and over one third of the drivers reported not stopping at a stop sign. All of these behaviors were found in higher frequency among males. The considerable prevalence of these behaviors among undergraduate students raises the question: In their eyes, are these behaviors considered a social norm or a deviance?

Introduction

Health risk behaviors are voluntary behaviors which lead to negative outcomes from a health perspective. A negative health outcome could be an injury, an illness or death. However, these behaviors could also have negative and problematic social outcomes for their

* Correspondence: Liat Korn, PhD, Researcher, Department of Health Management, School of Health Sciences, Ariel University, Ariel, Israel. E-mail: Liatk@ariel.ac.il.

implementer (1). The Problem Behavior Theory (PBT) explains that these behaviors are a product of an integration of risk factors which raise the probability of involvement in risk behaviors by providing a model for problematic behavior, broadening the possibilities of involvement in other risky behaviors, and magnifying the personal vulnerability of problematic behaviors. The model also introduces resilience factors which reduce the probability of involvement in risk behaviors by providing a model of positive social behaviors, by means of social and personal supervision and control, as well as a supportive social environment. Both risk and protective factors are present in all of our social and personal systems (2). According to this theory, health risk behaviors are related to each other and have a clustering effect.

Illegal drug use is a common behavior among young-adults including undergraduate students. Cannabis products (marijuana and hashish) constitute the most common drug in general and among undergraduate students in particular (3). A comprehensive study conducted in Israel on behalf of the Israel Anti Drug and Alcohol Authority (IADA) in 2003 examined undergraduate student's attitudes towards drug use as well as drug use rates in a representative sample (N=6,965) from twelve higher education institutes. Over 40% of the students reported experiencing illegal drug use. Close to one third of the students (30%) reported illegal drug use within the last year. Cannabis was found to be the most common drug used amongst the illegal drugs (4).

Excessive alcohol consumption is a growing phenomenon in the Israeli society. Studies in the field show an increase in excessive alcohol use and an expansion of the phenomenon in the various alcohol dimensions such as binge drinking and drunkenness. Binge drinking is defined as drinking five or more servings of alcohol within a few hours- that is, in one event. In research literature it is considered an extremely dangerous behavior, in which under the influence of such quantity of alcohol, judgment and response capabilities are significantly impaired (1, 5). Epidemiological data from various studies shows a significant increase in this behavior in recent years. Ezrahi, Rosiner, Nirel & Bar-Hamburger (6) reported an increase in beer drinking among young-adults aged 18-40 as well as a rise in reported drunkenness.

Cigarette smoking was also examined among young-adults in several studies, and has proved to be a problematic risk behavior among adolescents (7). More than one third of the sample (37.6%) aged 18-40 reported smoking cigarettes in 2009 (6), a lower incidence in comparison to 2005 (41.0%). Youth aged 18-24 reported smoking cigarettes at a higher frequency than the frequency in both of the older age groups (25-34 and 35-40) examined. The prevalence of male smokers (47.2%) was much higher than the prevalence of female smokers (28.0%). Approximately half of the student sample reported that they did not smoke or have ever smoked in the past. About 38% reported smoking cigarettes, and about a quarter reported smoking regularly (4).

Hookah (water-pipe) smoking is a health risk behavior which has expanded in Israel over the last decade and a half from the prevalence of zero to that which is higher than that of cigarette smoking among adolescents (1, 5, 8). Hookah experiencing prevalence stood at 37.7% of Israeli youth while cigarette experiencing prevalence stood at 27.7%. A study conducted on a representative sample of youth in Israel in 2002 found that those who smoke a hookah have a higher incidence of involvement in other risk behaviors in comparison to those who do not smoke hookahs, such as: suffering injuries, involvement in violence, involvement in risky sexual behaviors, cigarette smoking, alcohol consumption and drug use. The study findings indicate that it is important to view the behavior of hookah smoking among adolescents in Israel as a health risk behavior associated with the consumption of addictive substances and as a gateway for experiencing more serious risk behaviors (8). A different survey conducted in 2008, in the Arab sector, among adolescents in the city of Taybeh found an even higher incidence where 37.1% report smoking a hookah regularly- 55.0% among males and 17.4% among females. The probability of hookah smoking increased among undergraduate students with low academic aspirations and smoking parents (9). A survey conducted by the Anti-Drug and alcohol Authority also found that 27.0% of the adolescents and approximately 17.0% of the adults reported hookah smoking within the past month (6).

Academic dishonesty is an additional risk behavior commonly found among undergraduate students, which is attributed to copying and cheating on examinations, copying homework assignments and plagiarism of academic tasks (see for example: 10, 11). Subjects tend to view academic dishonesty as a normative behavior which is not considered immoral, but stress that this does not mean that students perceive this behavior as appropriate (10). With respect to gender differences, there are no consistent study findings which stand out. Some studies found that males copy on exams at a higher rate than females, while others found no significant gender differences (12).

Driving/moving Violations – the Israeli driver, especially the young driver, drives with a sense of immunity from traffic accidents, despite the high incidence, in practice, of involvement in road Accidents. Although young drivers are at the peak of their physical and mental power, their involvement in accidents is particularly high. The reason for this is most likely a combination of several factors: lack of experience (and therefore limited driving skills), underestimation of risk, overexposure to driving in dangerous situations (night driving, driving in a state of fatigue, driving after drinking alcohol, etc.), and an internal need as well as social pressure to demonstrate "masculinity" by taking risks while driving (13).

In international literature, significant gender differences were found with respect to driving. On average, males more than females, tend to drive faster, pass other cars more often, are more involved in drunken driving offenses and generally take more risks. Males are also more likely than females to be involved in serious car-accidents, especially accidents caused by traffic offenses such as speeding, driving under the influence of alcohol, etc. (13, 14). It was also found that Israeli men spend more hours driving and have a higher self-evaluation and higher self-confidence than women (13).

In summary: In this section we have listed various health risk and deviant behaviors among undergraduate students and young-adults in Israel: Illegal drug use, excessive alcohol consumption, cigarette smoking, hookah smoking, academic dishonesty and driving violations. Some of these behaviors (excluding driving violations and academic dishonesty) have been generally examined, especially among children and adolescents; e.g., in a study of the HBSC in Israel, headed by Dr. Yossi Harel-Fisch et al. (5), but few comprehensive studies have been conducted on these topics among undergraduate students. With respect to hookah smoking, for instance, we have found no studies which have been conducted among undergraduate students. The importance of examining these behaviors, as a whole, is derived from the conclusions of the Problem Behavior Theory mentioned above, which led us to examine the combination of these behaviors since the factors contributing to one risk behavior may also be explanative factors for a different risk behavior.

Our study

Our research goals of the current study are to examine the prevalence of various risk and deviant behaviors among undergraduate students. The study seeks to answer the following questions with reference to existing literature: Will risk behaviors be found in high frequency among undergraduate students? Are risk and daring behavior patterns more common among male students than among female ones? And, is it possible to predict cannabis use among those who exhibit other risk, daring or deviant behaviors?

Based on the literature review conducted, the hypotheses derived from the research questions are: The prevalence of males involved in risk, daring and deviant behaviors will be higher than the prevalence of females who report it. Additionally, as the PBT theory had determined, various risk behaviors will present in clusters. Risk behaviors will be found in high frequency among the undergraduate students examined, and cannabis use can be predicted by examining use of other health risk and deviant behaviors.

This study was based on a structured, self-reported anonymous questionnaire which was completed by undergraduate students at a large academic institute in Israel. The study questionnaire was based on two main sources: First, the CU (2003) Personal and Social Development Questionnaire, created by Professor Jessor (15) for the examination of risk and well-being behaviors of college students at the University of Colorado, Boulder, USA; Second, the Israeli Health Behavior in School-aged Children (HBSC) study, the Israeli part of a collaborative Cross-National Study headed by the WHO (1). Our complete questionnaire included questions on different topics as detailed: various socio-demographic questions; self-perceptions; self-esteem and body-image; psychosomatic symptoms; stress; social support; social relationships; academic studies; religion and security; excitement and daring behaviors; nutrition, diet and eating habits; exercise; dental hygiene; sexual behavior; cigarette smoking habits and smoking cessation; hookah smoking; alcohol consumption; reckless driving, and drug abuse. The questionnaire constructed for this study was mainly composed according to the American questionnaire used and was adapted to the student population in Israel. Due to the large quantity of topics presented in the questionnaire and due the desire to not excessively burden the students, the questions were divided into two columns. The most important core questions of each subject were asked in both columns, but different issues were expanded on in each of the columns. Column A expanded on issues of smoking, alcohol, drugs and driving. Column B expanded on issues of education, excitement seeking, eating habits, sexual behavior, religion and security. Each questionnaire column distributed comprised 16 pages.

Population and sample: A total of 1,574 undergraduate students participated in the study, representing 36% of all registered undergraduate students enrolled in an academic institution in Israel. The study was conducted in three faculties (Health, Nature and Social sciences) with their deans' approval. No sampling was, in fact, conducted in this study. Instead, all students present in the classroom who had agreed to complete the questionnaire participated in the study. The surveyors entered all classrooms in the three faculties. The response rate for the questionnaire stood at 93.5%. Of these, 768 completed column A questionnaire, 770 completed column B questionnaire, and 36 students were the pilot group for this study. The sample included 1028 females and 566 males, the average age of the sample was 27 (SD =

6.64). After logic cleaning and cleansing of the data file from significant multiple or missing values, the sample included 1519 subjects.

Research procedure: All students present in the classrooms received the questionnaires within the classroom. Overall the coverage percentage of the sample was 36.3% of students in the sampled departments. The questionnaire was distributed among the students during classes that they attended during April - May, 2009. Overall the surveyors entered approximately 70 classrooms. Questionnaire completion lasted, on average, 20-30 minutes. The three department heads of the faculties participating in the study helped coordinate the classrooms including the number of students attending, the lecturers and the study topic in order to arrange for the most convenient dates for distributing the survey, for the lecturers, the students and the research team. A telephone conversation was conducted between the principal investigator and the various lecturers in order to explain the study and its goals. Considerable cooperation was noted from the lecturers with respect to the completion of the study. Each meeting that was arranged by the principal investigator with a lecturer was followed by an additional reminder telephone call by the surveyor the day before entering the classroom. The surveying team received detailed instructions on how to carry out the questionnaires in the classrooms. Students were told that they do not have to complete the questionnaire if they are not interested in doing so.

Variables: the dependent variables in this study are health risk behaviors, driving violations, deviant behaviors and delinquency. These variables were tested against the independent variables: gender, age, ethnicity, religious background and family income. In addition, in order to examine the odds ratio, indexes were created for driving offenses variables as well as for deviation and delinquency (variable and index details in Appendix 1).

Findings

Table 1 presents the dependent variables in the study according to gender. The findings are presented in the table in percentages with standard deviations appearing in parentheses. The table indicates the prevalence of the subject sample according to reports on daring behaviors, health risk behaviors and driving offences. Overall it can be seen that among the deviant behaviors reported, reports on academic dishonesty are highest (25.1%). Of the reported driving offences, reports of speeding are most common (72.9%). With respect to all of the risk and deviant behaviors specified in the table, there is a higher prevalence of males in comparison to females in reporting these behaviors. The biggest gaps between genders were found in the category of binge drinking (42.7% and 17.4% respectively) and in the category of speeding (80.7% and 68.2% respectively).

Table 2 presents the results of predicting the probability of experiencing and regular smoking of cannabis, i.e., what are the chances of, for example, a male to smoke marijuana in comparison to a female. When the safety margin starts at a point greater than 1, the result is significant, and the smaller the range between two points is - the better the result is. Most of the odds ratios values presented in the table are significant (except for deviation and delinquency and ecstasy experiencing – with cannabis experiencing).

Table 1. Distribution of study measures by gender (percentages; ±SE)

	Measure list	N	Total	Females	Males
Deviation and Delinquency	Academic dishonesty	1302	25.1 (0.82)	24.1 (0.75)	27.1 (0.94)
	Shop lifting	1308	3.1 (0.34)	2.1 (0.26)	5.0 (0.46)
	Property damage	1308	3.4 (0.33)	1.8 (0.19)	6.6 (0.50)
	Drug sale or practice	1306	3.0 (0.42)	2.3 (0.35)	4.3 (0.53)
	Theft of something valuable	1308	1.3 (0.21)	0.7 (0.14)	2.5 (0.31)
	Hitting someone who said something I did not like	1308	3.7 (0.35)	2.5 (0.21)	6.2 (0.53)
Driving Offences	Not stopping at a stop sign	1107	35.3 (0.87)	33.1 (0.79)	38.7(0.97)
	Failure to keep distance	1102	57.8 (0.98)	54.8 (0.85)	62.6(1.12)
	Driving after drinking alcohol	1102	27.5 (0.84)	20.2 (0.65)	39.1(1.04)
	Speeding	1100	72.9 (1.34)	68.2 (1.22)	80.7(1.42)
	Driving through a red light	1104	8.2 (0.45)	6.9 (0.38)	10.2(0.55)
	Driving after using marijuana	1103	6.4 (0.55)	3.2 (0.36)	11.4(0.75)
	Not always wearing a seatbelt when a friend drives [1]	567	13.6 (0.57)	10.4 (0.44)	18.8(0.74)
	Not always wearing a seatbelt when I drive [1]	563	5.0 (0.41)	3.3 (0.30)	8.0 (0.56)
Health Risk Behaviors	Hookah smoking at least once a week	1192	7.5 (0.70)	4.1 (0.56)	13.3(0.85)
	Regular daily cigarette smoking [2]	341	22.9 (0.83)	19.9 (0.80)	27.3 (0.87)
	Alcohol binge drinking [2]	495	28.5 (1.09)	17.4 (0.69)	42.7(1.38)
	Getting drunk within the last month [2]	525	24.8 (0.91)	20.3 (0.69)	30.5(1.12)
	Any cannabis smoking experience	1265	25.3 (0.78)	22.5 (0.73)	30.5(0.86)
	Smoking cannabis once a week or more in the last month [2]	429	9.1 (1.27)	6.0 (1.11)	13.6(1.45)
	Experiencing ecstasy [1 2]	199	7.5 (0.75)	6.2 (0.29)	9.3 (1.10)
	N	---	---	1000	519

[1]Questions asked only in column A.

[2] filtered questions (from the sample of drivers or from those whom have experienced cannabis).

The table reveals strong predictors in the areas of: socio-demographic characteristics, driving offenses, deviation and delinquency and health risk behaviors. The table demonstrates that the odds of an undergraduate student to experiment with cannabis are higher if they are males (1.5 times higher) in comparison to females, older (1.9 times higher) in comparison to younger, single (almost twice as high) in comparison to married, and more secular (more than 5 times as high) in comparison to more religious. In addition undergraduate students of Ashkenazi (or Eastern European) decent are more likely to experiment with cannabis (1.72 higher) when compared to students of a Sephardic or Ethiopian decent, and those with a high family income are 1.6 times more likely to experiment with cannabis when compared to those with a low family income. The driving offense index also demonstrates that the probability of experiment with cannabis is 2.5 times higher among students whom have committed driving offenses than among those who have not committed any driving offenses. The examination of all risk behaviors shows that hookah smoking experience raises the probability of a student to experiment with cannabis (by more than 10 times) or use them regularly (more than 11 times). While the examination of ecstasy experiencing did not come out significant when compared with experiencing with cannabis (most likely due to the small number of students who reported it), the probability of a person whom has experienced ecstasy to use cannabis regularly is very high (more than 12 times higher) and is clearly significant in comparison to students who have not experienced ecstasy. The findings in the table do show that the essence of drug use in its whole is similar, and that the prospect of students who smoke, drink, get drunk or use ecstasy to experience and use cannabis as well, is high.

Table 2. Odds ratios of different variables in predicting experimentation and regular cannabis smoking

	Independent variables	Single experience of smoking cannabis OR (CI)	Regular use of cannabis OR (CI)
Socio-demographic Characteristics	Gender (0-Females, 1-Males)	1.52 (1.17, 1.97)	1.90 (1.42, 2.54)
	Age (0- 25 and younger, 1- 26 and above)	1.89 (1.46 ,2.45)	1.95 (1.46 ,2.60)
	Marital status (0-married, 1-single)	1.96 (1.45, 2.67)	2.37 (1.64, 3.43)
	Religiosity index (α= 0.85) (0-religious, 1- less religious)	5.40 (3.57 ,8.17)	5.09 (3.14 ,8.24)
	Ethnicity (0- Sephardic, Ethiopian 1- Ashkenazi, European decent)	1.72 (1.31, 2.26)	1.63 (1.20, 2.22)
	Family income (0- up to 7000 NIS per month, 1- over 7000 NIS per month)	1.65 (1.18, 2.31)	1.59 (1.09, 2.32)
Driving Offenses 8 items (α =0.61)	Driving offence index (0- none, 1 at least one)	2.50 (1.52, 4.41)	4.06 (1.95, 8.46)
Deviance and Delinquency (α =0.73)	Deviance and delinquency index (0- none, 1- at least one)	1.49 (0.98, 2.26)	1.76 (1.13, 2.76)
Health Risk Behaviors	Hookah smoking experience (0-no, 1- yes)	10.11 (6.53, 15.63)	11.41 (6.55, 19.88)
	Regular cigarette smoking (0-no, 1- yes)	4.69 (3.42, 6.44)	4.34 (3.08, 6.11)
	Alcohol binge drinking (0- no, 1- yes)	2.28 (1.50, 3.46)	2.84 (1.85, 4.36)
	Drunkenness in the last month (0- no, 1- yes)	2.55 (1.67, 3.91)	2.87 (1.85, 4.45)
	Experiencing ecstasy (0- no, 1-yes)	5.68 (0.75, 45.68)	12.69 (1.63, 98.50)

*CI= Confident Interval, OR= Odds Ratio

The table indicates that the independent variables show a higher probability for regular cannabis use to be preceded by other risk behaviors, than a one-time experience with it. This is especially noticeable with respect to the driving offenses index (2.50 versus 4.06) and ecstasy experiencing (5.68 versus 12.69). In other words, students who commit driving offences and experience cannabis are more likely to be regular cannabis users than those who experience cannabis only once. The table also shows that the deviance and delinquency index does not considerably increase the likelihood of students to experience cannabis.

Discussion

This study examined risk and deviation behavioral patterns among undergraduate students at a large academic institution in Israel. A major query arising, concerns the prevalence of these behaviors, and whether, due to their high frequency, they should be defined as a deviation or whether these behaviors are considered to be a social norm among the students. It was found that cheating on exams was reported by approximately one quarter of the students (25.1%) in comparison to few positive answers to the other questions pertaining to: shoplifting (3.1%), property damage (3.4%), sale of or dealing drugs (3.0%), theft of something valuable (1.3%) and hitting someone for saying something I did not like (3.7%). It may therefore be assumed that cheating on exams is not considered by students as a deviance, but is perceived as a common and legitimate enough behavior in comparison to the other deviant behaviors presented.

An analysis of the driving offenses index shows quite an interesting picture. Of the eight questions in this index, two offenses were answered at a very high rate. These were: Driving at an excessive speed (72.9%) and failure to keep distance (57.6%). It is apparent from this data that these two offenses are perceived as a normative behavior among most students. Two additional questions which were found to be “mainly normative" pertain to not stopping at a stop sign (35.3%) and driving after consuming alcohol (27.5%). It was interesting to see that the lowest prevalence was received in questions about not wearing a seat belt, driving through a red light and the use of marijuana while driving. From this, we can conclude that these behaviors are considered to be a deviation among the students, and the majority of them do refrain from executing them. In other words, it seems that among the students in our sample, not wearing a seat belt in a car is perceived to be more of a deviant behavior than driving after drinking alcohol or speeding. It is possible that the requirement to wear seatbelts, which was implemented in recent years, was internalized and accepted by the Israeli public. Therefore, it seems that it is possible to change deviant behavioral norms if an emphasis is put on preventing these behaviors, along with conducting campaigns for their prevention and using various law enforcement methods against those conducting them.

Another interesting finding pertains to the differences observed between the genders in this study. The study findings showed an unequivocal trend regarding differences in risk and deviant behaviors between the genders. The prevalence of males in all of the behaviors examined in the study was higher than the prevalence of females reporting these behaviors. The greatest disparities between the genders were found in the issues of binge drinking and of speeding. A gap of more than double exists between the genders on the issue of frequent cannabis use (13.6% among males compared to 6.0% among females) and binge drinking (42.7% and 17.4% respectively). The frequency of cannabis use, and these differences between the genders correlates with previous findings presented in the literature with respect to drug use, as shown by Ezrahi et al. (6; 12.3% of the males vs. 5.5% of the females). The large gaps between the genders are also expressed in the issue of alcohol consumption both in our study and in the work of Ezrahi et al., (6; 73.5% of the males vs. 54.9% of the females).

Additionally, the frequency of cigarette smoking and gender differences are similar both in the literature examined (4, 6) and in our study. The various daring and deviant behaviors examined also proved to be unfavorable towards the males. With respect to cheating on exams, no consistence stood out in the research literature pertaining to gender differences. Some studies found that males copy on exams more frequently than females, while others found no significant gender differences (12). The findings of this study do not shed new light on the issue and do not show significant differences between the genders in this respect. While, cheating on exams / homework was found to be higher among males in this study, the differences reported were insignificant (27.1% vs. 24.1% respectively). On the issue of driving offenses, however, clear differences emerged between the genders, as found in international literature. Studies have shown that males tend to drive on average faster than females. They also pass cars more often, are involved in more drunk driving offenses and generally take more risks than females. Males are also more likely than females to be involved in serious accidents, especially accidents caused by traffic offenses, such as speeding and driving under the influence of alcohol (13, 14). The current study findings support this data. The prevalence of males was higher than that of females in all driving offense examined (i.e., not stopping at the stop sign, failure to keep a distance, the combination of drinking and driving, cannabis smoking and driving, speeding, driving through a red light and not wearing a seat belt). The price paid by women in a patriarchal society is clear, however even the men pay the price- the price of risk. Males tend to take part in risk behaviors more than females in many fields - as is clearly evident in the present study, among others, in order to prove the superiority of the male gender.

Accordingly, and in order to determine whether a behavior is a deviation, we must examine the practices of a society in a given a time and place. If the behavior violates the practice, rule, law or norm acceptable it is a deviation. Drug use is considered a deviation in the Israeli society, the behavior deviates from the customary rules of conduct in the Israeli culture and by law is defined as illegal. However, students report that drug use is part of the young-adult culture in Israel and that to them, it is not considered a deviance, on the contrary, this is the acceptable norm and those who deviate from it experience peer pressure at times. Cannabis use is illegal in Israel and yet many believe that this law should be changed (16). For example, Bar - Hamburger (4) found that 25% of his sample reported that they are in favor of changing the law pertaining to the legalization of cannabis use, 42% of the students expressed their opinion that the law prohibiting its use should stay as it is, and the rest - 33% were indecisive. Many of the students who reported using drugs in practice favored legalizing their use. In general, young-adults and students do not perceive the use of cannabis products as a deviant or negative behavior (for example: 4, 16), and many of them do not attribute health risk to cannabis (6).

The data obtained in this study helps base the understanding of the reasons for the change observed in the extent of drug abuse among students and also gives a better understanding as to the characteristics of students who use drugs, while relating them to additional risk patterns. In addition, another unique importance of this study is that it presents, in a comprehensive manner, abundant information about various risk behaviors, beyond drug abuse, and in various aspects – behaviors which have a clear and significant relationship between them.

The study findings also try to explain cannabis smoking by means of different variables. The most significant variables for explaining experiencing marijuana are: a religious background, driving offenses, and health risk behaviors - especially hookah smoking. The probability of students experiencing cannabis were 5.4 times higher among the less religious students in comparison to the more religious ones; 2.5 times higher among students who also commit driving offenses; and more than 10 times higher among students who smoke a hookah. The deviance and delinquency index as well as the ethnic origin did not come out significant in the analysis.

The current study adds confirmation the Problem Behavior Theory (2) which shows that relationships exist between the different risk behaviors - cannabis use vs. driving offense, deviation and delinquency, hookah and cigarette smoking, alcohol binge drinking, and experiencing ecstasy. Strong causal and significant relationships were found for all of these in our study. According to the PBT, experiencing and using cannabis are explained by the strengthening of risk factors and the weakening of resilience factors in the personal and social environment. Indeed in our study, as expected, when the risk factors increased, so did the odds of students to experiment and use cannabis regularly. It seems that the content world of smoking and alcohol use considerably affect the likelihood of students to smoke cannabis.

This study has several limitations. First, the study is based on students whom are present in the classroom rather than on all students registered in the various programs. This may have a moderating effect on the degree of their involvement in risk and deviant behaviors. Second, despite the questionnaire being anonymous, the fact that it was distributed in an academic institute may have had a moderating effect on the subjects' responses as they may have feared for impact on their academic record. If these influences exist, it should be presumed that the scope and the severity of risk and deviant behaviors examined in this study are lower than in reality.

Overall, this study is a pioneering study which is meant to be used as a pilot of a larger study which will include a representative sample of students from a number of leading academic institutions in Israel and later, internationally as well.

Acknowledgments

We would like to thank the academic institution where this research was conducted, and to the Israeli Anti-Drugs Authority for the funding assistance and for its support; The students for their willingness to contribute to this research and for their patience in completing the questionnaire; Professor Jessor, from the University of Colorado, Boulder, for his contribution in guidance and theoretical instruction as well as for allowing us to use his research questionnaire and finally we want to thank Mrs. Yael Shaked for her comments and ideas.

References

[1] Harel Y, Molcho M, Tillinger E. Youth in Israel, health, well-being and risk behavior. Summary of findings from the third national study (2002) and trend analysis (1994-2002). Bar Ilan: Bar-Ilan University, 2003. [Hebrew]

[2] Jessor R, Turbin MS, Costa MF. Adolescent problem behavior in China and United State: A cross-national study of psychosocial protective factors. J Res Adolesc 2003;13(3):329-60.

[3] Bonny-Noach H. Between anti-language, slang and Argo- the Israeli drug users backpackers language. In: Bonny-Noach H, ed. Backpackers and drug abuse: A documentary, research, treatment and prevention perspective. Jerusalem: Bialik Publishers, 2008:260-87. [Hebrew]

[4] Bar-Hamburger R. Survey of attitudes and use of psychoactive drugs among students in institutes of higher learning in Israel. Jerusalem: Israel Anti-Drug Authority, 2003.

[5] Harel-Fisch Y, Korn L, Fogel-Grinvald H, Ben-David Y, Naveh S.Youth in Isreal, health, well-being and risk behavior. Summary of findings from the fifth national study (2006) and trend analysis (1994-2006). Ramat Gan: Bar-Ilan University, 2009. [Hebrew]

[6] Ezrahi Y, Rosiner I, Nirel R, Bar-Hamburger R. Illegal use of drugs and alcohol in Israel, 2009, Seventh national epidemiological survey. Jerusalem: Israel Anti-Drug Authority, 2009. [Hebrew]

[7] Turbin MS, Jessor R, Costa FM. Adolescent cigarette smoking: Health-related behavior or normative transgression? Prev Sci2000;1(3):115.

[8] Korn L. The nargila smoking phenomenon among teen-agers in Israel: A sociological analysis [Ph.D. thesis]. Ramat Gan: Bar-Ilan University, 2005.

[9] Korn L, Magnezi R. Cigarettes and nargila (water pipe) use among Israeli Arab high school students: Prevalence and determinants of tobacco smoking. ScientificWorldJournal 2008;8:517-25.

[10] Arnett JL, Arnett JJ, Feldman SS, Cauffman E. I'ts wrong, but everybody does it: Academic dishonesty among high school and college students. Contemp Educ Psychol 2002;27:209-28.

[11] Whitley EB. Factors associated with cheating among college students: A review. Res Higher Educ 1998;39(3):235-74.

[12] JordanEA. College student cheating: The role of motivation, perceived norms, attitudes, and knowledge of institutional policy. Ethics Behav 2001;11(3):233-47.

[13] Taubman-Ben-Ari O, Mikulincer M,Gillath O. From parents to children:Similarity in parents and offspring driving styles. Transport Res Part F Traffic PsycholBehav 2005;8:19-29.

[14] Simon F, Corbett C. Road traffic offending, stress, age, and accident history among male and female drivers. Ergonomics 1996;39:757-80.

[15] CU 2003. Personal and social development wuestionnaire. University of Colorado, Institute of Behavioral Science. URL: http://www.colorado.edu/ibs/jessor/questionnaires/questionnaire__guide _spsd2.pdf

[16] Bonny-Noach H. Construction of a social problem among Israeli drug users backpackers. In: Bonny-Noach H, ed. Backpackers and drug abuse: A documentary, research, treatment and prevention perspective. Jerusalem: Bialik Publishers, 2008:13-31. [Hebrew]

Appendix 1: Variable details

The *health risk behaviors* examined in this study are hookah smoking, cigarette smoking, alcohol consumption, marijuana smoking and ecstasy use. The Measure of hookah smoking at least once a week was built from the variable of hookah smoking frequency: "If you smoke a hookah, how often do you smoke a hookah these days?". The answer values to this question were: 1. I do not smoke. 2. Less than once a week. 3. At least once a week but not every day. 4. Every day. This measure included subjects who replied values 3 and 4. For the examination of regular daily cigarette smoking - subjects were asked to indicate whether the statements are applicable for them. This measure was based on the statement: "I smoke regularly and consistently throughout the day". The answer values to this question were: 1. Yes 2. To some extent. 3. No. This measure included subjects who replied value 1. The binge drinking measure was based on the question: "In the last month, how often did you drink five or more alcoholic drinks when drinking?" and the drunkenness measure was based on the question: "In the last month, approximately how many times did you actually get drunk?". The answer values to these questions were: 1. Never 2. Once. 3. Two - three times. 4. Once a week. 5.

Five to seven times. 6. Twice a week 7. More than twice a week. Subjects replying values of 2 to 7 were included in these measures. The measure of cannabis smoking experience was based on the question: "Have you ever tried marijuana/ hashish?" Answer values were: 1. No, never. 2. Yes, once. 3. Yes, more than once. This measure included subjects who replied values 2 and 3. Smoking marijuana once a week or more was based on the question: "Over the past month, how often have you used marijuana/ hashish?". The values ranged from 1 never to 7 every day. This measure included values 4-7 from once a week to daily. Ecstasy use experience was based on the question "Have you ever used the following drugs? If so, please indicate how many times you have used each drug during the last month." The values were: 0. No. 1. Yes, and an option of putting down the number of times they had used in the last month.

The *driving offenses indexes* were based on a series of questions as detailed: "Over the past month, how often did you: 1. pass a stop sign without coming to a complete stop? 2. Drive too close to the car in front of you? 3. Drive after drinking at least one whole bear, a glass of wine or something similar? 4. Drive more than 20 kilometers per hour above the speed limit? 5. Drive through a red light? 6. Drive after using marijuana?" The answer values to these questions ranged from 1. Never to 5. Ten times or more. Subjects replying answer values 2 (once or twice) to 5 (ten times or more) were included in these measures. Two additional measures on the use of seat belts were based on the questions: "When you are a passenger in a car that a friend is driving, do you use your seat belt?" And "Do you wear a seat belt when you drive?" The answer values for both questions ranged from 1. Always to 5. Almost never. Subjects replying answer values 2 (almost always) to 5 (almost never) were included in these measures.

Daring, deviant and delinquent behavior indexes were based on a series of questions as detailed: "Over the past month, how often did you: 1. Cheat on exams or homework? 2. Shop lift? 3. Caused damage or marked public or private property on purpose? 4. Sold or dealt drugs? 5. Stole something valuable such as a Palm pilot, a backpack, or a wallet from someone? 6. Hit someone because you did not like what they had to say?". Values for these questions ranged on a scale from 1. Never to 5. 5 times or more. Subjects replying values 2 (once) to 5 (twice or more) were included in these measures.

Independent variables: *gender* (male, female), The *age* category variable - determined by year of birth (age group distribution was determined by the median value - born in 1984 - distributing the sample to young people – up to age 26, and from age 26 onwards - adults). The variable of *ethnicity* was based on the question: "What ethnic background best describes you?". This question had eight response values as follows: 1. Ashkenazi/ Western Europe; 2. Spain/ Mizrahi. 3. Eastern Europe/ The Soviet Union / Russia. 4. Ethiopia. 5. Arab Israeli 6. Druze. 7. Bedouin. 8. Other. In the construction of the measure, categories were created for Jewish – those who replied values 1 to 4, and non-Jewish – those who replied values 5 to 7. The *marital status* variable included the categories 1. Single, 2. Single living with a partner. 3. Married. 4. Separated. 5. Divorced, 6. Widower. The Analysis included students from the categories 1 + 2 as single, and Category 3 - married. The *family income* variable was based on the question: "What is your family's average monthly income?" Response values were: 1. Less than - 7,000 NIS 2. Between 7,000 NIS and 9000 NIS, 3. Between 9,000 NIS and 13,000 NIS. 4.Between 13,000 NIS and 17,000 NIS. 5. Between 17,000 NIS and 25,000 NIS, and 6. Over 25,000 NIS.

Odds ratio analysis indexes: *Religiosity* index (α = 0.85) consisted of five questions as follows: 1. How important is it for you to be able to rely on what religion teaches when you have a problem? 2. How important it for you to believe in God, a higher power or a creator? 3. How important it for you to depend on your religious beliefs as a guide to everyday life? 4. How important it for you to be able to turn to prayer when you deal with personal problems? And Question 5 - How many times did you attend synagogue or other religious services during the last month? In questions 1-4 the students were asked to mark their answer from four values on a scale ranging from "very important" to "not important at all". In the fifth question they were asked to list the number of times from - 1.Never to 7. Eight times or more. For the creation of a secular - religious index, the five questions were put together and their values were divided to two according to the average value.

The *driving offenses* index (α = 0.61) consisted of eight questions which asked the respondent to mark frequencies within the last month on a scale of five responses ranging from "never" to "10 times or more", for the questions: 1. Not stopping at a stop sign 2. Not keeping a distance 3. Driving after drinking alcohol. 4. Speeding. 5. Driving through a red light 6. Driving after using marijuana 7. Not wearing a seat belt when a friend drives. 8. Not wearing a seat belt when I drive. For index creation purposes, these eight questions were put together, and the values were divided to 0 - no offense, and 1 - one or more offense.

The *deviation and delinquency* index (α = 0.73) consisted of five questions in which the subjects were asked to select, within the past month, how often, on a scale of five responses, ranging from "never" to "5 times or more", have they: 1. Shop lifted. 2. Caused property damage. 3. Sold or dealt drugs 4. Stole something valuable. 5. Hit someone because they did not like what they said. For index creation purposes, these five questions were put together and the values were divided to 0 – none of these behaviors, and 1 – at least one of these behaviors. The "cheating on exams" variable was omitted from the index because it lowered the reliability of items with results of under 0.6.

In: Mental Health from an International Perspective
Editors: J. Merrick, S. Aspler and M. Morad

ISBN: 978-1-62948-519-5

Chapter 16

Discordance among Chilean families

Julie Ma, MSW, Pilar Horner, PhD**, Yoonsun Han, MSW, Andrew Grogan-Kaylor, PhD, Jorge Delva, PhD and Marcela Castillo, PhD

School of Social Work, Michigan State University, East Lansing, Michigan, United States of America

Parent-youth agreement on parental behaviors can characterize effective parenting. Although discordance in families may be developmentally salient and harmful to youth outcomes, predictors of discordance have been understudied, and existing research in this field has been mostly limited to North American samples. This chapter addressed this literature gap by using data from a community-based study of Chilean adolescents. Analysis was based on 1,068 adolescents in Santiago, Chile. The dependent variable was discordance which was measured by the difference between parent and youth's assessment of parental monitoring. Major independent variables for this study were selected based on previous research findings that underscore youth's developmental factors, positive parental and familial factors and demographic factors. Descriptive and multivariate analyses were conducted to examine the prevalence and associations between youth, parental and familial measures with parent-youth discordance. There was a sizable level of discordance between parent and youth's report of parental monitoring. Youth's gender and externalizing behavior were significant predictors of discordance. Warm parenting and family involvement were met with decreases in discordance. The negative interaction coefficients between parental warmth and youth's gender indicated that positive parental and familial measures have a greater effect on reducing parent-youth discordance among male youths. Results support the significance of positive family interactions in healthy family dynamics. Findings from this study inform the importance of services and interventions for families that aim to reduce youth's problem behavior and to create a warm and interactive family environment.

* Correspondence: Julie Ma, Doctoral student, School of Social Work, Michigan State University, 254 Baker Hall, East Lansing, MI 48864 United States. E-mail: maju@msu.edu.

Introduction

Family relationships, especially parent-child relationships, have been a predominant theme in the field of adolescent development (1). Understanding of this parent-youth relationship is crucial to families, researchers and clinicians since many significant transformations occur to this relationship and family dynamics during adolescence (2). Furthermore, researchers observed that this important strength of parent-child connection is inherently stressful and at greatest risk during the child's adolescent years (2-4). Studies have reported that the level of disagreement between the parent and child increases during adolescence both in frequency and degree, relative to other time periods in the child's development (1). The increased conflictual relationship between parent and child during adolescence could be explained by two broad causes. The first explanation focuses on individual changes that children go through during puberty such as biological changes, increased social cognition and a growing need for independence (2). A second emphasis is on parenting stress that could be heightened by changes in family interactions caused by mid-life stress, career and parent's marital relations during the stage of adolescence (4). These changes may disrupt family integration and the well-accepted parent-child system that was more hierarchical in nature by replacing it with a more equal relationship. In addition, conflicts and disagreements are common because poor communications and unmet expectations are common during adolescence when parent and child adapt to new behaviors (4).

Literature has suggested that conflict between parent and child may increase the parent-youth disagreement on parental behaviors (4) and could potentially increase distress, reducing levels of intimacy in the parent-child relationship (5). Studies have reported that the increased parent-child disagreement during adolescence, specifically, perceptual differences in parenting that are measured by examining disagreement at the level of any particular parental behavior can be seen as problematic (6). Specifically, researchers have observed that high levels of disagreement in parent-child relationships can lead to undesirable increases in adolescents' internalizing and externalizing outcomes such as depression, anxiety and delinquency (6-7).

In addition, studies report that stress and conflict in the parent-child relationship could possibly indicate problems such as parent-child discordance and youth's negative adjustment (8-9) and could contribute to mental health problems (6). On the other hand, it has been reported that parental behaviors are most likely to produce intended consequences only if they are perceived or defined similarly by the child and the parent (8). The demonstrated significance of parent-child agreement in the family system (8-9), thus, is vitally important o study. Improving our understanding of the discrepancies between parents' and youth perceptions of the parenting behaviors (9) could suggest useful information for interventions concerning the wellbeing of youth and their families.

Among various parenting practices, it may be especially worthwhile to closely examine parental monitoring behavior in the context of parent-youth discordance. A large body of literature has suggested that parental monitoring, which represents parental awareness of youth's whereabouts and friends, is a particularly effective parenting strategy (10). Indeed, many empirical studies have demonstrated that adequately high levels of parental monitoring are associated with less delinquency, lower levels of substance abuse and antisocial behavior in youth (10-13). Parents may understand parental monitoring behaviors as necessary adult supervision. Conversely, youth may understand parental monitoring behaviors as intrusive and controlling (14). Researchers have suggested that these differences are likely to create discord and conflict in families (6) that could result in problem behaviors among youth. Therefore, due to such potentially differing appraisals of the level of parental monitoring, parent-youth discrepancies in the perceived levels of parental monitoring merit attention.

Prior literature have identified several factors that are associated with higher levels of youth-parent disagreement in level of parental monitoring. First, empirical findings have suggested the significance of youth characteristics such as gender, age, and problem behaviors in understanding predictors of discordance. In a study of middle class African American adolescents and their parents, Smetana and Gaines (15) reported more everyday conflict in families with adolescent female adolescents, and more unresolved conflicts with increased age of child. A meta-analytic review of studies of change in parent-child conflict suggested that the rate of parent-child confrontations decreased with youth's age, specifically between early adolescence and mid-adolescence, while the intensity of conflict increased during these times (3). A longitudinal study of youth by Guion and colleagues (6) reported the association between perceptual differences of parent-youth parenting behavior and internalizing problems such as depression and anxiety. The same study did not find a significant relationship between parent-child discordance on parental monitoring and externalizing behavior whereas Lippold and colleagues (7) reported a link between increased parental monitoring and level of youth's externalizing behavior such as delinquency and substance use.

Second, there is some suggestion within the research literature that there may be an association between the socio-economic status of the family (as measured by family income and parental education) with discordance. Tein and colleagues (8) reported that families with fewer disadvantages in socio-economic status that is measured through family income and education of parent had higher levels of congruence in the perceived level of monitoring. Moreover, Smetana and Gaines' (15) study suggested a link between family income and two biological parents in conflict resolution. Specifically, families with lower incomes, two biological parents and higher parental monitoring were more likely to resolve conflicts by the youth giving in to the parents.

Lastly, other researchers have indicated that positive and warm parenting could have an association with parenting styles such as parental monitoring (10, 16) and that an increased level of parental monitoring is associated with less delinquency (11). Furthermore, positive parent child relationships have been suggested as protective factors of family conflicts (17). In a longitudinal analysis, Fletcher, Steinberg and Williams-Wheeler (18) emphasize the importance of warm relationship between parent and adolescents in reducing adolescent delinquent behaviors. Moreover, Smetana (19) has suggested that a warm and responsive family environment and an interactive parent-child relationship encourage information sharing and reduce discord in families.

In sum, discordance between youth and parents concerning perceived levels of parental behavior provides meaningful information on parent-child dynamics as it points to areas of tension and disagreement in family life (2). Therefore, it is important increase our understanding in parent-child discordance. However, research in this field has also been limited to studies with North American samples (20) and understanding on the predictors of parent-child disagreement was lacking (8). To increase our knowledge in the predictors of discordance in parental monitoring, this paper addressed the following research questions with data from the Santiago Longitudinal Study, a National Institute for Drug Abuse (NIDA) funded study of adolescents conducted in Santiago, Chile. First, which family factors, youth factors and positive parenting factors predict higher levels of discordance in Chilean families? Second, what is the role of gender in moderating the relationship between these factors and the level of parent-youth discordance? Drawing upon evidence from existing literature, this study hypothesizes that there can be multiple indicators which predict youth-parent discrepancies in perceived levels of parental monitoring. Furthermore, we expect these associations to differ between male and female adolescents.

Our study

The analyses conducted for this study used cross-sectional data from the first wave (2008-2010) of the Santiago Longitudinal Study, a study of adolescents and their families in Santiago, Chile, funded by the National Institute on Drug Abuse (R01 DAD21181). The complete sample included 1,068 youth (mean age = 14.5, 51.5% male) from mid- to low-SES neighborhoods who completed a questionnaire with standardized measures that were pilot tested and validated with the population under investigation prior to conducting the study. The two-hour questionnaire was administered at the University of Chile Nutrition and Food Technology Institute (INTA) by Chilean psychologists and assessed a wide range of comprehensive topics at multiple levels, such as individual familial, and school and neighborhood characteristics. The questionnaire was administered in Spanish and was translated and back-translated and measures were pilot tested prior to the study with population under investigation. The analysis for the present study is based on 833participants.

Based on previous research findings (6-8, 11, 16-17), measures for this analysis were selected to examine which youth, family and parenting factors might have an impact on the level of discordance. In detail, youth level measures included demographic characteristics such as sex and age reported by the youth, and a behavioral problem scale. Family level measures used in this study included demographic variables such as education of parent, income, and whether both parents are present in the family. Warmth of parent was included in the analysis to understand the relationship between parents' parenting style and discordance. Level of family involvement was included to assess the effect of familial factors.

Discordance. The dependent variable was created by the absolute value of the difference in perceived levels of parental monitoring reported between youth and parents. Parental monitoring was measured using the Parental Monitoring Scale (21). Of the ten questions on this scale, only five were asked of both parents and children in this study. These five questions that asked both parents (a = 0.56) and youth (a=0.6) about how knowledgeable parents were on the youth's whereabouts were combined in this study to assess the level of discordance. Example questions included: "How often, before the child goes out, does the child tell the parent when (s/he) will be back? (How often, before you go out, do you tell your mom/dad or guardian when you will be back?)" and "If a parent or a sitter is not home, how often does the child leave a note about where (s/he) is going? (If your mom/dad or guardian are not at home, how often do you leave a note for them about where you are going?)." The response categories for these questions were 5 (All of the time), 4 (Most times), 3 (Sometimes), 2 (Hardly ever), and 1(Never).

Externalizing YSR problem scale. Youth externalizing behavior was assessed by the Youth Self Report (YSR) scale which is a standardized assessment of adolescent's behavior problems and social competencies (22). The externalizing problem scale (a = 0.85) is the sum of 15 questions on youth's delinquent behavior and 17 questions on aggressive behavior that are assessed on a Likert-type scale with response categories being 0 (not true), 1 (somewhat or sometimes true), 2 (very true or often true). Items on the scale that measured aggression included: "I am mean to others" and "I threaten to hurt people." Delinquency was measured by: "I hang around with kids who get in trouble".

Internalizing YSR problem scale. Youth internalizing problem was assessed by the YSR. The internalizing problem scale (a = 0.84) combined 13 questions on anxious depression and 8 questions on withdrawn depression. Example items that measured anxious depression included: "I am too fearful or anxious," "I feel worthless or inferior." Items that measured withdrawn depression included: "I am unhappy, sad, or depressed" and "I am withdrawn, does not get involved with others."

Warmth of parents. Among the 17 item scale that measures the youth's relationship with their parents, 9 questions that inquire about the quality of parent-child relationship were combined to assess the level of warmth of each parent (23). Items such as "When you and your mother spend time talking or doing things together, how often does she lets you know she really cares about you?" and "...acts supportive and understanding towards you?" measured the warmth of parents. These questions were reported by the participants with four options for responses, 4 (never), 3 (sometimes), 2 (often), 1 (always). Cronbach's alpha for this 9-item scale was 0.92 for mothers and 0.93 for fathers.

Family involvement. Family involvement was assessed by asking adolescents five questions (a = 0.73) that measured the level of positive family relationship (24). Some questions were: "Thinking about your family, about how many days in the past 4 weeks did your parents or other adults in your family spend time with you doing something fun?" and "...talk with you or listen to your opinions and ideas?" Response categories were 1 (no days), 2 (1 to 3 days), 3 (4 to 6 days), 4 (7 to 14 days) and 5 (15 to 28 days).

Demographic characteristics. Youth reported their gender and age. Gender was a dichotomous variable with males coded as "1" and females as "0". Age was a continuous variable that measured youth's age at the time of interview in years. Education of each parent was reported by the last school year that was completed. Parental income was the total monthly income of the mother and the father combined in the local currency of Chilean pesos.

This chapter presents a descriptive summary to depict the characteristics of the study sample. Second, this study uses multivariate analysis employing ordinary least squares (OLS) regression to examine the degree to which parental factors, child factors and familial factors predict higher levels of discordance. OLS regression is an appropriate method of analysis for this study as discordance is a continuous dependent variable.

Findings

Table 1 describes the demographic characteristics of our study sample. The mean of discordance was higher for male adolescents (0.91) than for female adolescents (0.78). Age ranged from 11 to 17 years old with a mean age of 14.28 years and a standard deviation of

1.43. The proportion of male (52%) and female (48%) youth was nearly the same. The average years of parent's education were 9.89 years and the average monthly income was 314,000 pesos (approximately 670 U.S. dollars). 68% of the families had both parents present in the household. The mean of externalizing YSR problem scale was 13.09 while it was 13.51 for internalizing YSR problem scale. The average of parental warmth was 27.93 with a range of 10.50 to 36, while mean of family involvement was 18.81 with a minimum of 5 and maximum of 25.

Table 1. *Descriptive Summary* (*N* = 833)

Variable	Mean	Standard Deviation	Minimum	Maximum
Discordance	0.85	0.68	0	3.80
Male	0.91	0.71	0	3.80
Female	0.78	0.64	0	2.80
Age (years)	14.28	1.43	11.92	17.75
Male	0.52	0.50	0	1
Education (years)	9.89	2.95	1	21
Income (1,000 pesos)	314	170	70	1,500
Both Parents	0.68	0.47	0	1
Externalizing Behavior	13.09	7.35	0	46
Internalizing Behavior	13.51	7.33	0	40
Parental Warmth	27.93	6.00	10.50	36
Family Involvement	18.81	4.13	5	25

Ordinary least squares regression

Results of the OLS analysis reported the predictors of discordance (Table 2). Table 2 contains information of four regression models that analyzed the relationship with youth factors, parental factors and familial factors on discordance. Model 1 described the association between youth variables and level of discordance in families. Gender was a significant predictor of discordance. Families in which the adolescent study participant was male displayed a higher level of discordance than those in which the adolescent study participant was female. Increases in externalizing behavior were also associated with increases in discordance. For example, a standard deviation increase in youth's externalizing behavior was associated with higher levels of discordance by 0.18 standard deviation units (= 0.27*0.68). However, internalizing behaviors did not have a significant relationship with discordance. Model 2 indicated that parents' income, education and having both parents in the family did not have a significant relationship with the level of discordance. Model 3 examined whether familial and parenting measures were inversely associated with discordance. Greater levels of family involvement and parental warmth were significantly associated with lower levels of discordance. Lastly, Model 4 described the relationship between all independent variables of interest and discordance. Similar to the results from the previous models, Model 4 indicated that youth gender (male adolescents) and higher levels of externalizing behavior were significant predictors of greater levels of discordance whereas increases in positive family measures such as family involvement and parental warmth were met with decreases in the level of discordance.

Table 2. Predictors of Discordance: Results of OLS Regression Models

Independent Variables	**Model 1**		**Model 2**		**Model 3**		**Model 4**	
	Coefficient	**Beta**	**Coefficient**	**Beta**	**Coefficient**	**Beta**	**Coefficient**	**Beta**
Youth								
Age	-0.011	-0.023					-0.027	-0.057
	(0.016)						(0.016)	
Gender	0.128**	0.095					0.137**	0.102
	(0.047)						(0.047)	
Externalizing Behavior	0.025***	0.270					0.020***	0.215
	(0.004)						(0.004)	
Internalizing Behavior	0.000	0.003					-0.002	-0.025
	(0.004)						(0.004)	
Parent								
Income			0.061	0.015			0.086	0.022
			(0.146)				(0.138)	
Education			-0.007	-0.030			-0.003	-0.014
			(0.008)				(0.008)	
Both Parents			-0.062	-0.043			-0.018	-0.012
			(0.050)				(0.048)	
Family & Parenting								
Family Involvement					-0.020**	-0.125	-0.014*	-0.086
					(0.007)		(0.007)	
Parental Warmth					-0.018***	-0.158	-0.015***	-0.134
					(0.005)		(0.005)	
Constant	0.604**		0.939***		1.728***		1.635***	
	(0.230)		(0.093)		(0.121)		(0.309)	
Observations	833		833		833		833	
R-squared	0.0815		0.0026		0.0620		0.1132	
Adjusted R-squared	0.0771		-0.0010		0.0597		0.1035	
F	18.37		0.71		27.41		11.67	

Note: † $p < 0.1$; * $p < 0.05$; ** $p < 0.01$; *** $p < 0.001$

In Table 3, we added the interaction term between positive parenting measures and youth's gender to Model 4. The significant negative interaction term between family involvement and youth's gender suggested that the effect of positive family environment on decreased levels of discordance was greater for male adolescents than for female adolescents when controlling for other independent variables (Model 5). Similarly, Model 6 suggested that the inverse association between parental warmth and discordance was larger among male adolescents than female adolescents.

Table 3. Predictors of Discordance: Interaction Models

Independent Variables	Model 5		Model 6	
	Coefficient	Beta	Coefficient	Beta
Youth				
Age	-0.026 (0.016)	-0.055	-0.027 (0.016)	-0.057
Gender	0.585** (0.209)	0.433	0.625** (0.212)	0.463
Externalizing Behavior	0.020*** (0.004)	0.214	0.020*** (0.004)	0.215
Internalizing Behavior	-0.002 (0.004)	-0.026	-0.002 (0.004)	-0.025
Parent				
Income	0.072 (0.138)	0.018	0.085 (0.138)	0.021
Education	-0.002 (0.008)	-0.010	-0.003 (0.008)	-0.015
Both Parents	-0.023 (0.048)	-0.016	-0.018 (0.048)	-0.012
Family & Parenting				
Family Involvement	-0.003 (0.008)	-0.018	-0.015* (0.007))	-0.092
Parental Warmth	-0.016*** (0.005)	-0.138	-0.007 (0.006)	-0.059
Interactions				
Gender*Family Involvement	-0.024* (0.011)	-0.351		
Gender*Parental Warmth			-0.017* (0.007)	-0.380
Constant	1.435*** (0.322)		1.418*** (0.322)	
Observations	833		833	
R-squared	0.118		0.119	
Adjusted R-squared	0.108		0.108	
F	11.03		11.11	

Note: † $p < 0.1$; * $p < 0.05$; ** $p < 0.01$; *** $p < 0.001$

Discussion

In line with the findings from existing literature, parents and their adolescent children in the community sample of Santiago, Chile, had low to moderate levels of agreement with each other on the parental behaviors. Findings of this study suggested that discordance is expected to be greater in families with male adolescents and with youth who have more externalizing problems. Moreover, the results confirmed the hypothesis that the effect of positive family environment and parental warmth would matter differently for male and female adolescents.

Gender was associated with level of discordance, age was not

Results of the multivariate analysis in this study suggested that gender was a significant predictor of discordance. Specifically, discordance increased in families with male adolescents. In addition, descriptive statistics indicated that families with male adolescents have a higher mean of discordance than families with female adolescents. These results suggest that the gender difference in discordance and its association with parent-child relationship could provide insightful information on family dynamics, specifically, parent-youth discordance. The gender difference in discordance could be explained by male adolescents' and female adolescents' distinguishable perceptions of parental behaviors. As an example, studies report that male adolescents perceive parental behaviors to be more controlling and dominant in comparison to female adolescents who are more likely to perceive parents to be warm and loving (25).

These different perceptions between male adolescents and female adolescents concerning the nature of parenting may be closely linked with the quality of parent-youth interaction or time spent together, which may determine the degree to which there is mutual understanding of their behaviors. Unlike gender, age was not a significant predictor of discordance in this study, a finding that was inconsistent with previous literature that reported positive association with youth's age and discord (3, 15). The reason that age was not a significant predictor of discordance may be partly due to the fact that the age of this study's sample is fairly clustered around the mean, with the majority of the ample youth being in the developmental stage of middle adolescence.

Externalizing behavior predicted discordance, internalizing behavior did not

Higher levels of externalizing behavior were positively associated with higher levels of parent-child discordance, a finding consistent with previous literature (9, 17). This may suggest that youths who are more aggressive and engage in delinquent behavior are likely to have a larger gap between youth's own and parents' own, assessment of parental monitoring behavior. In fact, the standardized beta coefficients of externalizing behavior were largest compared to other variables that were significant predictors of discordance.

Although a great amount of literature support the significant relationship between parent-youth discordance and youth's externalizing problem scale, the direction of this association is not clear. In other words, it is uncertain from this study whether the difference in youth's and parent's perception of parenting behavior is the result of youths "acting out," or is the cause of the youth's problem behavior. In contrast to the significant relationship between externalizing behavior and discordance, internalizing behavior did not have an association with discordance. This could be explained by the fact that externalizing behavior is more expressive and salient than internalizing behavior in the parent-child relationship (10).

Parents' income, education, living with both parents were not predictors of discordance

Previous findings reported that family disagreement increased in single-parent families, families with lower income and in families with less parental education (8, 15). Smetana and Gaines (15) have reported income-related discrepancies in family outcomes such as long-term values and level of tolerance and argue that these income-related discrepancies could possibly result in varying levels of discordance in families. Nonetheless, demographic variables of parents such as income, education and having both parents present in the family were not significantly related to discordance in this study. This may be partly due to the design of this study, which primarily sampled youth from low SES neighborhoods. As a result, the small amount of variation across youth in these demographic variables may have led to effect sizes that were not statistically significant in the analyses.

Warm parenting style and family involvement were protective factors

In line with previous literature (17-19), increases in warm parenting and family involvement were significant predictors of lower levels of discordance. The association between positive parenting and lower parent-youth discordance could be explained through communication and parental knowledge that is increased with parental warmth and in a warm family environment. Standardized beta coefficients showed that parental warmth has a greater relationship with discordance than family involvement.

Youth's gender moderates relationship between protective factors and discordance

The gender and family involvement interaction as well as gender and parental warmth interaction was significant, indicating that the effect of positive family measures on discordance changes with youth's gender. In detail, the protective effect of family involvement and parental warmth on discordance was greater for male adolescents than for female adolescents. This gender difference could be due to the discrepancy in discordance between male adolescents and female adolescents, with male adolescents reporting higher level of parent-youth discordance than female adolescents that could more possibly have a greater impact by parents' positive parenting practices.

Limitations and future work

In conclusion, this study demonstrated that youth's gender, externalizing behavior and positive parenting style is a significant predictor of parent-youth discordance in level of parental monitoring. Furthermore, the interaction between gender and positive parenting style was significant, confirming our initial hypotheses that the effect of warm parenting and family interaction on the level of discordance would be different for male adolescents and female adolescents. Notwithstanding, these findings should be noted with the following study limitations in mind. First, parent's report on parental monitoring is mostly obtained by mothers. Therefore, understanding of the family dynamics is limited than if we had reports from both mothers and fathers, or at least a wider representation of mothers and fathers. Second, generalization of this study's findings should be based on the characteristics of this study's population which are low-income adolescents and their families in Santiago, Chile. Finally, the cross-sectional design makes it impossible to examine causal, and even, temporal inferences among the variables examined in this study. Notwithstanding these limitations, this study's use of extensive family and parenting characteristics, and various analyses conducted, contributes to the literature on parent-child discordance, especially in the Latin American context. More broadly, this study that examined factors that predict the level of parent-child discordance on parental behaviors can aid more objective research and interpretation by taking the significant effect of these predictors into account (8). Furthermore, by being able to better understand parent-youth relationship, this study may contribute to designing more effective interventions, and have meaningful implications to practitioners and clinicians working with families.

Acknowledgments

This study received support from US National Institute on Drug Abuse (R01 DAD21181) and the Vivian A. and James L. Curtis School of Social Work Research and Training Center, University of Michigan. We are grateful to the families who participated in the Santiago Longitudinal Study.

References

[1] Steinberg L. We know some things. Parent-adolescent relationships in retrospect and prospect. J Res Adolesc 2001;11(1):1-19.

[2] Smetana JG, Campione-Barr N, Metzger A. Adolescent development in interpersonal and societal contexts. Annu Rev Psychol 2006;57:255-84.

[3] Laursen B, Coy K, Collins WA. Reconsidering changes in parent-child conflict across adolescence: A meta-analysis. Child Dev 1998;69:817-32.

[4] Montemayor R. Parent and adolescents in conflict: All families some of the time and some families most of the time. J Early Adolesc 1983;3:83-103.

[5] Davies PT, Windle M. Gender-specific pathways between maternal depressive symptoms, family discord, and adolescent adjustment. Dev Psychol 1997;33(4):657-68.

[6] Guion K, Mrug S, Windle M. Predictive value of informant discrepancies in reports of parenting: Relations to early adolescents' adjustment. J Abnorm Child Psychol 2009;37(1):17-30.

[7] Lippold M, Greenberg M, Feinberg M. A dyadic approach to understanding the relationship of maternal knowledge of youths' activities to youths' problem behavior among rural adolescents. J Youth Adolesc 2011;40:1178-91.

[8] Tein J-Y, Roosa MW, Michaels M. Agreement between parent and child reports on parental behaviors. J Marriage Fam 1994;56(2), 341-355.

[9] Feinberg ME, Howe GW, Reiss D, Hetherington EM. Relationship between perceptual differences of parenting and adolescent antisocial behavior and depressive symptoms. J Fam Psychol 2000;14(4):531-55.

[10] Pettit GS, Laird RD, Dodge KA, Bates JE, Criss MM. Antecedents and behavior-problem outcomes of parental monitoring and psychological control in early adolescence. Child Dev 2001;72(2):583-98.
[11] Griffin KW, Botvin GJ, Scheier LM, Diaz T, Miller NL. Parenting practices as predictors of substance use, delinquency, and aggression among urban minority youth: Moderating effects of family structure and gender. Psychol Addict Behav 2000;14(2):174-84.
[12] Lansford JE, Criss MM, Pettit GS, Dodge KA, Bates JE. Friendship quality, peer group affiliation, and peer antisocial behavior as moderators of the link between negative parenting and adolescent externalizing behavior. J Res Adolesc 2003;13(2):161-84.
[13] Simons-Morton B. Social influences on adolescent substance use. Am J Health Behav 2007;31(6):672-84.
[14] Pettit GS, Laird RD. Psychological control and monitoring in early adolescence: The role of parental involvement and prior child adjustment. In: Barber BK, ed. Intrusive parenting: How psychological control affects children and adolescents. Washington, DC: American Psychological Association, 2002:97-124.
[15] Smetana JG, Gaines C. Adolescent-parent conflict in middle-class African American families. Child Dev 1999;70(6):1447-63.
[16] Smetana J, Daddis C. Domain specific antecedents of psychological control, Parental monitoring, and adolescent autonomy: The role of parenting beliefs and practices. Child Dev 2002;73:563-80.
[17] Formoso D, Gonzales NA, Aiken LS. Family conflict and children's internalizing and externalizing behavior: protective factors. Am J Commun Psychol 2000;28(2):175-99.
[18] Fletcher A, Steinberg L, Williams-Wheeler M. Parental influences on adolescent problem behavior: Revisiting Stattin and Kerr. Child Dev 2004;75:781–96.
[19] Smetana JG. "It's 10 o'clock: Do you know where your children are?" Recent advances in understanding parental monitoring and adolescents' information management. Child Dev Perspect 2008;2(1):19-25.
[20] Ingoldsby B, Schvaneveldt P, Supple A, Bush K. The relationship between parenting behaviors and adolescent achievement and self-efficacy in Chile and Ecuador. Marriage Fam Rev 2004;35(3):139.
[21] Patterson GR, Capaldi DM. Psychometric properties of fourteen latent
[22] constructs from the Oregon Youth Study. New York: Springer, 1998.
[23] Achenbach TM, Rescorla LA. Manual for the ASEBA school-age forms and profiles. Burlington, VT: University Vermont, Research Center Children Youth Families, 2001.
[24] Conger RD, Ge X. Conflict and cohesion in parent-adolescent relations: Changes in emotional expression from early to mid-adolescence. In: Cox M, Brooks-Gunn J, eds. Conflict and cohesion in families: Causes and consequences. Mahwah, NJ: Erlbaum, 1999:185-206.
[25] Riley AW, Green BF, Forrest CB, Starfield B, Kang M, Ensminger ME. A taxonomy of adolescent health: Development of the adolescent health profile-types. Med Care 1998;36(8):1228-36.
[26] Lanz M, Scabini E, Vermulst AA, Gerris JR. Congruence on child rearing in families with early adolescent and middle adolescent children. Int J Behav Dev 2001;25(2):133-9.

In: Mental Health from an International Perspective
Editors: J. Merrick, S. Aspler and M. Morad

ISBN: 978-1-62948-519-5

Chapter 17

United States: Mental health issues in an adolescent medicine clinic patient population

Abdel Salous, MSci[1], Linah Al-Alem, MSci[2,3] and Hatim A Omar, MD, FAAP*[4]

[1]University of Kentucky College of Medicine MD/PhD Program
[2]Department of Molecular and Biomedical Pharmacology
[3]Obstetrics and Gynecology, University of Kentucky College of Medicine
[4]Division of Adolescent Medicine, Department of Pediatrics, University of Kentucky College of Medicine, Lexington, Kentucky, United States of America

The correlation between exposure to forms of violence and development of mental disorders in victims is well established. The purpose of this chapter was to identify mental health problems in an adolescent medicine clinic population in Lexington, Kenrucky and to investigate potential correlation of mental disorders with psychosocial factors. Data were gathered from the charts of 169 adolescent clinic patients (age 10-22) seen in the clinic for mental health care and analyzed using Excel. Of the patient population, 68% were urban, whereas 32% were rural. In terms of gender, 40% of the patients were male and 60% were female, 80% were white, 13% black, and 7% had other racial back-ground(s). The most prevalent mental disorders in this group were depression 32.12%, 13% with generalized anxiety disorder, 8.2% with an attention deficit disorder (including ADHD), and 5.76% with an adjustment disorder. The abovementioned demographic trends showed that depression continues to be the most common mental health problem in this population regardless of gender, ethnic origin, or economic status. This finding highlights the need for availability of mental health support to this patient population. Further work is needed to spotlight the most significant psychosocial factors and root causes of mental health conditions in this age group.

* Correspondence: Hatim A Omar, MD, FAAP, Professor of Pediatrics and Obstetrics/Gynecology, Children's Miracle Network Chair, Chief, Division of Adolescent Medicine and Young Parents Program (J422), Kentucky Children's Hospital, UK Healthcare, Department of Pediatrics,University of Kentucky College of Medicine, Lexington, KY 40536, United States. E-mail: haomar2@uky.edu.

Introduction

By the year 2020, adolescents representing individuals in the 10 to 22 year-old age range are expected to compose 14% of the United States population (1). Adolescence is a challenging transition phase with physical, cognitive, and emotional changes, all of which can have a significant impact on mental health (2). Epidemiologic data from the World Health Organization show that 20% of all adolescents worldwide have one or more mental or behavioral health problems (3). In addition, up to 50% of all adult mental disorders have been shown to have their onset in adolescence (3). This early onset of disease becomes more critical when a common mental disorder like depression is expected to show a rising trend during the coming 20 years of their lives (3). Moreover, although the incidence of depression peaks during middle age, depression is increasingly being recognized during adolescence and young adulthood (4).

Approximately 20% of depressives end their lives by committing suicide (5). With respect to adolescents, suicide attempt rates were highest among adolescents 15-19 years old (6). In addition, completed suicide remains among the top three causes of death in the population aged 15-34 years in both males and females (3). Other mental disorders, such as adjustment disorders, lead to psychosocial impairment, problems with the legal system, and restlessness (7). As for attention deficit and hyperactivity disorders, these in turn have a negative impact on scholastic performance, social relationships, and social behavior (8). Overall, the effect of mental disorders on society accounts for over 15% of the burden of disease in the United States, surpassing the disease burden caused by all cancers (9). In economic terms, children with mental health disorders impose a greater load on their parents to cut work hours, to quit work, and to spend more time arranging their child's care compared with children with other healthcare needs (10).

The causes of mental disorders in adolescents are complex and may evolve from a wide variety of psychosocial stressors, physical injuries, developmental changes, exposure to various forms of abuse, genetics, and cultural influences (4, 11-13). To better characterize the relative impact of the various psychosocial factors on the development of mental disorders, this study examined and reported on a sample of an outpatient adolescent clinic patients in Lexington, Kentucky. The patients were recipients of either counseling or medical services for mental disorders for which they were diagnosed. Specifically, the study sought to describe retrospectively this patient population with respect to demographic profile, age, gender, racial background, socioeconomic status (SES), marital status, educational level, and prevalent mental disorders. The descriptive analysis in this paper is deemed to give rise to further investigation of the most significant psychosocial factors that precipitate the onset of mental disorders in adolescents.

Our study

Medical chart review was conducted for 174 patients, who received counseling or therapy for diagnosed mental disorders. Patients received psychological therapy services regularly on an outpatient basis for mental health. In addition, medical services were provided for other physical conditions patients presented with at the time of the visit. The patients' data were entered into a spreadsheet program for further analysis. Patients were excluded from the study if they did not meet the age requirements (10-22 years) at the time of data collection and if their charts lacked documentation regarding mental disorders or conditions. With all exclusions, the final sample size was 169 patients. The different variables were entered in separate columns, grouped, codified, and analyzed statistically using Excel functions.

Findings

The age range of the patients included in the study was 10-22 years at the time of the study. The mean age was 15.6 years and the median age was 16 years, while the mode value for age was 17 years (see table 1). As expected, most of the patient population was urban (68%). The remaining 32% came from the surrounding rural areas such as Montgomery, Anderson, and Jessamine counties in addition to others (table 2). In terms of gender, 40% of the patients were male and 60% were female (see table 2).

Table 1. Age profile of subjects in the study (n=169)

Age Range	Min	Max	
	10	22	
Age distribution	Mean	Median	Mode
	15.6	16	17

As expected, the majority of the patient population was urban (68%). The remaining 32% came from the surrounding rural areas such as Montgomery, Anderson, and Jessamine counties in addition to others (table 2). In terms of gender, 40% of the patients were male and 60% were female (see table 2).

Table 2. Demographic characteristics of subjects in the study (n=169)

Geographic Distribution	Urban	Rural		
	68%	32%		
Gender Distribution	Female	Male		
	60%	40%		
Socioeconomic Status*	High	Low		
	61%	39%		
Ethnic Background**	White	Black	Other	
	80%	13%	7%	
Marital Status	Single	Married	Other	
	98%	1%	1%	
Educational Level***	High School	Middle School	College	Other
	67%	23%	5%	5%

*The insurance plan was documented as an indicator of socioeconomic status (SES). High SES patients were carriers of a private insurance plan while low SES patients were carriers of other non-private insurance plans such as state medical assistance or no insurance. **Other includes Hispanic, mixed racial origin and unspecified racial origin. ***Other includes dropouts, home schooling, and other educational arrangements

The type of in insurance plan was documented as an indicator of SES either as high or low. Of all patients, almost two-thirds carried an insurance plan reflecting high SES, with the remainder reflecting a low SES. The latter patients either received financial assistance or were carriers of other non-private insurance.

Ethnic background showed that the vast majority of patients were white, 13% black, and the rest had other racial backgrounds, including Hispanic and mixed racial back-ground. With regard to marital status, almost all patients reported their status as single, with only 1% as married and 1% as other. The educational profile showed that two-thirds of the patients were in high school, almost one-quarter in middle school, and only 5% in college. The remaining 5% included dropouts and patients with other educational arrangements including home schooling.

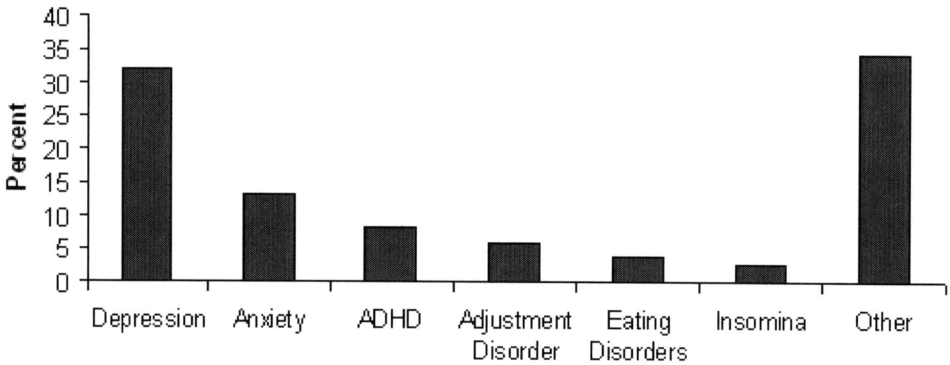

Figure 1. Prevalence of mental disorders (n=169).

Mental disorders

Figure 1 shows that the most prevalent mental disorders in this group were depression, generalized anxiety, ADHD, and adjustment disorders in the listed order; 32.1% of the patients were diagnosed with a depression disorder, whereas 13.0% were diagnosed with a generalized anxiety disorder; 8.2% of patients had an attention deficit disorder (including ADHD), and 5.8% had an adjustment disorder. Eating disorders, including both bulimia and anorexia nervosa 3.9%, and insomnia accounted for 2.7%. The remaining mental disorders grouped under "other" included anger management, Asperger's syndrome, bipolar disorder, conversion disorder, obsessive-compulsive disorder, pain disorder, panic disorder, post-traumatic stress disorder, and trichitillomania (see figure 1).

Discussion

The goal of this study was to characterize a representative outpatient adolescent population receiving treatment for mental health. The mean, median, and mode values for age shown in table 1 are indicative of a higher incidence of mental health disorders during high school age.

The higher incidence of mental health disorders in urban areas, as represented by two-thirds of the patients (table 2), may reflect the additional stressors of urban life as compared with rural settings. Alternatively, the proximity of urban dwellers to the urban healthcare facility may play a role in this distribution. In turn, this could indicate a greater need for mental health services in this sector of the adolescent population. This demographic trend could also be attributed to the insufficiency of medical services in rural areas.

The ratio of female to male patients (table 2) points to a higher prevalence of mental disorders among women versus men. This trend is in agreement with mood disorder rates of 5% to 12% for men and 10% to 25% for women ages 15 years and older (14). An alternative explanation for this trend is that women could have a higher susceptibility than do men to psychosocial factors. For example, violence, socio-economic disadvantage, low income, low or subordinate social status and rank are all psychosocial factors that affect women disproportionately compared with men (15). In addition, women are more vulnerable to forms of abuse and associated development of mental disorders (15, 16). Additionally, according to the National Survey on Drug Use and Health (17), compared with men, women with substance abuse disorders are more likely to seek treatment.

As for SES, almost two-thirds of the patients had private insurance plans, whereas low SES patients were carriers of medical assistance plans or no insurance. The potential correlation between SES and types of mental disorders poses an interesting question to be explored in future studies.

The racial breakdown shown in table 2 roughly parallels the national racial distribution—75% white, 12% African American, 3.6% Asian, and 2.4% with mixed racial back-grounds (18). Although the racial diversity closely matches the national averages, it is important to recognize the wider variation that may exist in other communities. For example, rural communities and inner city communities may deviate significantly from these trends. The educational profile clearly shows that high school students were the major recipients of mental health services in this clinic. The most prevalent mental disorder in this group was depression, followed by anxiety disorders. Unfortunately, the prevalence of mental disorders in adolescents has not been as well documented as that for adults (2).

This study sought to provide a brief description of an adolescent patient population receiving mental healthcare services in an outpatient clinic. This goal was accomplished by reporting on the demographic characteristics and the most prevalent mental disorders in this patient sample. We conclude that mental health issues are a significant problem in adolescents, with depression as the most common disorder. Access to mental health care is therefore crucial to help prevent consequences (such as suicide) and to help teens grow into healthy adults.

Acknowledgments

The authors would like to thank Dr. Marlene Huff, Dr. Kimberly McClanahan, Ms. Elizabeth Johnson, and Ms. Heidi Smith for their help in data collection and advice. This chapter is a revised and adapted version of an earlier publication: Salous A, Al-Alem L, Omar HA. Trends in mental health of an adolescent medicine clinic patient population.

Int J Adolesc Med Health 2008;29(1):9-14.

References

[1] Kolbe L. Adolescent health: population as patient. Adolescent health leadership forum. Elm Groove, IL: Am Acad Pediatrics, 2003. URL: http://www.aap.org/advocacy/ahproject/AHLPopulationasPatient LKolbe.pps.

[2] Satcher D. Mental health: A report of the surgeon general. Prof Psychol Res Pr 2000;31(1):5-13.

[3] The World Health Organization. The world health report. Mental health: New understanding, new hope. Geneva: WHO, 2001:19-41.

[4] Lewinsohn PM, Hops H, Roberts RE, Seeley JR, Andrews JA. Adolescent psychopathology: I. Prevalence and incidence of depression and other DSM-III-R disorders in high school students. J Abnorm Psychol 1993;102 (1):133-44.

[5] Goodwin FK, Jamison KR. Suicide. Manic-depressive illness. New York: Oxford Univ Press, 1990:227-46.

[6] Suicide Prevention Resource Center (2004). United States Suicide Fact Sheet. URL: http://www.sprc. org/stateinformation/PDF/statedatasheets/sprc_national_data.pdf.

[7] Pelkonen M, Marttunen M, Henriksson M, Lonnqvist J. Adolescent adjustment disorder: precipitant stressors and distress symptoms of 89 outpatients. Eur Psychiatry 2007;22(5):288-95.

[8] Lauth GW, Heubeck BG, Mackowiak K. Observation of children with attention-deficit hyperactivity (ADHD) problems in three natural classroom contexts. Br J Educ Psychol 2006;6(Pt 2):385-404.

[9] National Institute of Mental Health (2008). Mental health statistics. URL: http:// www.nimh.nih.gov/health/statistics/index.shtml.

[10] Busch SH, Barry CL. Mental health disorders in childhood: assessing the burden on families. Health Aff 2007; 26(4):1088-95.

[11] Fischer T, Koch P, Saager C, Kohut GN. The radio-radial external fixator in the treatment of fractures of the distal radius. J Hand Surg [Br] 1999;24(5):604-9.

[12] Kessler RC, Davis CG, Kendler KS. Childhood adversity and adult psychiatric disorder in the US National Comorbidity Survey. Psychol Med 1997;27(5):1101-19.

[13] MacMillan HL, Fleming JE, Streiner DL, Lin E, Boyle MH, Jamieson E, et al. Childhood abuse and lifetime psychopathology in a community sample. Am J Psychiatry 2001;158 (11):1878-83.

[14] Waraich P, Goldner EM, Somers JM, Hsu L. Prevalence and incidence studies of mood disorders: a systematic review of the literature. Can J Psychiatry 2004;49(2):124-38.

[15] The World Health Organization. Gender and women's mental health: Gender disparities and mental health: The facts. URL: http://www. who.int/mental_health/prevention/genderwomen/en/.

[16] Sanci L, Coffey C, Olsson C, Reid S, Carlin JB, Patton G. Childhood sexual abuse and eating disorders in females: findings from the Victorian Adolescent Health Cohort study. Arch Pediatr Adolesc Med 2008;162(3):261-7.

[17] Substance Abuse and Mental Health Services Administration. National survey on drug use and health, 2004. URL: http://www.oas.samhsa. gov/NSDUH/2k4nsduh/2k4Results/2k4Results.pdf.

[18] US Census Bureau, 2000. URL: http://www.census.gov/.

SECTION THREE:
ACKNOWLEDGMENTS

In: Mental Health from an International Perspective
Editors: J. Merrick, S. Aspler and M. Morad
ISBN: 978-1-62948-519-5

Chapter 18

About the editors

Joav Merrick, MD, MMedSci, DMSc, born in Copenhagen, is professor of pediatrics, child health and human development affiliated with Kentucky Children's Hospital, University of Kentucky, Lexington, Kentucky, United States and the Division of Pediatrics, Hadassah Hebrew University Medical Center, Mt Scopus Campus, Jerusalem, Israel, the medical director of the Health Services, Division for Intellectual and Developmental Disabilities, Ministry of Social Affairs and Social Services, Jerusalem, the founder and director of the National Institute of Child Health and Human Development in Israel. Numerous publications in the field of pediatrics, child health and human development, rehabilitation, intellectual disability, disability, health, welfare, abuse, advocacy, quality of life and prevention. Received the Peter Sabroe Child Award for outstanding work on behalf of Danish Children in 1985 and the International LEGO-Prize ("The Children's Nobel Prize") for an extraordinary contribution towards improvement in child welfare and well-being in 1987. E-mail: jmerrick@zahav.net.il

Shoshana Aspler, RN, BScN, MPH, is Chief Community Nurse, Health Services, Office Medical Director, Division for Intellectual and Developmental Disabilities, Ministry of Social Affairs and Social Services, Jerusalem and affiliated with the National Institute of Child Health and Human Development in Israel. She is a specialist in disaster medicine and has published in the areas of disaster medicine, intellectual disability and public health issues. E-mail. shoshiasp@walla.com

Mohammed Morad, MD, FRCP (Edin), MRCPS(Glasg) is specialist in family medicine, now working as the medical director of the Yaski Community Medical Center, Ben Gurion University of the Negev, Clalit Health Services, Beer-Sheva, a university affiliated community medical center. He is a senior lecturer in family medicine affiliated with the Department of Family Medicine, Division of Community Health and Center for Multidisciplinary Research in Aging at the Faculty of Health Sciences, Ben Gurion University of the Negev, Beer-Sheva, Israel. Associate director of the National Institute of Child Health and Human Development in Jerusalem, Israel, professor of pediatrics at the Department of Pediatrics, University of Kentucky, Lexington, Kentucky, United States and 2011-2012 he spend a year as the leading general practitioner responsible for out-of-hours primary care service in the NHS Lanarkshire area in Scotland. Before Scotland he worked as the medical director of a large medical specialist center for the south of Israel in the city of Beer-Sheva operated by the Clalit Health Services (150 medical specialists, 300 support staff and 250,000 annual visits). Publications on Bedouin health, health aspects, spiritual health and aging in persons with intellectual disability, and presenter on public health topics, health policy and services for the disadvantaged at national and international conferences. E-mail: morad62@gmail.com

In: Mental Health from an International Perspective
Editors: J. Merrick, S. Aspler and M. Morad
ISBN: 978-1-62948-519-5

Chapter 19

About the National Institute of Child Health and Human Development in Israel

The National Institute of Child Health and Human Development (NICHD) in Israel was established in 1998 as a virtual institute under the auspicies of the Medical Director, Ministry of Social Affairs and Social Services in order to function as the research arm for the Office of the Medical Director. In 1998 the National Council for Child Health and Pediatrics, Ministry of Health and in 1999 the Director General and Deputy Director General of the Ministry of Health endorsed the establishment of the NICHD.

Mission

The mission of a National Institute for Child Health and Human Development in Israel is to provide an academic focal point for the scholarly interdisciplinary study of child life, health, public health, welfare, disability, rehabilitation, intellectual disability and related aspects of human development. This mission includes research, teaching, clinical work, information and public service activities in the field of child health and human development.

Service and academic activities

Over the years many activities became focused in the south of Israel due to collaboration with various professionals at the Faculty of Health Sciences (FOHS) at the Ben Gurion University of the Negev (BGU). Since 2000 an affiliation with the Zusman Child Development Center at the Pediatric Division of Soroka University Medical Center has resulted in collaboration around the establishment of the Down Syndrome Clinic at that center. In 2002 a full course on "Disability" was established at the Recanati School for Allied Professions in the Community, FOHS, BGU and in 2005 collaboration was started with the Primary Care Unit of the faculty and disability became part of the master of public health course on "Children and society". In the academic year 2005-2006 a one semester course on

"Aging with disability" was started as part of the master of science program in gerontology in our collaboration with the Center for Multidisciplinary Research in Aging. In 2010 collaborations with the Division of Pediatrics, Hadassah Hebrew University Medical Center, Jerusalem, Israel around the National Down Syndrome Center and teaching students and residents about intellectual and developmental disabilities as part of their training at this campus.

Research activities

The affiliated staff have over the years published work from projects and research activities in this national and international collaboration. In the year 2000 the International Journal of Adolescent Medicine and Health and in 2005 the International Journal on Disability and Human Development of De Gruyter Publishing House (Berlin and New York) were affiliated with the National Institute of Child Health and Human Development. From 2008 also the International Journal of Child Health and Human Development (Nova Science, New York), the International Journal of Child and Adolescent Health (Nova Science) and the Journal of Pain Management (Nova Science) affiliated and from 2009 the International Public Health Journal (Nova Science) and Journal of Alternative Medicine Research (Nova Science). All peer-reviewed international journals.

National collaborations

Nationally the NICHD works in collaboration with the Faculty of Health Sciences, Ben Gurion University of the Negev; Department of Physical Therapy, Sackler School of Medicine, Tel Aviv University; Autism Center, Assaf HaRofeh Medical Center; National Rett and PKU Centers at Chaim Sheba Medical Center, Tel HaShomer; Department of Physiotherapy, Haifa University; Department of Education, Bar Ilan University, Ramat Gan, Faculty of Social Sciences and Health Sciences; College of Judea and Samaria in Ariel and in 2011 affiliation with Center for Pediatric Chronic Diseases and National Center for Down Syndrome, Department of Pediatrics, Hadassah Hebrew University Medical Center, Mount Scopus Campus, Jerusalem.

International collaborations

Internationally with the Department of Disability and Human Development, College of Applied Health Sciences, University of Illinois at Chicago; Strong Center for Developmental Disabilities, Golisano Children's Hospital at Strong, University of Rochester School of Medicine and Dentistry, New York; Centre on Intellectual Disabilities, University of Albany, New York; Centre for Chronic Disease Prevention and Control, Health Canada, Ottawa; Chandler Medical Center and Children's Hospital, Kentucky Children's Hospital, Section of Adolescent Medicine, University of Kentucky, Lexington; Chronic Disease Prevention and

Control Research Center, Baylor College of Medicine, Houston, Texas; Division of Neuroscience, Department of Psychiatry, Columbia University, New York; Institute for the Study of Disadvantage and Disability, Atlanta; Center for Autism and Related Disorders, Department Psychiatry, Children's Hospital Boston, Boston; Department of Paediatrics, Child Health and Adolescent Medicine, Children's Hospital at Westmead, Westmead, Australia; International Centre for the Study of Occupational and Mental Health, Düsseldorf, Germany; Centre for Advanced Studies in Nursing, Department of General Practice and Primary Care, University of Aberdeen, Aberdeen, United Kingdom; Quality of Life Research Center, Copenhagen, Denmark; Nordic School of Public Health, Gottenburg, Sweden, Scandinavian Institute of Quality of Working Life, Oslo, Norway; The Department of Applied Social Sciences (APSS) of The Hong Kong Polytechnic University Hong Kong.

Targets

Our focus is on research, international collaborations, clinical work, teaching and policy in health, disability and human development and to establish the NICHD as a permanent institute at one of the residential care centers for persons with intellectual disability in Israel in order to conduct model research and together with the four university schools of public health/medicine in Israel establish a national master and doctoral program in disability and human development at the institute to secure the next generation of professionals working in this often non-prestigious/low-status field of work.

Contact

Joav Merrick, MD, MMedSci, DMSc
Professor of Pediatrics, Child Health and Human Development
Medical Director, Health Services, Division for Intellectual and Developmental Disabilities, Ministry of Social Affairs and Social Services, POB 1260, IL 91012 Jerusalem, Israel.
E-mail: jmerrick@zahav.net.il

In: Mental Health from an International Perspective
Editors: J. Merrick, S. Aspler and M. Morad
ISBN: 978-1-62948-519-5

Chapter 20

About the book series "Health and human development"

Health and human development is a book series with publications from a multidisciplinary group of researchers, practitioners and clinicians for an international professional forum interested in the broad spectrum of health and human development. Books already published:

- Merrick J, Omar HA, eds. Adolescent behavior research. International perspectives. New York: Nova Science, 2007.
- Kratky KW. Complementary medicine systems: Comparison and integration. New York: Nova Science, 2008.
- Schofield P, Merrick J, eds. Pain in children and youth. New York: Nova Science, 2009.
- Greydanus DE, Patel DR, Pratt HD, Calles Jr JL, eds. Behavioral pediatrics, 3 ed. New York: Nova Science, 2009.
- Ventegodt S, Merrick J, eds. Meaningful work: Research in quality of working life. New York: Nova Science, 2009.
- Omar HA, Greydanus DE, Patel DR, Merrick J, eds. Obesity and adolescence. A public health concern. New York: Nova Science, 2009.
- Lieberman A, Merrick J, eds. Poverty and children. A public health concern. New York: Nova Science, 2009.
- Goodbread J. Living on the edge. The mythical, spiritual and philosophical roots of social marginality. New York: Nova Science, 2009.
- Bennett DL, Towns S, Elliot E, Merrick J, eds. Challenges in adolescent health: An Australian perspective. New York: Nova Science, 2009.
- Schofield P, Merrick J, eds. Children and pain. New York: Nova Science, 2009.
- Sher L, Kandel I, Merrick J, eds. Alcohol-related cognitive disorders: Research and clinical perspectives. New York: Nova Science, 2009.
- Anyanwu EC. Advances in environmental health effects of toxigenic mold and mycotoxins. New York: Nova Science, 2009.

- Bell E, Merrick J, eds. Rural child health. International aspects. New York: Nova Science, 2009.
- Dubowitz H, Merrick J, eds. International aspects of child abuse and neglect. New York: Nova Science, 2010.
- Shahtahmasebi S, Berridge D. Conceptualizing behavior: A practical guide to data analysis. New York: Nova Science, 2010.
- Wernik U. Chance action and therapy. The playful way of changing. New York: Nova Science, 2010.
- Omar HA, Greydanus DE, Patel DR, Merrick J, eds. Adolescence and chronic illness. A public health concern. New York: Nova Science, 2010.
- Patel DR, Greydanus DE, Omar HA, Merrick J, eds. Adolescence and sports. New York: Nova Science, 2010.
- Shek DTL, Ma HK, Merrick J, eds. Positive youth development: Evaluation and future directions in a Chinese context. New York: Nova Science, 2010.
- Shek DTL, Ma HK, Merrick J, eds. Positive youth development: Implementation of a youth program in a Chinese context. New York: Nova Science, 2010.
- Omar HA, Greydanus DE, Tsitsika AK, Patel DR, Merrick J, eds. Pediatric and adolescent sexuality and gynecology: Principles for the primary care clinician. New York: Nova Science, 2010.
- Chow E, Merrick J, eds. Advanced cancer. Pain and quality of life. New York: Nova Science, 2010.
- Latzer Y, Merrick, J, Stein D, eds. Understanding eating disorders. Integrating culture, psychology and biology. New York: Nova Science, 2010.
- Sahgal A, Chow E, Merrick J, eds. Bone and brain metastases: Advances in research and treatment. New York: Nova Science, 2010.
- Postolache TT, Merrick J, eds. Environment, mood disorders and suicide. New York: Nova Science, 2010.
- Maharajh HD, Merrick J, eds. Social and cultural psychiatry experience from the Caribbean Region. New York: Nova Science, 2010.
- Mirsky J. Narratives and meanings of migration. New York: Nova Science, 2010.
- Harvey PW. Self-management and the health care consumer. New York: Nova Science, 2011.
- Ventegodt S, Merrick J. Sexology from a holistic point of view. New York: Nova Science, 2011.
- Ventegodt S, Merrick J. Principles of holistic psychiatry: A textbook on holistic medicine for mental disorders. New York: Nova Science, 2011.
- Greydanus DE, Calles Jr JL, Patel DR, Nazeer A, Merrick J, eds. Clinical aspects of psychopharmacology in childhood and adolescence. New York: Nova Science, 2011.
- Bell E, Seidel BM, Merrick J, eds. Climate change and rural child health. New York: Nova Science, 2011.
- Bell E, Zimitat C, Merrick J, eds. Rural medical education: Practical strategies. New York: Nova Science, 2011.
- Latzer Y, Tzischinsky. The dance of sleeping and eating among adolescents: Normal and pathological perspectives. New York: Nova Science, 2011.

- Deshmukh VD. The astonishing brain and holistic consciousness: Neuroscience and Vedanta perspectives. New York: Nova Science, 2011.
- Bell E, Westert GP, Merrick J, eds. Translational research for primary healthcare. New York: Nova Science, 2011.
- Shek DTL, Sun RCF, Merrick J, eds. Drug abuse in Hong Kong: Development and evaluation of a prevention program. New York: Nova Science, 2011.
- Ventegodt S, Hermansen TD, Merrick J. Human Development: Biology from a holistic point of view. New York: Nova Science, 2011.
- Ventegodt S, Merrick J. Our search for meaning in life. New York: Nova Science, 2011.
- Caron RM, Merrick J, eds. Building community capacity: Minority and immigrant populations. New York: Nova Science, 2012.
- Klein H, Merrick J, eds. Human immunodeficiency virus (HIV) research: Social science aspects. New York: Nova Science, 2012.
- Lutzker JR, Merrick J, eds. Applied public health: Examining multifaceted Social or ecological problems and child maltreatment. New York: Nova Science, 2012.
- Chemtob D, Merrick J, eds. AIDS and tuberculosis: Public health aspects. New York: Nova Science, 2012.
- Ventegodt S, Merrick J. Textbook on evidence-based holistic mind-body medicine: Basic principles of healing in traditional Hippocratic medicine. New York: Nova Science, 2012.
- Ventegodt S, Merrick J. Textbook on evidence-based holistic mind-body medicine: Holistic practice of traditional Hippocratic medicine. New York: Nova Science, 2012.
- Ventegodt S, Merrick J. Textbook on evidence-based holistic mind-body medicine: Healing the mind in traditional Hippocratic medicine. New York: Nova Science, 2012.
- Ventegodt S, Merrick J. Textbook on evidence-based holistic mind-body medicine: Sexology and traditional Hippocratic medicine. New York: Nova Science, 2012.
- Ventegodt S, Merrick J. Textbook on evidence-based holistic mind-body medicine: Research, philosophy, economy and politics of traditional Hippocratic medicine. New York: Nova Science, 2012.
- Caron RM, Merrick J, eds. Building community capacity: Skills and principles. New York: Nova Science, 2012.
- Lemal M, Merrick J, eds. Health risk communication. New York: Nova Science, 2012.
- Ventegodt S, Merrick J. Textbook on evidence-based holistic mind-body medicine: Basic philosophy and ethics of traditional Hippocratic medicine. New York: Nova Science, 2013.
- Caron RM, Merrick J, eds. Building community capacity: Case examples from around the world. New York: Nova Science, 2013.
- Steele RE. Managed care in a public setting. New York: Nova Science, 2013.
- Srabstein JC, Merrick J, eds. Bullying: A public health concern. New York: Nova Science, 2013.

- Thavarajah N, Pulenzas N, Lechner B, Chow E, Merrick J, eds. Advanced cancer: Managing symptoms and quality of life. New York: Nova Science, 2013.
- Stein D, Latzer Y, eds. Treatment and recovery of eating disorders. New York: Nova Science, 2013.
- Sun J, Buys N, Merrick J. Health promotion: Community singing as a vehicle to promote health. New York: Nova Science, 2013.
- Pulenzas N, Lechner B, Thavarajah N, Chow E, Merrick J, eds. Advanced cancer: Managing symptoms and quality of life. New York: Nova Science, 2013.
- Sun J, Buys N, Merrick J. Health promotion: Strengthening positive health and preventing disease. New York: Nova Science, 2013.
- Merrick J, Israeli S, eds. Food, nutrition and eating behavior. New York: Nova Science, 2013.

Contact

Professor Joav Merrick, MD, MMedSci, DMSc

Medical Director, Health Services, Division for Intellectual and Developmental Disabilities, Ministry of Social Affairs and Social Services

POBox 1260, IL-91012 Jerusalem, Israel

E-mail: jmerrick@zahav.net.il

SECTION FOUR: INDEX

Index

A

B

C

D

E

F

G

H

I

J

K

L

M

N

O

P

Q

R

S

T

U

V

W

Y